MIND, BRAIN & HUMAN POTENTIAL

Brian Lancaster is a Senior Lecturer in Psychology at
Liverpool Polytechnic where his research encompasses both
brain science and the psychology of religion. In addition
to lecturing in both England and Israel, he has extensive
experience in leading groups and workshops. His published
works include poetry as well as academic articles.

Mind, Brain & Human Potential

*The Quest for an
Understanding of Self*

BRIAN LANCASTER

ELEMENT

Shaftesbury, Dorset • Rockport, Massachusetts

Published in Great Britain in 1991 by
Element Books Limited
Longmead, Shaftesbury, Dorset

Published in the USA in 1991 by
Element Inc
42 Broadway, Rockport, MA 01966

Cover design by Max Fairbrother
Designed by Roger Lightfoot
Typeset by Selectmove Ltd, London
Printed and bound in Great Britain by
Dotesios Ltd, Trowbridge, Wilts

British Library Cataloguing in Publication Data

Lancaster, Brian
  Mind, brain and human potential :
  the quest for an understanding self.
  I. Title
  158.1

ISBN 1-85230-209-7

Contents

Acknowledgements

I would like to give my thanks to all those who have aided me in bringing this work into the light of day. Thanks in particular to my wife, Irene, for constructive criticism in the crucial early stages of my preparation of the manuscript. My colleague at Liverpool Polytechnic, Tony Shelton, and Susan Blackmore of Bristol University both read the work with an academic eye and gave helpful comments for which I am grateful. Grammatical accuracy was advanced through my father's enduring influence. Finally, these acknowledgements would not be complete without a mention of S. C. Chayim, who brought into focus one or two points of common interest.

Introduction

> If I am not for myself, who is for me? When I am for myself, what
> am I? And if not now, when?[1]

These famous words belong to Hillel, the great teacher of Judaism
who lived some 2000 years ago at the beginning of the Common
Era. Superficially, they are directed towards our ethical conduct.
One should be self-reliant, but not self-centred. Taken more
deeply, they convey an essential paradox concerning the nature
of the self. The juxtaposition in this aphorism of the two Hebrew
words, *ain*, meaning nothing, and *ani*, meaning I, is itself a
pun. The one thing that is perhaps the firmest for us to hold
on to, our very sense of being an 'I', becomes, through the
merest rearrangement of letters, a void – 'no-self', as the Buddhist
teaching has it. Understood in this light, the last sentence ('If
not now, when?') becomes a profound challenge to our inner
make-up. The apparent firmness of 'I' obscures something of our
spiritual nature. 'I' holds us to the past and conditions our future;
it represents our security in the endless flow of time. But if we
could awake to true consciousness of the moment *now*, without
clutching to past or future, then, and only then, might we uncover
the limitless root of our being. Knowledge arises where the finite
connects with the infinite in self.

This book may be viewed as a commentary on this aphorism
of Hillel. What is 'I', and what is the 'self'? Perhaps more words
have been expended on these questions over the ages than on any
other issue. Knowledge of self, whether in the guise of ancient
oracles or in that of contemporary therapeutic approaches to the
individual, has been presented as the key which unlocks true
wisdom. The quest for an understanding of self is perhaps one

which unites us over history with our forebears. It is, moreover, a quest that bridges all the various qualities of human endeavour. Religion, and more especially religious mysticism, may be viewed in juxtaposition to the sciences of neurophysiology and psychology in this context. Modern physics as well as ancient philosophy and literature jostle for place in the ongoing drama of the human quest to know oneself.

Whilst all these areas of enquiry have their place in this book, it is primarily a book about the human brain. Over this century the lens of science has been focused ever more powerfully on the brain, and we have begun to unravel its secrets. How have such advances helped us in the quest to understand the self? What have our endeavours to understand the brain added to those introspective and intuitive insights into the nature of mind gleaned over the ages by philosophers and mystics? How has modern science advanced the universal human imperative to know oneself? These are the central questions around which the themes of this book cohere.

Throughout the book I have tried to convey something of the challenge of integrating what are often puzzling bits of information thrown up by experiments in the area of brain science and by studies on patients who have suffered some form of brain damage. I have tried to see how far we can go in mapping our experience of mental life on to the brain. And I have tried to interweave observations about the brain with the overarching perennial philosophy, the framework that places humanity beyond the indignity of the merely mechanical. This book is not a textbook of brain function; it is an exploration of the hinterland between science and religion in the quest to understand the self.

It is, accordingly, a book about the mind. That the mind is related to brain function there seems little doubt. But how exactly the physical matter of the brain is related to our sphere of experience, the mind, is still something of a mystery. Central to this mystery is the relationship between consciousness and the unconscious. In the wake of Freud's great insights into the mind, this notion of a distinction between the conscious and unconscious sides to the person has filtered into general knowledge. But there may be something of a mistaken outlook here. The distinction tends to be viewed as more static than it really is; and the unconscious becomes some kind of personal psychological dustbin, to be opened at our peril. These views have come about partly through a distortion of Freud's theories, but also partly as a consequence of Freud's particular approach. As with many pioneers, Freud tended towards a rigid schematization of his subject matter.

I believe that our understanding of the brain today gives greater insight into these issues. As will become clear, the key to the relationship between conscious and unconscious processes is an understanding of 'I', the very centre of our everyday experience.[2] Through the pages of this book a model of the mind is advanced, a model that focuses on the nature of 'I'. The questions asked are, fundamentally, *which* brain processes generate 'I', *why* is there any need for such processes to exist in the first place, and *how* do they give rise to this sense of 'I'?

Chapter 1 addresses the mystery of consciousness itself and clarifies my use of terminology in this complex area. What, for example, is the difference between consciousness and awareness? How may we meaningfully define mind? We have a general, intuitive understanding of these terms, but it is not easy to specify their precise meaning. If there is doubt as to their meaning, we inevitably encounter further difficulties in relating them to aspects of brain function. This chapter, then, lays the foundation of the entire work. The human brain is undoubtedly the soil of the human mind, but is there perhaps some intangible quality of mind which is not limited to the brain substance itself? Such a question takes us beyond brain science into a consideration of matter in general and the insights into reality gleaned through modern physics. Perhaps, as argued in this chapter, consciousness is somehow intrinsic to reality as a whole, and not merely a property of the brain.

Returning to the more immediate properties of the mind, I argue in Chapter 2 that the human mind is most fundamentally characterized as displaying a quest for meaning. The brain actively organizes its world. Perception, the process whereby the brain maintains contact with the objective world, is not a simple translation of sensory data into the neuronal language of the brain. It is a process directed to making sense of the world in relation to our cumulative prior experience. We are limited, not only by the resolution of our senses, but also by the conservatism of 'I' – that is, we tend to perceive what we are set to perceive on the basis of our expectations. The first stage in my formulation of a model of the mind is laid here, in an attempt to explain the way in which these perceptual processes operate.

Central to this model is the role of memory. Given that we perceive according to prior experience, memory becomes the cornerstone of perception. Memory is, furthermore, the 'taproot of mind', for without memory what kind of mind could there be? In Chapter 3, neurological cases where there has been impairment of memory are discussed. At the extreme, an amnesic patient may lose the very core of their conscious self, the sense of identity. This sense of identity is 'I', an apparent continuity in our experience of self in relation to the world around us.

Even in the normal individual, however, this apparently continuous 'I' may not be so firm as we think. In this chapter on memory, evidence is presented which questions the common-sense notion that there is something substantial and never-changing about 'I'. It is proposed here, and further elaborated in Chapter 4, that 'I' comes about as a moment-to-moment output from memory. Information is stored in memory together with an index, or 'tag', of the 'I' that previously experienced that particular bit of information. Throughout our daily lives, such 'I-tags' are continually being activated and updated. The result is an ever-changing flux of 'I-tags', called in this work the *identity plane*.

Generally speaking, however, we do not experience ourselves as a flux of 'I's. Our sense is that of being a *unified 'I'*, continuous over time. This experience of self as a single character passing through time as the stream of consciousness lies at the heart of everyday experience. In Chapter 4 the origination of this unified 'I' is examined in detail. A specialized module in the brain's left hemisphere, which has been called the *interpreter*, generates this 'I' as a kind of final common path in the identity plane. The interpreter is just what its name implies; it interprets operations elsewhere in the brain by providing them with a focus, a cause. 'I' *is* this cause, but it is a cause constructed retrospectively, a kind of *post hoc* hypothesis. 'I' gives only the illusion of control in the mind. In fact 'I' comes about as a satisfying solution to the quest for meaning; it gives a sense of continuity in time and a unified focus to what would otherwise be a multiplicity of 'I'. It is indeed these qualities of unification and continuity which give us the crucial sense of meaning in our experience.

For all these strengths, 'I' is, as mentioned above, a retrospective construct and as such constitutes a limitation on our ability to be genuinely in touch with the present. 'I' gives us security, but at a price – the price of losing contact with a greater wholeness of being. In the final section of Chapter 4, transcendence of the identity plane is discussed. It seems that full realization of human potential may only come about through direct experience of a region beyond the identity plane, called here the *higher plane*.

These issues are further discussed in Chapter 5, which considers the way in which different levels of the brain relate to different levels in our experience of self. The self is not a fixed entity, tied to one specific region of the brain. Rather, with evolutionary development of the brain so has the sense of self developed. This survey of the 'archaeology of self' provides a framework to the various alterations in self that may be experienced when the security of 'I' is eclipsed.

Why do we dream? Chapter 6 describes the challenging relationship between changes in brain activity associated with rapid eye movement sleep and the experience of dreaming. Once again we are drawn to a consideration of the brain–mind relationship. In this chapter a framework is established for understanding the inter-relationships between the physical, psychological and spiritual spheres pertaining to self. Dreaming itself is viewed as a process concerned with organizing the 'I-tags' relating to memories. The chapter opens out further to explore the nature of imagery, not only in the dreaming associated with sleep but also in the context of meditative and visionary experience. It is argued that imagery can play a central role in the expansion of consciousness which accompanies explorations of the various levels of self. Imagery or visualization entails a 'letting go' of those control processes which reinforce the habitual nature of 'I'.

Chapter 7 returns to a fuller consideration of the higher plane in the context of volition, free will and responsibility. If 'I' is not really the instigator of action, being only a retrospective construct of the interpreter, how can we hold individuals responsible for their actions? The issue here is really the nature of the person. Here, then, the implications to society of our search for an understanding of self come under scrutiny. The higher plane is viewed as the true conscious base of personhood, even though the individual person may not be conscious of it! In matters of law, as, for example, in matters medical, we must focus on the whole person.

A further discussion of memory brings back the more intra-personal focus. In literature the power of recollection to herald a deep awareness of self has been explored more than once. In particular, Marcel Proust has incisively examined such experience, and his work is discussed here in relation to the concept of the higher plane of mind.

Finally, in Chapter 8 the centrality of imagination is explored. Together with memory, imagination defines what mind is. In the simplest sense imagination involves the ability to go beyond sensory data to perceive meaning, whilst in the deepest sense imagination brings us into the orbit of the transpersonal sphere through its role in promoting detachment from 'I'. Imagination is the faculty that places us most fully 'in the image of God'.

I

Consciousness, Mind and Brain

PROLOGUE

The primal centre is the innermost light, of a translucence, subtlety and purity beyond comprehension. . . . Beyond this point nothing can be known. Therefore it is called beginning.[1]

In both mythical and scientific thinking, light is the metaphor most commonly employed to convey the nature of consciousness.[2] It is not difficult to see why. As we become conscious of an object it is indeed as if the object has emerged from darkness. In a more subtle sense, not only does the polarity of light and darkness epitomize the distinction between conscious and unconscious, but the invisibility of the very agent – that is, light – which renders visibility possible, constitutes a paradox that well serves to equate with the paradox of consciousness attempting to define itself. As we reach out to grasp the precise nature of light, or of consciousness, we find that some indefinable quality always seems to evade us. So the metaphor is indeed a powerful one.

Beyond the use of metaphor all we can really say is, *consciousness is*. Consciousness is the ground of our existence as beings seeking knowledge. It seems to me impossible for us to specify in any objective sense where it comes from and what sustains it. Certainly we know consciousness from the inside but we cannot subject it to the direct scrutiny of external instruments, as is required for scientific understanding.

The problem for us is that living, as we do, in the scientific age, we expect a tangible answer to questions concerning the nature of consciousness and the genesis of the human mind; and the brain looms up front, such mysteries apparently just beyond the sensitivities of our current investigative techniques. And, so the argument would go, with technological progress we may expect scientific answers in this area. But, of course, no matter how sophisticated the techniques (and under the influence of the new technology current techniques are already incredibly complex) the most we can do is observe the manner in which the brain handles *information*. Insights into the nature of consciousness and the mind remain as interpretations of scientific data. And here lurks the danger of individual scientists projecting their own predilections on to those interpretations.

Such is the minefield we enter with a book concerning mind and brain. In this book we will be examining aspects of current understanding of brain processes and venturing to distil a model of the mind. Further than this, we wish to consider what it means to seek the highest within us, as the phrase 'human potential' implies. In all this we will draw on the fruits of science but, as already implied, the interpretations are always open to discussion. Such is the challenge of brain science.

Science, then, has its place and, as we shall see, has advanced our ability to specify in detail the particulars of brain processes which we may reasonably correlate with processes of the mind; how activity in the visual cortex at the rear of the brain, for example, underlies the process of seeing. But science has no monopoly on this topic. When it comes to the most human part of ourselves, perhaps logical thinking will always play second fiddle to analogical thinking.

Thus it is that we return to light. And the reverberation of meaning brings creation and knowledge together. 'Let there be light' is not only the central image of creation myths, the spark which mysteriously galvanizes the void into seeds of the formed, but is also the phrase which best epitomizes the nature of mind itself. It is a clarion call to knowledge as the anthropocentric focus of our story of creation, for 'only in the light of consciousness can man know'.[3] And the implication is that the act of knowing recapitulates the act of creation. We can never, of course, know the world objectively as a totally detached observer. We know *our* world, a world we create. Creating and knowing are interlocked, and consciousness may be understood as the common principle shared by them. These three, creativity, the quest for knowledge and consciousness, seem to be the key characteristics of mind.

And then (to continue in the vein of analogical thinking), in the Hebrew Bible version of such world stories, Adam and Eve are cast out of the garden. The human condition is, accordingly, not only one of knowing, but more incisively one of knowing that you know: 'And the eyes of both of them were opened, and they knew they were naked.'

First, then, there is consciousness and the ability to know. Second, there emerges the sense of self, a feeling of separation (the symbol of nakedness emphasizing the new-found realization of boundaries) and reflective awareness. A necessary third inevitably follows: the memory of the loss. A ubiquitous trace of the golden age engenders the 'quest', the imperative to return and challenge the 'revolving, flaming sword which keeps the way of the tree of life'.

Thus is light the origin and en-light-enment the goal of the human mind:

> . . . at the beginning of religious history, we are given the archetype of 'the Shining One' which in almost endless variations is common to all great spiritual traditions. Krishna, Buddha, Moses, Christ, Muhammad, all these were figures of light, their bodies shone, so their disciples assure us, and they were sources of light, on all levels of meaning. . . . When heart and head, feeling, consciousness and intellect unite. . . , then the way is open for the influx of the divine light.[4]

The theme may be traced out in the intricacies of the original Hebrew of the bible.[5] The clothing which God made for Adam and Eve as He cast them out of Eden was of skin (Genesis 3:21). In mystical understanding this is not referring to animal skins as cover but to the actual human bodily skin. That is to say that, prior to this event, Adam and Eve possessed no materiality: they were beings of light. Thus, the Hebrew for light and for skin (*aur*) differ only in the (unsounded) first letter. The word for light begins with *alef*, a letter symbolizing unity. In the word for skin, *alef* is replaced by *ayin*, a letter symbolizing multiplicity. Before the episode with the fruit, Adam and Eve were at one with the transcendent realm they inhabited; this is the meaning of 'Eden'. Subsequent to the episode, the veil of separation descended, and their life in the mundane world began.

Furthermore, the same linguistic root as in the word for 'skin' has the meaning 'to awaken'. Thus, the teaching derived from the Genesis story calls us to awaken from our 'slumber' in the material level of mind in order to re-enter the transcendent sphere.

Such teaching finds its counterpart within psychology in those schools that encourage the individual towards an expansion of the conscious realm of mind in the search for realization of human potential:

> Underlying all rebirth symbolism is the transcendent function. Since this function results in an increase of consciousness (the previous condition augmented by the addition of formerly unconscious contents), the new condition carries more insight, which is symbolized by more light. It is therefore a more enlightened state compared with the relative darkness of the previous state.[6]

For the French thinker Maritain, such a view does not adequately capture the symbolism of light as it relates to the human psyche. For him, every image or idea of which we become aware is a product, in the first place, of the *illuminating intellect* identified with the spiritual unconscious.

> We possess in ourselves the Illuminating Intellect, a spiritual sun ceaselessly radiating, which activates everything in intelligence, and whose light causes all our ideas to arise in us, and whose energy permeates every operation of our mind. And this primal source of light cannot be seen by us; it remains concealed in the unconsciousness of the spirit.[7]

Here we will leave our prologue. The ambivalence of light as symbol of mind is the central ambivalence we find in addressing the question of human potential. Is the light of enlightenment to be identified with the light of reason, growing ever brighter as we become more conscious, or is it to be found by journeying into the unconscious, where the spark of simple being glows more strongly the more we turn away from the complexity of consciousness? This is, in effect, the unstated question of the biblical narrative. Can we not, to adapt a proverb, have our fruit and know it? After all, what is the tree of knowledge for if not to spur humankind on? But, in point of fact, there was never any command not to *touch* it.

A QUESTION OF SCALE

There are three terms which are central to this book. They are *consciousness*, *awareness* and *mind*. Each is familiar to us in everyday parlance and, as such, would seem to require no introduction. On the other hand, each has given rise to a tangled web of definitions, not only meaning different things to different authors, but seeming to imply different things in different times. It is essential, therefore, that the reader should have a clear picture of how I intend to use these terms. This first chapter is directed to that aim, and to the related aim of establishing a framework which will enable us to 'see the wood for the trees' in the survey of brain science that makes up the body of this book. Put simply, we wish to establish what brain science can, and what it cannot, tell us about the mind.

The problem, of course, arises because all three of the above terms refer to facets of private experience. No one can point to a slab of consciousness on the table and describe it accordingly! Indeed, we cannot even witness it in another person. Ultimately, it is an act of faith to assume that anyone other than ourselves is conscious. We infer, on the basis of our own experience, that equivalence of appearance, of expression and of action implies some degree of equivalence of inner experience.

A related problem centres on the intangibility of mind. It was the seeming impossibility of reconciling the 'stuff' of mind with that of physical matter that led Descartes to his famous dualism. For Descartes, the only compatibility between *res extensa* (matter), and *res cogitans* (mind), was achieved by the agency of God. In and of themselves, mind and matter can have no relationship.

Such a position may seem somewhat extreme in the light of contemporary brain science. However, whilst there can be little doubt that studying the brain does cast light on the nature of mind, there persists a mystery when we try to explain the connection. Whichever philosophical position we may adopt, most of us would agree that at some point an extra something, a peculiar quality – be it called consciousness, awareness or simply Being – has to come into the equation. The question is, can this extra quality be a product of the complex machinery of the brain, or is it somehow beyond matter, more of a spiritual quality?

Following Descartes, we can say that thought is the life of the mind. Our survey of brain science will cast light on the mechanisms of thought and related processes in perception, memory and emotion. But again, should we equate mechanism with mind? A machine can perform computations, but in common language we distinguish such computations from thought. When the machinery of the brain computes information, why do the results sometimes enter the conscious mind as thought? For this first chapter, then, it is not how we think, nor even what we think, that is the problem. *That* we think is the problem. How can it be that the workings of an electrochemical machine, the human brain, should be equated with the richness of experience we call consciousness? And, further, is it possible that free will, which is so central to our experience, should be in reality no more than a product of complex biological interactions? It is in these questions that we encounter the mystery of the mind.

In their attempts to unravel this mystery, authors have generally looked to tangible things by which they may begin to explain the nature of consciousness and mind. And it is here that we encounter the question of scale, for there are essentially three kinds of tangible things that have been examined in connection with consciousness, each of which introduces a difference of scale into the discussion. These three are, in order of increasing scale, the machine, the brain and the universe as a whole.[8]

Each of these three foci gives rise to a school of thought. We may designate them the *cybernetic, biological* and *universal* schools. Each one is a world apart from the next, so much so that representatives of each find difficulty in understanding the very foundation of a school of thought other than their own. The fundamental differences in approach are manifest in the representative statements that follow.

> *Cybernetic*: 'We can design our new machines as we wish, and provide them with better ways to keep and examine records of their own activities – and this means that machines are potentially capable of far more consciousness than we are.'[9]
> *Biological*: 'Conscious awareness . . . is interpreted to be a dynamic emergent property of cerebral excitation. As such, conscious experience becomes inseparably tied to the material brain process with all its structural and physiological constraints.'[10]
> *Universal*: 'The external world and consciousness are one and the same thing.'[11]

We have here, then, a hierarchy of belief. Consciousness is variously a property of machines (if sufficiently complex), a property of biological systems (again, the necessary complexity may restrict it to the human brain – but there are differing views on this) or a property of the universe.

Cybernetics, a term coined by Norbert Wiener in 1948, refers to the science of machines as goal-directed and purposive, and is the precursor of the current interest in artificial intelligence. There can be little doubt that a machine that is able to 'reflect' upon its activity, to learn from its mistakes, is deserving of the term 'intelligence'. However, in my opinion it is not appropriate to employ the term 'consciousness' in this machine context, as does Minsky in the above quotation. I would say that consciousness is not a property which can emerge from complexity or from information systems *per se*.

It follows, then, that the consciousness I associate with brain processes is not a function of the brain's complexity alone. The brain is not only a super-complex machine. The obvious next step would be to state that the brain generates consciousness, not simply as a result of its complexity of function, but primarily because it is a biological machine. Thus we arrive at the second level in our hierarchy of approaches.

However, at first sight this ignores the universal position. For if consciousness is to be equated with the 'external world', the computer, if sufficiently complex, should qualify as conscious in a way no different from the brain. After all, they both exist in the real world. It would, of course, be possible to dismiss the universal view, leaving the eminently sensible and straightforward biological viewpoint that brains are conscious because they are both complex (at least in the case of human brains) and alive. Nothing else in the universe would qualify as conscious, and the major question to be considered would be which, if any, other animals possess sufficiently complex brains. Unfortunately I do not believe that the universal view can be so easily dismissed. Let us examine it further.

The view that consciousness or mind is universal is one that shades rapidly into religious belief. Thus the Christian theologian Teilhard de Chardin:

> It is impossible to deny that, deep within ourselves, an 'interior' appears at the heart of beings, as it were seen through a rent. This is enough to ensure that, in one degree or another, this 'interior' should obtrude itself as existing everywhere in nature from all time. Since the stuff of the universe has an inner aspect at one point of itself, there is necessarily a *double aspect to its nature*, that is to say in every region of space and time – in the same way, for instance, as it is granular: *co-extensive with their Without, there is a Within to things.*[12]

Teilhard de Chardin goes on explicitly to identify this universal 'within' with consciousness.

In most traditions of religious and/or philosophical thought where mind is conceived of as a universal phenomenon, it is ultimately identified with the divine. Thus, for example, Spinoza held that mind is one aspect (the other being space) of the only possible substance – God. For Aristotle, human thinking – the life of the mind – is a reflection of the perfect activity of the deity whose 'thinking is a thinking on thinking'.[13]

In the last analysis, we come round to the place of personal experience. The universal view probably has its roots in mystical experience, and the profoundly moving quality of such experiences will, despite criticism of their subjectivity, always give rise to powerful arguments. The view that individual consciousness fades in the face of a transcendent unity characterized by non-differentiated awareness is common to mysticism across all cultures.

> The most important, the central characteristic in which all *fully developed* mystical experiences agree, and which in the last analysis is definitive of them and serves to mark them off from other kinds of experience, is that they involve the apprehension of *an ultimate nonsensuous unity in all things*, a oneness or a One to which neither the senses nor the reason can penetrate. In other words, it entirely transcends our sensory-intellectual consciousness.[14]

Such experiences are reported not only by those who have cultivated some form of spiritual discipline and may be expected to be particularly receptive, but also by many who, unsuspecting, have been taken unawares by such a 'vision' of reality.

> One day as I was walking along Marylebone Road I was suddenly seized with an extraordinary sense of great joy and exaltation as though a marvellous beam of spiritual power had shot through me linking me in rapture with the world, the universe, life with a capital L, and all the beings around me. All delight and power, all things living, all time fused in a brief second.[15]

This is one of many contemporary examples which have been collected by the Religious Experience Research Unit at Oxford. Surveys conducted by the Unit have demonstrated that we are not talking here about a tiny minority of latent 'mystics'. Rather the experience of being in the presence of something greater than oneself is reported by 36 per cent of the British public and is, accordingly, designated 'the common experience'.[16] In America, the proportion of adults reported as having had mystical experiences is 43 per cent.

One reason, then, to uphold the universal view is that it accords with the personal experience of a significant minority. Although it is still a majority who are without such experiences, it may be that the normal operation of mind acts to shield us from the collective base to consciousness. This is certainly the view of the world's major spiritual traditions. Thus, the lack of 'spiritual' experiences in the majority of individuals does not imply that the minority are somehow deluded.

The alternative view is that the experience of being 'at one' with the universe is explicable in psychological terms which have nothing to do with any continuity between the individual and the universe as a whole. Freud, for example, considered that 'oceanic feelings', as he called such experiences, represented nothing more than a regression to the kind of unconscious states experienced as an infant. We reach something of an impasse here, since we are in the realm of interpretation. The meaning of an experience may be one thing to the individual experiencing it, and another thing to the person classifying it. In other words, as far as experience alone is concerned, people will read from it a perspective that best accords with their general scheme of things. On the basis of psychological evidence, then, it is difficult to draw a firm conclusion as to whether we should accept or reject the universal viewpoint.

There is, however, a further reason for serious consideration of the universal view – that it accords with a scheme of reality as revealed by modern physics.

A WORLD IN A GRAIN OF SAND

It is no accident that the individual whose words I selected to represent the universal view above, Schrödinger, is one of the 'fathers' of quantum mechanics. Much has been written on the relationships between the worldview of modern physics and that of mysticism.[17] At the centre of the various parallels that may be drawn lies the realization that our implicit assumptions about physical reality are as illusory according to the physicist, as are those about mental reality according to the mystic. As far as physical reality is concerned,

> The real problem is that we are used to looking at the world simply. We are accustomed to believing that something is there or it is not there. Whether we look at it or not, it is either there or it is not there. Our experience tells us that the physical world is solid, real, and independent of us. Quantum mechanics says, simply, that this is not so.[18]

In other words, the infinite chasm that demarcated mind from matter, at least since Descartes, has been found to be a chimera.

Broadly speaking, there are two 'doors' through which consciousness has been accommodated within the world scheme as revealed by modern physics. These two are the concept of complementarity and the hypothesis of different orders of reality.

Complementarity is the idea introduced by Niels Bohr in the 1920s to account for some seemingly irreconcilable observations concerning the behaviour of light. Light behaves as a set of waves in one experimental situation, but as a train of particles in another. So what exactly is the nature of light? The answer, according to Bohr, and generally confirmed by subsequent studies, is that light has no reality independent of the set-up used to measure it. The wave-like properties and particle-like properties are only in some form of potentiality until the light is observed. This raises some intriguing questions concerning whether light can exist independently of some form of observer in the universe or, indeed, whether we, as observers, could exist independently of light. In Bohr's words, '. . . an independent reality in the ordinary physical sense can be ascribed neither to the phenomena nor to the agencies of observation'.[19]

Complementarity, then, is the concept advanced to describe the relationship between the two states (and subsequent studies demonstrate that the principle holds generally at the quantum level, not just with regard to light). Light is not a wave, nor a particle, nor an amalgam of the two, but may be either, depending on the conditions of observation.

Now the apparent relevance of this to the relationship between the mental and the physical realms is striking and has been explored by several authors, starting with Bohr himself. Thus it has been asserted that the mind and the brain are equivalent to wave-like and particle-like properties in complementary relationship to one another; it all depends whether you are observing from the inside or from the outside. More recently, Deikman has suggested that awareness is the complementary aspect of the organization of the biosystem.

> I would like to suggest that awareness, as distinct from the contents of awareness, is not a special form of sensation, with a particular receptor organ or some other neurological system responsible, nor is it any kind of neural response at all. Rather than being the product of a particular neural circuit, awareness is the *organization* of the

biosystem; that is, awareness *is* the 'complementary' aspect of that organization, its psychological equivalent.[20]

Complementarity is, at least, a useful analogy to the apparent duality of mind and matter. The issue is, however, whether it explains that duality. Further, the principle of complementarity makes appeal to a third entity, the observer, to resolve the relationship between the complementary pair. What is the third entity that resolves the complementarity between organization and awareness in this scheme of Deikman's? This problem may not be capable of simple solutions without an exploration of the second 'door' mentioned above, whereby consciousness has been introduced by physicists into the scheme of things – the notion of different orders of reality.

I stated above that the two properties of light are only in some form of potentiality until the light is observed. Without further consideration of the nature of such potentiality, this hardly helps us comprehend what light essentially is. How does potentiality translate into actuality, and is such potentiality in any sense real? An attempt to answer such questions has been made by proposing that there are two distinct orders of reality. The potentiality of light's properties *is* real, but its reality takes a form of holism which cannot be known directly in the order of reality we encounter through observation.

Such a theory has been formulated by Bohm. He notes three classes of phenomena which are accepted within quantum mechanics but seem to contradict our view of everyday reality. In general, these phenomena go against the common-sense view of events and objects as being separate and interacting via mechanistic laws. He describes these three classes of phenomena as follows.

1. Movement is in general *discontinuous*, in the sense that action is constituted of *indivisible quanta* (implying also that an electron, for example, can go from one state to another, without passing through any states in between).
2. Entities, such as electrons, can show different properties (e.g. particle-like, wave-like, or something in between), depending on the environmental context within which they exist and are subject to observation.
3. Two entities, such as electrons, which initially combine to form a molecule and then separate, show a peculiar non-local relationship, which can best be described as a non-causal connection of elements that are far apart.[21]

In other words, events occur at the microscopic (quantum) level which would make our hair stand on end were they to happen in the macroscopic level of experience. As Davies puts it, '. . . quantum theory demolishes some cherished commonsense concepts about the nature of reality. By blurring the distinction between subject and object, cause and effect, it introduces a strong holistic element into our worldview.'[22] The question is, how to bridge the divide between these two levels, the microscopic and the macroscopic; how can we hold on to our everyday view of things as intrinsically separate in time and space whilst at the same time accepting that under the surface, as it were, all things are apparently interconnected in some sea of holism?

The answer, according to Bohm, is simply to accept that these are, in fact, two separate orders of reality. The underlying order, the sea of holism as I called it, he terms the *implicate order*. It is characterized by 'undivided wholeness'. The second order of reality, which derives from the implicate order, he calls the *explicate order*, 'in which . . . each thing lies only in its own particular region of space (and time) and outside the region belonging to other things'.[23] So the order presented to our senses is secondary to the implicate order which includes, and, Bohm implies, goes beyond, the holism unearthed by quantum mechanics.

The relationship between these two orders Bohm specifies as one of *unfoldment* and *enfoldment*. The explicate order is continually flowing out of the implicate order through unfoldment and, in turn, flowing back through enfoldment. These processes constitute a ceaseless holistic flux which is termed the *holomovement*. It is the fundamental ground of all explicit reality: '. . . the holomovement which is "life implicit" is the ground both of "life explicit" and of "inanimate matter", and this ground is what is primary, self-existent and universal.' 'Our basic proposal was then that *what is* is the holomovement.'

The relevance of Bohm's proposals to the task of unifying the strands of quantum theory remains an open question. Do the peculiarities of the microphysical level become any the less problematic when a separate order of reality is advanced to accommodate them? As a non-physicist I would say that the strength of Bohm's theory lies, first, in its inclusiveness and, second, in its accord with that intuitive world view shared by platonic philosophers, shamans and mystics, in which a reality underscoring the (illusory) reality of the senses is advocated.[24]

My concern here is not with quantum mechanics *per se*, but with the relevance it may bear for our understanding of consciousness. For Bohm, the implicate order is itself the resolution of the divide between consciousness and matter. We have, in effect, a threefold scheme in which mind and matter are two aspects of the explicate order. They are separate, but necessarily linked at the implicate level which becomes the third feature in Bohm's scheme. It is a 'more comprehensive, deeper, and more inward actuality [which is] neither mind nor body but rather a yet higher-dimensional actuality, which is their common ground and which is of a nature beyond both'.[25] Just as the separation between objects, or between waves and particles, disappears in the holomovement at the implicate level, so the distinction between mind and matter is similarly overcome. Thus, 'In the implicate order. . . mind enfolds matter in general and therefore the body in particular. Similarly the body enfolds not only the mind but also in some sense the entire material universe.'

In effect, then, Bohm has fleshed out a view that has been articulated by many – that a common ground lies behind the apparent duality of mind and matter. William James held such a view, using the term 'pure experience' to refer to this common ground or 'primal stuff. . .of which everything is composed'.[26] Jung comes close to Bohm's position in conjecturing a *psychoid* base to the collective unconscious which 'manifests itself as a psychic as well as a physical energetic phenomenon'.[27] And in the world's spiritual traditions the One that gives life to the illusory duality of mind and matter is encountered in a plethora of enigmatic words.[28]

Whatever version of the 'common ground' view we may prefer, and notwithstanding the confusion of terminology (awareness, consciousness, pure experience, energy, inwardness – all seem to have their advocates!), it does present itself as the logical conclusion from the explorations of physicists over recent decades. As the Nobel prize-winning physicist Eugene Wigner puts it:

When the province of physical theory was extended to encompass microscopic phenomena, through the creation of quantum mechanics, the concept of consciousness came to the fore again: it was not possible to formulate the laws of quantum mechanics in a fully consistent way without reference to the consciousness. . . . The very study of the external world led to the conclusion that the content of the consciousness is an ultimate reality.[29]

DEFINING OUR TERMS

In the previous sections we have seen the evidence for the universal view I introduced earlier. Consciousness, it is suggested, is an ultimate reality, a property built in to the universe, perhaps even a factor presaged in the big bang itself.[30] The evidence is drawn from the psychology of spiritual experience and from modern physics. A third, and related, reason for accepting the universal view emphasizes the *simplicity* of consciousness.

This may initially seem strange. After all, we are accustomed to revelling in the sophistication of the human brain and the complexity of its output. For many, in particular proponents of the biological view, consciousness is the pinnacle of that output, and therefore a product of indescribable complexity. As Bloom and Lazerson put it in a recent text, 'The human cortex is probably more intricate in structure and more complex in function than anything else known to us. Its mechanisms . . . are alike in all of us. Yet the operations of these ensembles of neurons creates in each of us a unique consciousness, a self unlike any other.'[31]

This point of view, relating consciousness to the brain's complexity, is to be contrasted with the view expressed by those familiar with so-called 'higher states of consciousness' which emphasizes the simplicity of consciousness:

> Pure consciousness is utterly simple. Meditation makes it possible to reach to this simplicity and hold it. Consciousness resting in itself could be compared to the flame of a candle. Every time a thought or feeling arises, and your consciousness attaches to it, it is as if the flame breaks up and scatters, diminishing the power of that central focus.[32]

It is my belief that such 'pure consciousness' is, as its simplicity suggests, not a product of biological complexity. On the contrary, as has often been suggested,[33] the complexity of the brain tends to insulate us from the reality of pure consciousness surrounding us. As all meditation systems seem to concur, we 'tune in' to pure consciousness by stilling the fruits of the brain's complexity – those thoughts and images that tumble across the screen of the mind.

It therefore follows that attempts to explain consciousness in terms of biological, or indeed informational, systems are doomed to failure because it is, in fact, not generated by such systems. As the universal view suggests, *consciousness is intrinsic to reality and is*

brought into being by the processes inherent in the origin of the universe.
Yes, there is a mystery, but it is not the mystery of the brain. It is
the mystery of creation and of life itself.

In order to avoid further confusion, it is essential for us to realize
that the term 'consciousness' is commonly being used in at least
two different ways. First, it refers to the ground of being, 'pure'
consciousness, which is entirely non-personal. It is in this sense that
the universal view holds consciousness to be a property of reality,
beyond the individual brain.

Second, consciousness refers to a personal experience, 'my'
consciousness and 'your' consciousness. When we use the term
'consciousness' in this second sense, what we are really indicating is
the portion of the mind upon which we reflect, the accessible mind.
In this sense, as the philosopher Hume emphasized, consciousness
is nothing but the contents illumined; thus I may say that I am
conscious of this or that piece of information, or of certain aspects
of my psychological make-up. In the former sense, however, there
can be no contents, for as soon as there is knowledge *of*, there is no
longer pure consciousness. Thus it is that the mystics have spoken
of voiding the mind of specific contents, since pure consciousness
is identified with the goal, or at least a stage towards the goal, to
which mysticism is directed.

In the words of the Christian mystic Eckhart: '. . . when I cease
projecting myself into any image, when no image is represented
any longer in me, and when I cast out of myself and eject whatever
is in me, then I am ready to be transported into the naked being of
God, the pure being of the spirit'.[34] It is surely in this former sense,
'pure being' in Eckhart's terms, that we must understand Teilhard
de Chardin's designation of the 'Within' of things as consciousness.

Now, whatever the merits of the use of the term 'consciousness'
in the former of these two senses, as in 'pure consciousness', it is
probably best, in order to avoid confusion, to avoid it. For in the
post-Freudian age the terms 'conscious' and 'unconscious', used in
the latter of the above senses (that is, accessible versus inaccessible
contents of mind) have entered the common vocabulary.

The point is not simply academic. In discussing the nature of
mind and, in particular, the meaning of human potential, we
will delve quite deeply into issues concerning the conscious and
unconscious realms of mind. It seems to me an unfortunate
consequence of perceptions of Freudian theory that we tend to
think of the unconscious as somehow 'beyond us', almost apart
from us. It is not. In fact, it is almost certainly not one thing

anyway, and to think of it as somehow compartmentalized off is misleading. The crucial factor is not which compartment of the mind is active, but which 'I' within us is doing the observing at a given time. But in this we are anticipating ideas to be discussed in later chapters.

It is vital that we recognize the continuity between so-called conscious and unconscious processes. The continuity comes in their both being 'conscious' in the former of the two senses described above. In a textbook on states of consciousness, Jeffrey expresses the point as follows: 'The Unconscious is not unconscious, only the Conscious is unconscious of what the Unconscious is conscious of'. He is surely correct in this statement, but there has to be something wrong with the terminology when such confusion reigns! Similarly, we commonly use the phrase 'regaining consciousness' to mean waking up or coming out of a coma. Whereas the universal view implies that pure consciousness simply is, always.

In the light of these problems, I propose to refer to the universal phenomenon not as consciousness (as I have so far) but as *Being*. In using this term, I wish to stress its dynamic quality of becoming, over the static fact of existence. I overcome the confusion inherent in Jeffrey's statement, therefore, by stating that Being permeates both the conscious and the unconscious mind.

Now, where Being begins, and ends seems to me an unanswerable question. To return to an issue raised earlier, I cannot envisage that a machine could possess Being; therefore it could not be conscious. In this matter of terminology, convention slides rapidly into belief. My demarcation between humans and machines in this regard is a belief, and I freely admit that the specification of terminology is secondary to that belief. As for the limits of Being, I would have to include the whole of the Biosphere as including this mysterious inner quality. What about inanimate matter in general? Is there Being in a stone? And if a stone, why not a computer? As I said, the question becomes unanswerable.[36]

Central to the discussion in this chapter is the earlier question as to what brain science can and cannot tell us about mind. It is my opinion that brain science is in principle unable to tell us anything about Being. We will not, I feel sure, find it lurking inside specific brain cells, nor in particular brain processes. It is of a different order of reality. But brain science does, as we shall see, inform us of the mechanisms of the human mind. It furnishes many vital pieces of the jigsaw which hint at the ways in which the processes we know only from the inside – perception, memory, emotion and so on – work. And, as we shall discover, it provides a foundation for recognizing the limitations of habitual modes of operation and the potential for growth afforded by alternate strategies of mentation.

Having discussed what I regard as the central mystery, that of Being, I turn now to a consideration of other terms pertaining to the mind. Again, the important point is not the specific meanings of words; that is only convention, and, to some people, my usage may breach convention as they hold it. The important point is the recognition of distinctions between one quality and another. Thus, *awareness* seems to me the closest we can come to experiencing Being. But when we have particular contents to our experience, thoughts, images and so on, it is more appropriate to talk of *consciousness*. I may be conscious of this or that, but if the mind is completely stilled, with no discernible content, there is only awareness. As Deikman put it: 'Upon reflection you will find that thoughts can cease for a brief while, that there can be silence and darkness and the temporary absence of images or memory patterns – any one component of our mental life can disappear, but awareness, itself, remains.'[37]

Whilst Being is universal, I envisage that awareness only comes about with the evolution of a nervous system. In some way (and again, I am here firmly in the speculative realm) the nervous system focuses, or directs, Being. It enables the organism to *experience* its world.

Consciousness refers to representational awareness. The Latin derivation of consciousness implies 'with knowledge', and knowledge is impossible without the ability to represent that which is known. Such representative awareness holds for what we call the unconscious, as well as the conscious, mind. The distinction we make between the two is really a question of accessibility, and is only relevant when the next term is introduced. Where humans differ, I believe, from other creatures is in the representation of *self*. The sense of personal identity, or 'I', becomes the centre of our experience, and whatever is not accessible to 'I' is unconscious. As we will discover in later chapters, each of us in fact harbours a multiplicity of 'I'. The unified sense of 'I' is only a superficial feature of the human mind. This sense of personal identity, or *self-consciousness*, is dependent on the uniquely human faculty of language.

Representation, then, is the key to understanding what consciousness is. There could be no representation without information storage, which brings us, finally, to mind. Memory is indispensable to mind; there has to be some form of memory enabling storage of past forms. This introduces the dimension of time, and I think that a working definition of mind could be advanced as follows. *Mind* refers to the organization of Being over time. Being itself reduces to neither structure nor process, it simply is; but mind ceases to be when its structures (connections in memory) and processes (imagination and thought) themselves cease.

Mind, then, emerges when Being encounters a storage medium, as happens in the brain. However, it would be a mistake to think that the brain is the only such storage medium. A tree, for example, is itself (and, more especially, its DNA) a vessel for storing its 'treeness'. There are those who hold that the very fabric of the universe is itself a storage medium. If that were so, then mind as well as Being would be universal – 'Mind at Large', in Aldous Huxley's famous phrase.

We are, however, moving ahead of ourselves into complex ideas which will require further substantiation. For the present, the framework described above is provided as a basis for a model of mind. In summary, memory gives mind its *structure*, and thought flows as the *process* of mind. Neither one of these exists without the other. Memory effectively includes the flow of thought, as thought includes the structural connections of memory. They are the two necessary poles of Being in its actualization as mind.

2

Perception: Gateway to the Mind

Go, go, go, said the bird: human kind
Cannot bear very much reality.
T. S. Eliot, *Four Quartets*

WHAT'S IN A NAME?

The hallmark of the human mind is undoubtedly its quest for meaning. Meaning, like many of the terms discussed in Chapter 1, is somewhat difficult to pin down. To my way of thinking, it is bound up with consciousness. In a simple sense, any conscious representation of some event could be assigned the status of meaning. Thus the vibration of its web that triggers a spider to catch a fly is a meaningful event to the spider *to the extent that the spider is conscious* in the sense defined in Chapter 1. If we assume that the spider's nervous system includes in some form a representation of those vibrations of its web, then the condition defined in Chapter 1 is met since I defined consciousness as representational awareness.

The foregoing sense of the word 'meaning', however, does not really accord with a more common-sense view. In general, meaning is conveyed when we are *conscious of the intention or significance of some event*. In this sense meaning comes about through reflection on the contents of consciousness. Meaning is the corollary of self-consciousness.

I am inclined to the view that both these senses of the term 'meaning' are valid. The important point as far as my use of the term is concerned is its necessary relation to consciousness. Therefore, just as there is a distinction between consciousness and self-consciousness, there must also be a distinction between the two connotations of meaning as discussed here. These two connotations are perhaps best conveyed by referring to them as *direct meaning* and *reflective meaning*.

Meaning, further, builds towards knowledge. Knowledge takes us beyond the particular to appreciate the patterns of forces which underlie and govern the perceptible in our world. And knowledge it is which fuels the twin paths to human advancement – the urge to power and the drive to self-transcendence.

Thus it is with the story of the first brothers, Cain and Abel. The character of each relates to the derivation of his name: Cain from the Hebrew root *kana*, to acquire, Abel from *hevel*, meaning vapour or breath. These brothers portray, in archetypal language, the two options available to the human mind in its quest to know the world, options which manifest already at the perceptual gateway to the mind.

The first of these two options is the kind of knowledge which involves separation from the object; knowing the object as a 'thing' to be acquired, controlled and manipulated. It involves an active grasping of the object in terms of familiar frames of reference and intended actions. The second kind of knowledge is arrived at by fusion with the object, knowing it from the inside. This involves a more passive reception of the object's qualities which defy analysis along familiar lines. The physicist Eddington well caught the nature of this second form of knowledge by referring to it as *intimate knowledge*. He contrasted this with the other form, which he called *symbolic knowledge*.

Whilst different authors may use differing terms to describe these two styles of knowing the world,[1] there is broad agreement on the distinguishing characteristics. The first mode is dualistic, ego-enhancing, and proceeds through conceptualization; the second is direct and associated with a lowering of ego boundaries – we may actually feel ourselves fusing with the object. Confronted with, for example, a tree, we will normally see it in the conceptual mode. Occasionally, however, it may simply impress itself upon us, moving us as its beauty unfolds. It touches the poetic within us and, if we are inclined to spiritual values, we may verbalize the experience as one of seeing the 'soul' of the tree, or the 'hand of the divine in nature'.[2]

That Cain symbolizes the former of these two modes seems straightforward enough, for the mode is characterized by the motivation to acquire. The world of our senses becomes perceived egocentrically, in other words what is this object *to me*, how can *I* make use of it? As we will see later in this chapter, questions of this kind are being asked all the time in the split second, preconscious processing which leads to perception.

The notion that breath symbolizes the second mode may take further consideration. Breathing epitomizes our possibility of direct, unclouded contact with the world, for there is no separation between the air within and that without. Furthermore, as a focus for awareness in many schools of meditation the breath stills the mind to the point at which the grasping quality of mind falls away, the point where the mind may know itself.

Besides teaching about the continual struggle between these modes within us, the biblical story symbolically intimates how the first mode, having overpowered the second, becomes the means to civilization as we know it. The last-mentioned of Cain's descendants are Jabel, Jubal and Tubal-Cain. As spelt out in Genesis 4: 20–22, these three represent the three pillars on which civilization stands: agriculture, culture and toolmaking respectively. Whilst, clearly, civilization gave immeasurable benefits to developing humankind, the complete submission of the 'way of Abel' was a high price to pay. And therefore, in this language of symbolism, neither Cain nor Abel becomes the ancestral line from which we are descended. The foundation to our mentality was *Seth* (Hebrew root = foundation), because neither of the two extremes is best adapted to the world we inhabit. Whilst the benefits of the acquiring mode are legion, we ignore the inward mode at our peril. The middle way symbolized by Seth offers us potential access to the sense of harmonious integration which can emerge from the appropriate deployment of both modes.

The story is, of course, peculiarly appropriate to the environmental crisis looming upon us today.

GRASPING THE WORLD

The quest for meaning mentioned above is built in at the very forefront of our mind, in the mechanism of perception. The act of perception is itself a quest for meaning, even though we may think of it as the everyday meaning confronting us at every turn. And, as a consequence of this quest, we create the world we perceive, for the meaning is in us, not in the world.

For the newborn infant, however, there is no 'everyday

meaning'. In William James's famous phrase, babies are confronted by the 'blooming, buzzing confusion' coming through their senses. And it is in the powerful motivation of the infant to acquire meaning that we can best observe the dynamic, grasping aspect of perception – the forerunner of the 'Cain mode' as we find it in the adult.

The brain is an active organizer of its world. Observing the infant on the outside, all its movements and sounds can be seen as means to the end of maximizing the stimulation received in return. Dancing limbs are means to maximize the stimulation of touch; vocalizations are triggers to further sensory stimulation, this time from fellow humans around the infant. Chance discoveries, such as the coincidence of nourishment with specific visual and olfactory inputs, become the ground for future perceived meaning.

But it is on the inside that the motivation to maximize sensory input can be best specified. Drawing on the results of many studies of the newborn child's visual system, Haith concludes that the primary goal of visual activity over the first weeks of life is to 'keep the firing rate of visual cortical neurones at a high level'.[3] It seems that normal development depends upon the brain receiving as rich a level of stimulation as possible.

Haith's ideas largely derive from studies on infants' eye movements. The logic of such studies is straightforward: eye movements are indicative of visual attention and therefore can yield information about the strategies by which the newborn child begins to establish visual contact with the world. The general approach in these studies was instigated by Fantz,[4] who employed an experimental arrangement whereby two screens were situated above a baby acting as the subject. Two different pictures were presented, one on each screen, and Fantz simply measured the length of time that the infant looked towards each picture. The picture fixated for the longer duration was presumably the more 'attractive' in some way to the infant. In general, when confronted with a choice between two patterns, one containing more lines (higher contour density) than the other, the pattern with more lines was preferred. With very young infants, the 'meaning' of the picture seemed to have little or no impact; it was the relative contour density that determined their picture preference.

More detailed studies of eye movements by Haith and others

have demonstrated that the newborn child's eyes:

1. are active in the dark, scanning the visual field in a controlled way;
2. scan more broadly if the field is light but blank (no contours);
3. scan narrowly in the presence of a contour, engaging in movements that repeatedly cross the contour.

In summary, the infant's eye movements appear to be programmed to (i) locate contours and (ii) cross them. Such patterns of eye movements are observed with infants as young as two days old.

The efficacy of this 'rule' of operation for the developing infant should be clear. The contours in the visual field define the presence of objects; they are the information-giving aspects of the visual world. Thus the rules by which the infant's eyes look are tailor-made to maximize exposure of the developing infant's maturing visual system to the most informative features of the world.

When infants' eyes move towards contours and subsequently explore those contours by repeated crossings, it is not, however, the infants' recognition of the contours, or their meaning, that motivates them. How would the newborn child 'know' what to look for? These movements are, according to Haith, simply a direct consequence of the brain's in-built motivation to seek stimulation. It is a profound biological imperative that is at work here. The brain demands to be fed with maximal stimulation. The infant, then, is born not with any ability to make sense of the world, but with a powerful motivation to seek out the *means* to make sense of the world. Here we may observe the origins of the quest for meaning.

The arguments in support of this claim depend on an understanding of the physiology of the visual cortex. In brief, as indicated in figure 2.1, most cells in the visual cortex respond maximally to contours and their responses are strongest when the cell is first stimulated and when the stimulus disappears.[5] In addition, some cells only respond when contours are *moving* across the region of the visual field to which they are sensitive. Armed with this information, we can explain the eye movement data once we accept Haith's central assumption that the brain demands maximal stimulation. Quite simply, moving the eyes to cross contours repeatedly will generate more brain activity than simply keeping the eyes fixed on or around a contour.

These 'rules' by which the baby's visual system operates can give us an insight into more global concerns with regard to

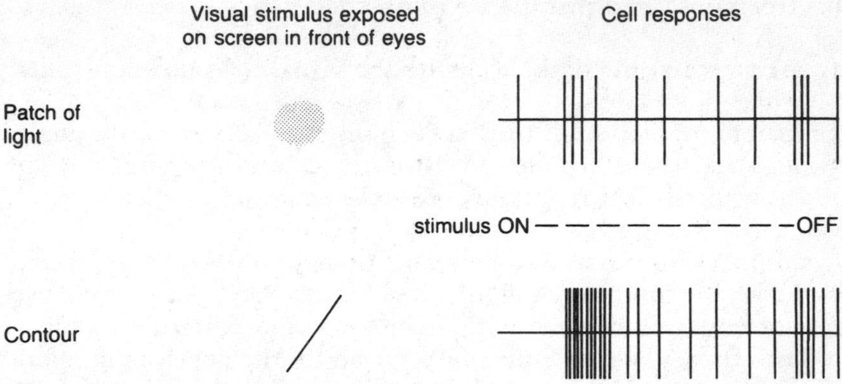

Figure 2.1: Responses of a neurone in the visual cortex. The degree of the cell's activation is reflected in the frequency of spikes recorded. Although a response is seen to a patch of light, the response is greater to a contour.

human potential. In effect, these rules epitomize the urge to exploration which characterizes the human mind. The baby's eyes are never stationary, passively awaiting stimulation. The system is spontaneously active, seeking out the means maximally to stimulate the brain. The baby's eyes are, in effect, merely tools subservient to the infant brain's primary quest, which is to be kept active. As the infant grows into first a child and then an adult the quest may change in emphasis, becoming more explicitly a quest for meaning. But in principle the means are the same: to seek out that which enriches the individual's knowledge of their self and their world. For the infant's visual system this is achieved via the direct biological imperative we have described – that the brain demands maximum activity in a simple quantitative sense. For the adult, however, it is the bounds of their world, their sense of scale, that exploration seeks to extend. And this depends not only on the quantity of the input (in terms of ideas as well as perceptions) but on the state of the individual; their state of consciousness and their ability to detach from habitual patterns of seeing and responding. Just as the infant instinctively explores with no understanding of an end result in store, so too as adults it is the search that matters. The real reward, as many an inventor or explorer can testify, comes not primarily in the discovery but in the search itself. 'We shall not cease from exploration . . .', says T. S. Eliot, for if we do, surely, we will have abandoned what it is to be human.

In the infant, then, the dynamic nature of the perceptual process is manifest by the brain, as it were, grasping for stimulation.

What about the adult? The answer is that the brain still grasps for stimulation, but it is no longer the immediate activation of the visual cortex that is important. Rather, it is in the higher stages of perceptual processing, stages in which the brain actively creates representations of the world it inhabits, that the brain grasps for meaning.

The evidence for the above assertion is twofold. First, we can point to the consequences of denying the brain its normal sensory input, so-called sensory deprivation studies. Second, we can draw on studies of the kind of errors that the perceptual system makes when something goes wrong, due either to brain damage or to those quirks of the sensory input that we call illusions.

The interest in sensory deprivation began in the 1950s due to concern over the ways in which prisoners of the Chinese during the Korean War were 'brainwashed'. It seemed that isolating an individual from normal contact with the world via the senses played a part in generating a state in which the mind was malleable and susceptible to ideas that would normally be strongly resisted. Sensory deprivation studies were, then, an attempt to investigate such mental changes in a controlled fashion.

These studies deprive the individual of normal input by reducing the presence of dynamic, patterned stimulation at the senses. Sound is obscured by white noise (a meaningless mixture of all frequencies of sound), sight by using a *ganzfeld* (a uniform white field in front of the eyes), touch by cotton muffs and so on. A general observation in these studies is that the subject experiences visual disturbances. Heron, Doane and Scott reported that subjects hallucinated after one day of deprivation.[6] The hallucinations typically started simple in form (rows of dots, mosaics and so on), later becoming more complex (scenery, people, bizarre architecture and the like).

Perhaps the most dramatic technique was the water tank method developed by Lilly and Shurley. Subjects were immersed in a water tank at uniform temperature, blindfold, and with auditory input restricted on account of materials around the tank to inhibit vibration. Approximately a third of these subjects reported hallucinations, commencing within three hours of immersion. Examples ranged from hearing non-existent dogs barking to seeing 'in the darkness before me a field of golden toadstools, with the sunlight brightly reflected from the stem of one'.[7]

There is some debate as to whether these reports reflect actual hallucinations or simply a rise in imagery/daydreaming activity in the subject. The question is one of definitions and need not unduly concern us here. Certainly, as concluded in a review by Reed, 'there is ample and consistent evidence that [sensory deprivation] subjects experience after-images, misperceptions, illusions, daydreaming, fantasizing and imagery of various types'.[8] It seems, then, that when its input is impoverished the brain compensates by stepping up its construction of meaning, this meaning being experienced by the subject perhaps as hallucination, but more generally as imagery.

Later we shall be considering imagery in some detail. Realization of human potential does seem to involve conscious and controlled exploration of imagery. For the moment, let us conclude that everyday perception involves a reconstruction of meaning. There seem to be two phases to the process of perception. First, the sensory input is analysed and broken down into its basic features. Second, on the basis of these features, the brain creates a representation of the input. The representation embodies the sensory input's meaning and our relationship to it. The place of sensory deprivation research is to draw our attention to the nature of the balance between these two stages, by indicating that when the input side is inhibited the creative side increases by way of compensation. The brain resists a vacuum.

A WORLD OF ILLUSION

Any difficulty in understanding the process of perception is surely attributable to the fact that we can be directly conscious only of the end result. We cannot access those component processes that must be going on within the many brain regions devoted to perception. Introspectively, it seems that perception is an immediate and faithful translation of the world out there. That it is not so simple a process becomes apparent when we reflect upon the limitations of our perceptual system and the nature of illusion.

The drive to perceive is, as implied in the previous section, the drive to construct a meaningful world. This is a drive that is central to the mind's very existence and extends beyond perception into all our thinking and general psychological balance. In general, meaning emerges when data are brought together and found to constitute a whole. The data find their place within a theory that is constructed to explain them. So it is with perception. The data – raw packets of energy falling on our various senses – become incorporated within a constructed image of the world.

General support for this perspective comes from the kinds of perceptual mistakes our brains make when the signals incoming from the senses are at all unclear (faint sounds in a noisy background, or dim objects at dusk, for example). We have all had experiences of the kind that Shakespeare describes in *A Midsummer Night's Dream*:

> Or in the night, imagining some fear
> How easy is a bush supposed a bear.

The raw sensory data are accommodated within a 'theory', in this case a theory which takes account of our fear of the dark. The perceptual image is thus an interpretation imposed on sensory data. In the split second that it takes for sensory input to reach consciousness, that input is transformed according to our quest for meaning.

Whilst we have all heard that 'seeing is believing', the psychology of perception should persuade us that believing may in fact condition seeing. The distinction between thinking and perceiving is not so great as we imagine. The flexibility we allow ourselves in thought determines how open we may be in our perceptions. Prejudice in thought, on the other hand, may become entrenched in a prejudiced vision; we may actually perceive the object of our prejudice in a negative light. The seeds of a vicious cycle are thus laid.

The history of science reveals many instances of misperceptions attributable to preconceived ideas, such as this example from the development of brain science.[9] Towards the end of the seventeenth century three individuals turned the power of the recently discovered miscroscope on the cortex of the brain to discern its composition. Malphighi (1628–94) considered the cortex to be comprised of 'glands'; Ruysch (1638–1731) thought it was made up of blood vessels; while Leeuwenhoek (1632–1723) settled for 'globules'. All three may be considered reasonable descriptions when we remember that the discovery of the electro-chemical nature of the neurone was some two centuries away. However, the discrepancies between their interpretations testify to the weakness of the visual evidence as they undoubtedly saw it through their primitive microscopes.

The common base to their observations was the accepted doctrine of their day that the cortex secreted 'animal spirits'. What they saw under the microscope was as much due to their belief in this doctrine as it was to the magnified brain structure. As we have implied, 'believing is seeing'! Thus, glands and blood vessels were known to be involved in secretion, and globules contain the secretions themselves. The evidence for 'animal spirits' was, as far as they were concerned, staring them in the face.

Our understanding of perception has been advanced by the study of visual illusions. Far from relaying a faithful translation of the input, each stage in the visual pathway modifies the signals it passes on. These modifications are normally an aid in subsequent interpretation of the signals. Illusions ensue when the modifications become inappropriate due to the artificiality of the picture we are looking at. The importance of illusions, then, is to draw our attention to the ways in which incoming signals are processed within the act of perception. Aspects of the perceptual process of which we are normally unaware may become known by their effects in illusions.

The illusion depicted in figure 2.2a, for example, draws our attention to the kinds of processes occuring in the visual cortex at the back of the brain. It is evidently the presence of the crossing lines which causes the parallel lines to appear oriented at an angle to each other. But why? In the visual cortex specialized cells respond to contours at specific orientations. One cell responds maximally to a line at a given orientation, a different cell to a line at a different orientation. These cells are arranged so that adjacent cells in the cortex respond maximally to lines with adjacent orientations – one, say, to 90 degrees, the next to 91 degrees, and so on through the full 360 degrees. The illusion comes about because adjacent cells, or groups of cells, mutually inhibit one another. In effect, the responses to the crossing lines cause those to the parallel lines to become skewed (see figure 2.2b). The point is that these inhibitory effects occur all the time in an advantageous way by sharpening up the cortex's ability to differentiate between one orientation and the next. Our visual system would be less efficient without such automatic processes. Yet these processes are not 'faithfully translating' the retinal image; they operate on the image in order to facilitate the search for meaning, which is the primary goal of the system.

The detection of the orientation of contours is just one of the many analytical processes carried out in the visual cortex. These analytical processes are referred to as *feature detection*. Specific groups of cells are set to respond when a particular feature is present in the visual input. Thus, for example, a cell which functions as a 'colour' detector is tuned to respond to specific

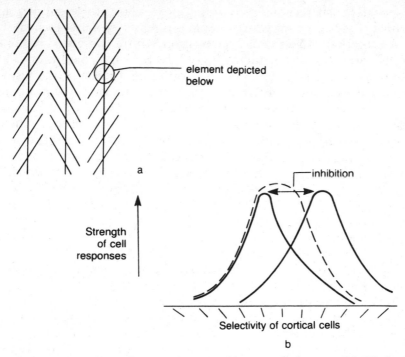

Figure 2.2a: The Zöllner Illusion. The vertical lines are, in fact, parallel. The basic element of the illusion comprises the cross-over of two lines as in the ringed section. The angle at which they intersect produces inhibition between cortical orientation-detecting cells, as depicted in figure 2.2b. In figure 2.2b the dotted plot represents the responses we would expect if the vertical line were being viewed without any crossing line. The solid plot depicts the actual responses to both lines, taking the inhibitory effects into account. The overall effect is that the vertical line gives rise to maximum output from cells whose preferred response is slightly off vertical.

wavelengths of light. One cell may be triggered by red light, another by blue, and so on. Furthermore, these feature-detecting cells are activated only when their feature is present in a precise area of the visual field. When we realize how many millions of such cells make up the visual cortex, each with a specific area and specific feature to which it responds, we can begin to envisage the way in which the brain builds up a kind of mosaic description of the visual scene from moment to moment.

Such feature detection is an essentially passive process. If the appropriate trigger feature is present in the appropriate position in the visual field, then the neurone fires – a simple, all-or-none response. Such responses continue even when, for example, an animal is asleep or anaesthetized (assuming its eyes are opened).

A remarkable degree of organization within the visual regions of the brain has been increasingly revealed by anatomical and physiological means. For example, differing aspects of the visual input are analysed in different regions: orientation of contours in one, directions of movement in another, colour in a third,[10] facial features in a fourth.[11] At the neuronal level, the neurones which respond to specific features of the visual input are arranged in a precise, systematic fashion, so that columns of cells are found all having the identical orientation of lines as their trigger stimulus.[12] We can begin to understand how the visual input is broken down and how, on account of the highly ordered arrangement in the visual cortex, its piecemeal analysis via this process of feature detection proceeds. To use computer terminology, the subroutines of visual analysis have precise addresses. What we do not yet understand, however, is how the brain puts it all together again, how the brain reintegrates the whole.

Such reintegration is surely the stage of the perceptual process in which the creative construction of meaning discussed above comes about. Whilst precise detail of the brain mechanisms involved eludes us for the time being, we can nevertheless usefully discuss this constructive stage of perception in more psychological terms.

The point may be illustrated by reference to the famous Müller-Lyer illusion (figure 2.3a). Simple as this illusion seems, it is generally agreed that there is more than one factor involved. Known physiological mechanisms may account for some of the misperception of the lengths of the vertical lines. Such mechanisms involve retinal and cortical processes including the kind of inhibition mentioned above. However, studies have shown that some 60 per cent of the effect cannot be accounted for in these terms.[13] At our present level of understanding we cannot specify the brain processes responsible for the full effect of this illusion. What we can do is explain it in terms more cognitive than physiological.

One of several cognitive approaches is that of Gregory, who has argued that the misperception is explicable in terms of 'inappropriate constancy scaling'.[14] He suggests that in the act of perceiving the figure we interpret it in relation to our experience with perspective. Such experience holds that objects do not really shrink in size as their distance from us increases, even though their image size on the retina does become smaller. Consequently, a

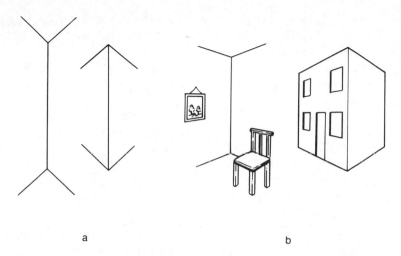

a   b

Figure 2.3a: The Müller-Lyer Illusion. The two vertical lines are, in fact, the same length. The 'arrow heads' induce an illusion of extent.
Figure 2.3b: An illustration of the way in which the line elements of the illusion figure may relate to the orientation of contours in a real scene projected in two dimensions. In this situation the contours depict perspective.

compensation for perspective size changes is included in normal perception. This size compensation is designated *constancy scaling*, and results in more distant objects becoming relatively stretched in size in the act of perception (figure 2.4). In the case of the Müller-Lyer figure, then, the configuration of line elements cues the system to the presence of perspective, and scaling automatically ensues so that the apparently more distant shaft of the outgoing figure is stretched in size. As stated earlier, we are only conscious of the output; we have no access to the perspective and scaling operations hypothesized to be occurring.

A second illustration may clarify the point. The full moon is perceived as being considerably larger on the horizon than when it is high in the sky. (Should you doubt this assertion, then check it out for yourself next time absence of cloud cover permits. It is a striking effect!) The difference is not one of objective size, but largely concerns the context within which the moon is perceived. When on the horizon, it is perceived in the context of the objects in the scene leading to the horizon; there are ample cues to perspective. Our perceptual system

Figure 2.4: The effects of constancy scaling. The second figure is the same size in both illustrations. The disproportionate appearance is attributable to the scaling process, which 'stretches' the size of the more distant figure in the first illustration. This scaling process evidently depends upon the perspective features from which the figure has been detached in the second illustration.

assumes the moon to be in the plane of the distant horizon and stretches its size according to the principle enunciated above. When, on the other hand, the moon is high in the sky, the absence of progressive cues to distance means that the scaling mechanism is not engaged and we perceive a smaller moon.

What emerges from both examples is the way in which interpretation follows on the heels of visual analysis. In the case of the Müller-Lyer illusion, analysis of the lines and their orientations *automatically* prompts interpretation in relation to prior experience with perspective. But we are not conscious of the perspective cued by the lines; we see the figure as being perfectly flat. In other words, we perceive a compromise between what we may think of as two stages of the perceptual process. The first stage comprises feature analysis of lines actually present, and the second involves constructing an image which somehow fits that analysis. The drive to perceive meaning is bound up with the second of these two stages, and, as we shall see, takes us into a consideration of memory. For the constructed image embodies our split-second interpretation of the sensory input, which in turn derives from information stored as a result of previous experience. Memory is thus the cornerstone of perception.

As a final illustration, consider figure 2.5. Cortical analysers, being passive in the sense described above, cannot respond to what is not there on the page before your eyes. The contour of the upper triangle (which we clearly see), is therefore only a product of the constructive process. The contour is included within the perceived image because the interpretation – that the figure shows two superimposed triangles – fits. Evidently the sensory data are interpreted as depicting two triangles, and consequently the necessary contours are constructed. We are back at the point that 'believing is seeing'. And perception is a gateway to the mind not only in the literal sense that it comes first, but also in the metaphorical sense that it becomes a microcosm to the nature of mind. All too easily we accept what 'fits', both about the world around us and about ourselves, and our quest for meaning ceases.

Of course, the rigidity implied by all this cannot be the whole story, otherwise we could never learn to perceive anything new. Whilst it is correct to state that perception tends to be a conservative process, fitting incoming stimuli into pre-established pigeonholes as they are analysed, we are nevertheless able to stretch our perceptual repertoire. Thus, for example, doctors not only learn what X-ray or CAT scan images mean, but also begin to see the images themselves in ways which are more organized. The learnt interpretation becomes incorporated

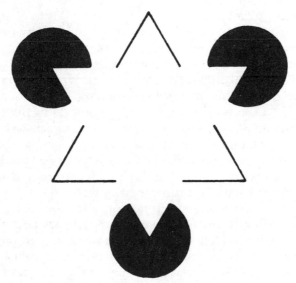

Figure 2.5: Kanizsa's Triangle. The figure gives rise to enhanced brightness and illusory contours.

in the perceptual process, giving rise to a more efficient system.

Such perceptual learning depends on active exploration. In a series of studies, Held[15] demonstrated that perceptual learning does not take place if we remain passive. He studied our ability to adapt to a distortion of the visual input brought about by wearing prisms. The prisms were arranged in such a way that images entering the eyes were displaced horizontally. The question at issue was whether the subjects would learn to orient themselves correctly to the world around them – whether they could overcome the prismatic displacement.

In one study, two groups of subjects were given different conditions whilst wearing the prisms. One group went for a walk on an outside path; subjects in the other group were taken for a walk on the same path in a wheelchair. Thus, whilst both groups would see similar things, the groups differed in the extent to which the visual images coming through the subjects' eyes would be related to their own movements. The first group were active, their own movements dictating what they would see. The second group were passive; what they would see depended not on their own movements, but on the direction in which the helper pushed the wheelchair. Results indicated a difference between the two groups in their degree of adaptation to the distortion induced by the prisms. The active group showed greater adaptation than did the passive group.

Such a result seems hardly surprising. It is obvious simply from watching developing children that they build up their knowledge of the world, at the perceptual as well as at the intellectual level, through active involvement. Play is not merely an amusing distraction, it enables the infant to become an active manipulator of the world. Infants place objects in their mouths, or watch intently as they move them around, always bridging across sensory and motor modalities, for that is what seems to lie at the root of the enjoyment of play. Children derive pleasure from extending their world view. And each such extension is insistently tested out in the rough and tumble of action.

But is such overtly active interaction with the world the only path to human development? Have we not left out of our discussion the 'way of Abel'? That effective manipulative conquest of the world grows out of childhood play is certainly the case. But is there not another kind of play, the play of the imagination (also a development of childhood play), which enables us all to embrace a richer adaptation to our world?

THE WAY OF ABEL

> The purpose of rhythm, it has always seemed to me, is to prolong the moment of contemplation, the moment when we are both asleep and awake, which is the one moment of creation, by hushing us with an alluring monotony, while it holds us waking by variety, to keep us in that state of perhaps real trance, in which the mind liberated from the pressure of the will is unfolded in symbols.[16]

In the prolonged 'moment of contemplation' we move from the grasping mode I associated earlier with Cain to the more direct, receptive mode associated with Abel. The rhythm which Yeats, in the above quotation, views as central to contemplation, surrounds us at every turn. We are creatures of rhythm and we live in a world dominated by rhythm. We may slip into a contemplative trance by following the rhythm of our own breath, or perhaps the rhythm of ripples on a lake. To be effective, a hypnotist must cultivate vocal rhythm. Indeed, the response to rhythm is amongst our most primitive instincts. The rhythm may be that of a mantra, pulsing into the depths of our mind, or of prayer, or indeed of a dance. It is, above all, the rhythm of poetry for, as mentioned earlier, it is the poetic within us that responds to the moment of contemplation.

> Thus, when it comes to poetry, we must admit that in the spiritual unconscious of the intellect, at the single root of the soul's powers, there is, apart from the process which tends to knowledge by abstract ideas, something which is preconceptual or nonconceptual and nevertheless in a state of definite intellectual actuation. . . . such a thing is knowledge in act, but nonconceptual knowledge.[17]

I shall argue that the moment of contemplation is the moment of perception prolonged in a stage that normally precedes the final conscious percept. In other words, the moment of contemplation brings about an awareness of normally preconscious material.

As has been said, the meaning we perceive in the world is the meaning extracted from stored representations. A crucial stage of the perceptual process involves a preconscious search of these representations to locate that which most closely fits the current sensory input. The final stage amounts to a limitation of the possibilities inherent in the input when the major representation is matched to the input. All other accessed representations are normally inhibited as we become conscious of the particular object. Thus, for example, if looking at a cat, the brain accesses stored images of associated items – other breeds, perhaps other animals, or symbolic associations such as images of a sensual nature, and so on. But all this is attenuated, even before we could become conscious of the variety of such images, when the brain 'locks on' to the correct image. We see the cat for what it is – or, rather, for what it means to us – in an apparently effortless moment. Some insight into the complexity of this process can be obtained when we are confronted with a situation in which the brain is unable immediately to lock on to the correct percept. For example, when peering at some unknown form, such as a clump of leaves at dusk, we may 'see' a variety of possibilities in succession. It appears perhaps as a bird, or a mouse, or even something more sinister, before becoming fixed in our mind for what it actually is. Further evidence for this notion of a preconscious search of representations will be discussed later in connection with subliminal perception.

Contemplation, it seems to me, retraces the path of this preconscious search. Quite simply, during the moment of contemplation the inhibition of competing representations is suspended as we become conscious of material brought forward by this search through the memory store.

It is worth noting at this juncture that the imagery generated through contemplation offers the opportunity to explore the structure of memory itself. The structure of memory embodies not only the fluidity in objects' meanings (as manifest, for example, through metaphor) but also the fluidity of *our own meaning to ourselves*, since the organization of our memory is very much the organization of our personality. The way we react in a given situation, for example, is largely a product of the evaluation attached to the memory images preconsciously activated by the situation. We will see in later chapters that the key to realization of human potential is, as recognized in ancient times, knowledge of self. By consciously exploring the form taken by our imagery generated during contemplative or meditative states we can expand our identity, becoming conscious of memory structures which had previously lain outside our conscious grasp.

In the case of outwardly directed contemplation, what we experience as direct, or intimate, knowledge of the external object derives from internally generated imagery which may exaggerate the object's qualities and our relationship to it. Readers could explore this point for themselves simply by contemplating an object and, subsequently, examining the nature of the imagery that occurred. Deikman conducted a study of these phenomena.[18] He recorded the perceptual distortions experienced by subjects during 'experimental meditation', in which subjects were instructed to contemplate a blue vase for a prolonged period. Subjects saw the vase as more vivid or 'luminous', or they became aware of additional features: 'I began to feel this light going back and forth', reported one subject. Others reported the vase moving with a life of its own, and yet others felt themselves merging with the vase.

There is, then, no great mystery surrounding intimate knowledge. The intimacy, as it were of knowing the object from the inside, is not set apart from the normal processes that enliven perception in all our minds. The 'inside' is not the inside of the object out there. Rather, it is the inside of our minds, and the freshness of vision possible at such times arises through the sense that there is always more to the object than appears to exist in the present moment. The associative process is endless, and, if followed to a hypothetical, absolute, end would result in all things merging together in a kind of primordial idea. As Blake expressed it, 'If the doors of perception were cleansed, everything would appear to man as it is, infinite.'

We arrive at the question of reality orientation. In everyday perception, in the grasping mode, the richness of associations is held at bay as we see the object for what it immediately means to us. We assume that to be its reality. The mysticism of Blake, on the other hand, derives from the view that the object's reality lies in its totality which emerges only with its deeper fusion with everything else. Perhaps, adopting the notion that all things are connected in the implicate order (as discussed in Chapter I), we could go along with Blake. Since our consciousness also is founded in the implicate order, contemplation would imply retracing our connection to things. In the implicate order we and the object are, indeed, one. Imagery would then be the form that our mind places on such union as it unfolds into the explicate domain.

The focus of the reality question concerns the nature of memory. It is axiomatic in what has already been said that there could be no perception without memory. We generally think that the objects we perceive are real and that memory involves merely secondary representations of those objects. But since we can only ever know objects via their representations, it is impossible to distinguish objective reality from the 'reality' of memory. This leads us towards the philosophical viewpoint of Plato – that, fundamentally, reality comprises the ideal forms of objects. The question is whether memory is only a personal matter or whether memory constitutes some kind of transcendent reality. If the latter, then objects have their ultimate reality in this transcendent sphere in which the reverberation of what we recognize as associations takes place. The real object *is* its meaning in some kind of collective memory, or mind. These are complex issues to which we shall return. Let us note for the time being that, whilst many associations are personal and may be considered trivial, some take on larger dimensions and constitute *symbols*. Hence Yeats's reference to the mind unfolding in symbols. We may not all be poets, but we all are capable of recognizing the power of symbols. It is certainly not an uncommon experience to be moved by the shift in scale that the symbol works in our mind.

Contemplation, then, detaches us from the automatic function of mind which normally limits perception to our immediate needs in the world. When imagery takes the mind's centre stage – 'in that state of perhaps real trance', as Yeats put it – material that immediately 'fits', be it about ourselves or about objects around us, may be placed on hold and new possibilities explored. It enables us to stretch the yardstick by which we measure the world. It is important to realize that our orientation to reality is not as rigid as we might generally think.

In his *A Defence of Poetry*, Shelley captures the point with characteristic precision: 'Poetry defeats the curse which binds us to be subjected to the accident of surrounding impressions. . . . It creates anew the universe, after it has been annihilated in our minds by the recurrence of impressions blunted by reiteration.'[19]

The creativity of perception is the same creativity as we will meet elsewhere in the context of understanding human potential. In the passage already cited on page 35, Maritain writes of 'the spiritual unconscious of the intellect . . . the single root of the soul's powers'. Whether or not we embrace such overtly religious terms, we find more and more evidence for the notion that the basic principle of the psyche is the creative imagination (see Chapter 8). Be it in the construction of images to match with current sensory input in the moment of perception, or in the mindplay we call dreams, or, indeed, in the musings of the creative artist, it is in the preconscious mind that creativity unfolds. And that is where we must look to investigate our full potential.

IMAGERY AND PERCEPTION

The interactions between imagery and perception, explored in the previous section, may be placed on a firmer foundation by reference to evidence that imagery shares brain mechanisms with perception. Such evidence would seem to bear out the proposal that the imagery ensuing from contemplation relates to the normally automatic, preconscious search of images that takes place during perception. I will examine the evidence in this section.

Segal[20] conducted some experiments to confirm an early observation by Perky in 1910 that, under appropriate conditions, subjects are unable to distinguish between images that are generated from within (imagery or visualization) and images derived from outside (perception). Segal asked subjects to visualize a given scene or object. On half of the occasions a simple coloured geometric design was projected, around the threshold for recognition, on a screen in front of the subject. The result was that a significant number of subjects' visualizations included assimilations from the projected image. For example, when instructed to visualize a packet of cigarettes several subjects reported visualizing a menthol brand when the projected image was of a green square. When there was no accompanying projected image, such brands were never reported in subjects' imagery. Similarly, when asked to visualize a bicycle with an accompanying projected design consisting of nine red dots, the visualized image was of a bicycle covered with rust spots.

The key issue was whether subjects would fail to realize the external, 'objective', derivation of some of their imagery, as had been the case in Perky's study. Although the results were not so clear-cut as Perky's, they did support the same conclusion – that externally derived images may be confused with images which are purely internal in origin. At least in the early stages of each trial, subjects whose imagery clearly displayed evidence of assimilation from the external image believed their imagery to be coming purely from within their mind's eye.

Segal reinforced this conclusion by demonstrating that the threshold for perceiving an image from the outside is raised when the subject is visualizing an equivalent image. The implication from these studies is that visualization is tying up some of the mechanisms involved in normal, externally directed perception.[21]

Such an implication is, of course, fully consistent with my earlier emphasis on the constructive nature of perception:

> . . . for the sensory input does not depict an external stimulus, it merely gives clues out of which the observer constructs a personal experience. Sensory input is always present, and whether a conscious subjective image approximates an external stimulus and so is called a 'perception' or fails to match any consensually valid external stimulus and so is called an 'image' or 'hallucination', the process involved in both experiences is similar. Both the 'perceptual' experience and the 'imagery' experience are in fact constructions.[22]

More recently, both Shepard and Finke have produced further evidence of a psychological nature for the involvement of visual mechanisms in imagery.[23] Finke's work is noteworthy in our present context since it extends the observations discussed earlier (page 34) concerning perceptual adaptation to the distortions induced by wearing prisms. As we noted, Held demonstrated that subjects must explore their visual circumstances actively for any adaptation to come about. Finke's study demonstrated that adaptation may also be facilitated by imagery. In the sense we are considering, then, exploration through imagery can be just as effective in influencing the visual system as is active exploration through physical movement.

To my mind, the strongest evidence for establishing a connection between imagery and perception derives from studies examining the activity of the brain directly. Farah[24] points to three classes of relevant observations. First, studies of regional cerebral blood flow have shown that, when a subject is engaged in a visualization task, the supply of blood to the rear of the brain (where the visual areas are situated) is increased by comparison with the resting state. Since it is known that blood flow to a region of the brain increases in proportion to the region's activity level, it appears that visualization activates specifically the visual areas of the brain, the very areas active during normal visual perception.

The second class of observations is electrophysiological. When a visual stimulus (such as a letter) is repeatedly flashed to a subject, we can record a pattern of electrical activity from the scalp which embodies the brain's response to the stimulus. Such a pattern is called an event related potential (ERP). ERPs have proved invaluable in establishing which parts of the brain are involved, and how they are involved, in the brain's perceptual activity. Analysing the differences between ERPs when subjects were, or were not, engaged in concurrent imagery indicated an effect of imagery in the ERP localized over the visual cortex at the rear of the head. Again, imagery was demonstrated to share mechanisms with visual perception.

Finally, the effects of localized brain injury (due, for instance, to strokes) also point to the shared mechanisms of imagery and perception. In cases where damage has given rise to specific perceptual deficits, the patient generally loses the ability to generate imagery related to the lost perceptual ability. In one case, for example, a patient had sustained brain damage which gave rise to a rather bizarre perceptual problem: he was generally able to recognize non-living things, but had great difficulty in recognizing living things. The same pattern of loss was evident in the patient's imagery abilities. On testing these, recall of non-living things was significantly higher than was recall of living things. A second example concerns brain damage resulting in the loss of ability to recognize faces. This is a quite specific disorder, clinically known as *prosopagnosia*, and patients may retain the ability to perceive other objects with very little impairment. Again, testing for imagery reveals specific impairment in imagery involving faces compared to imagery of other objects.

Another example may be culled from the rather bizarre syndrome known as *neglect*. This refers to a condition characterized by the patient's neglect of one half (usually the left half) of visual space. Such patients deny the presence of objects, even their own limbs, on the left side. If asked to copy a picture, a patient may, for example, produce a drawing which faithfully reproduces the right half of the target picture but completely leaves out the left. The patient regards the task as completed and shows no awareness of the missing section. These patients are not 'blind' to the left side in any simple sense. What seems to be happening, according to Bisiach,[25] is that they have difficulty in representing the left half of space. It is a central impairment involving brain processes concerned with attention, not a peripheral impairment.

Bisiach and his colleagues asked neglect patients to visualize themselves at one end of a famous piazza familiar to them. They were asked to describe the buildings around the piazza. The patients performed quite well with buildings to the right of the piazza, but omitted those to the left. Thus the neglect apparent in perceptual tasks applied also to imagined scenes. Again, some degree of equivalence between imagery and perception was evident.

From all these examples it would be difficult to contend with the conclusion that visual perception and imagery are directly inter-related in terms of their underlying brain mechanisms. This conclusion lends strong support to my earlier discussion of contemplation. As imagery relating to some particular object or scene unfolds in our mind's eye, it is the substructure of perception that is being uncovered. Armed with this evidence, I am now in a position to describe more fully the model of perception hinted at in the previous section.

MODELLING THE MIND

The history of psychology is very much the history of models of the mind. We have the Freudian model, the Jungian model, a whole host of cognitive models, and so on. It should be apparent from our discussion so far that the mind operates very much by building models. The act of perception is itself an act of building and comparing models – in other words, representations – of our world. This propensity of the mind to build models brings an unavoidable paradox in its wake. In our attempts to understand the mind we generate theoretical models of the very structure that compels us to build models in the first place! But then, the whole notion of mind desiring to know itself is unique, being perhaps the only defining hallmark of mind that could stand up to scrutiny.

It is not only to psychology that we need turn to view man's models of the mind. From astrology to the design of cities we can usefully observe the outward projections of the structures and processes of the human mind. The mandala is well known to be, at one and the same time, both a model of the universe and a graphical embodiment of the essence of mind, the self. When we read 'here be dragons' beyond the limits of the known world in ancient maps, we can recognize the mind modelling itself. For it is inherent in the nature of mind that it should clothe the unknown. In more recent times such territory became 'complexes of the unconscious'. The latter term has a more scientific ring to it than does jargon about some leviathan. The real challenge is to substitute explanation for myth. Although not the only viable form of explanation, description of mental phenomena in terms of observable brain processes promises a secure foundation to a model of the mind. Here, then, is one of the challenges facing modern psychology: to generate a model of the mind which can explain, in terms of known brain processes, the psychic realities embedded in the myths of bygone ages. The model of the mind presented in this book is advanced as an approach to such a challenge. But it is only an approach. It would be presumptuous indeed to suggest that the great panorama of human experience could be fully explained in terms of our current understanding of the twitchings of the fifty billion or so nerve cells comprising the human brain.

As stated earlier, by calling this chapter 'Gateway to the Mind' I wish to imply not only that perception comes first, but also that perception constitutes a microcosm of the operation of mind. Consequently, the model presented here to describe the perceptual process will become the seed around which broader issues raised in subsequent chapters cohere.

Any model of perception must accommodate, first, the way in which hierarchical feature-detecting mechanisms drive the process, and, second, the commonalities between imagery and perception discussed in the previous section. In parallel to these two considerations the model presented here incorporates two stages. These are:

(i) an externally driven stage to the process in which feature-detecting cells respond to sensory input, and

(ii) an internally driven stage in which the brain constructs a meaningful image.

Figure 2.6 presents the model. In the first stage the detection of key features generates a *neuronal input model*. The neuronal input model consists of the total pattern of activity in the banks of feature-detecting cells, in other words a kind of neuronal code representing the features (line elements, colour, movement and so on) present in the current sensory input.[26] As the neuronal input model is generated, a search of stored schemata (memory images) ensues, activating those that possess features in common with the model. It is envisaged that this search amounts to a broad sweep through the network of associations in memory.

At the end of the first stage a comparison between the accessed schemata and the present input model is made. Normally, under unambiguous circumstances, a ready match is rapidly forthcoming and the search terminates. This match constitutes the pivotal point of the whole process. It is the event which gives rise to conscious recognition as generally understood. As will become clearer through subsequent chapters, it is the point at which an 'I' connection to the sensory data is established. When the circumstances are ambiguous, however, such as reduced visibility

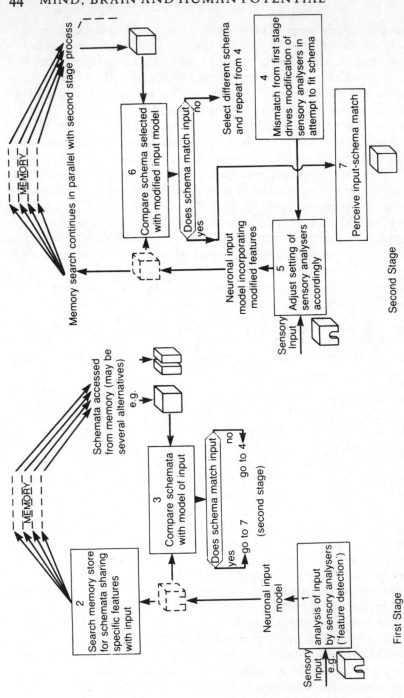

Figure 2.6: A Model of Perception.

or camouflage, the search may take longer. Under such conditions the individual may become conscious of the search itself in a way that is not the case under normal circumstances.

The processes of searching for the appropriate schema and matching it to the current input constitute the quest for meaning discussed earlier. As we shall see when we discuss memory more fully in Chapter 3, the schema embodies our relationship to the object in the widest sense. By matching input to schema the meaning built up through previous experience becomes the determining factor in our vision of the world. As Oatley has put it, 'The way we see is in terms of our human purposes in the environment.'[27]

It is proposed that the mechanism by which input is matched to schema involves the backward neuronal connections which have been described in the brain's sensory systems.[28] Such connections function to enable a 'higher' area to influence the way in which a 'lower' area responds to visual stimuli. Indeed, all the senses themselves are influenced by such backward connections. Such efferent fibres, as they are called, are known to influence, for example, the responses of the cochlear nucleus and the geniculate nucleus, which send auditory and visual signals respectively to their receiving areas in the brain. It would therefore be wrong to think of the brain as a one-way system for analysis of sensory information. On the contrary, it is a highly interactive system. The mechanism thus exists for the input to be modified within certain parameters to make it 'fit' the schema. Such is the hypothesized second stage of the present model.

It is important to realize that the two stages are not necessarily sequential. The analyse–search–match complex of operations is envisaged to involve much brain activity in parallel. For example, as the neuronal input model is being generated, the memory search will already have commenced. Competing schemata will, accordingly, be undergoing comparison to the input model at the same time as more complex features of the input are being generated in the input model. In reality, the search will be predetermined by expectancy – in other words, we are already expecting to see the likely course of events as soon as we have taken in the initial situation. As we see a brick hurtling towards a window, for example, schemata concerning broken glass are already being activated even before the brick strikes. The memory process is as much involved in predictions of the likely course of events as it is in the immediate response to the input in the present moment. So the two stages captured in figure 2.6 are laid out sequentially only for ease of understanding. It is impossible to freeze what must, of course, be a highly dynamic, inter-active process. This point concerning the inadequacy of capturing a frozen moment of such dynamic psychological processes should be borne in mind when viewing all similar figures in later chapters.

We may usefully employ this model of perception to clarify the relationships and differences between the four kinds of 'perceptual' experience depicted in figure 2.7. Each of these experiences includes the stage involving a search of memory schemata. Where they differ is in the extent to which the input analysis and matching stages are involved. As far as normal perception is concerned, as we have seen, all three stages take place, and the match of a specific memory schema to the current input model inhibits further processing of schemata (figure 2.7a). Contemplation differs in that such inhibition is limited; some of the schemata associated with the input also reach consciousness (figure 2.7b). Images which are generated through visualization or hallucination are, by definition, independent of sensory input,[29] and, accordingly, the analysis stage is absent. The difference between these two is that hallucinations result from a false 'match' and the subject therefore experiences the image as deriving from the external world. The hallucinated image is 'really there' as far as the subject is concerned, whereas images generated through visualization are clearly known to be subjective. In fact, the distinction between these two is not quite so clear-cut as this implies. Sometimes a hallucinating patient will 'see' or 'hear' images as coming from the external world, whilst recognizing that they are not actually 'real'. On the other hand, in some individuals with exceptional imaging ability there may be some degree of confusion between visualized images and external objects. A famous case studied by Luria, for example, had difficulty reading the time from a clock on account of interference from residual images of previous encounters with the clock.[30]

The model, then, helps us to understand this variety of 'images of reality', ranging from the poetic to the literal, from the insane to the mystical. But the model is not complete. For the present we have simply labelled some processes as 'preconscious' and some as reaching 'consciousness'. But what exactly happens when an image becomes 'conscious'? How may we reconcile this model with the ideas concerning consciousness discussed in Chapter 1?

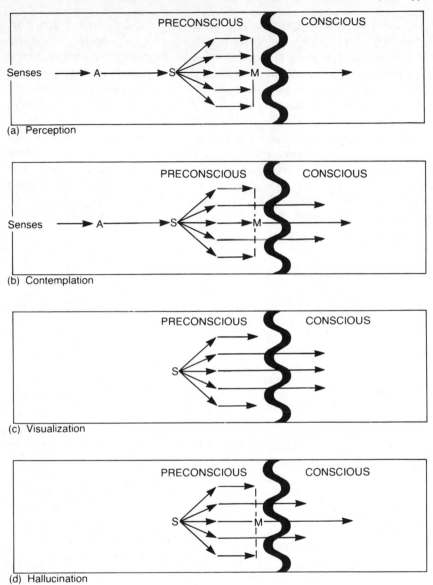

(a) Perception

(b) Contemplation

(c) Visualization

(d) Hallucination

Figure 2.7: Images of reality – true and false. A = analysis, S = search, M = match. See text for explanation.

The central feature missing from figures 2.6 and 2.7 is undoubtedly our *image of ourselves*, our sense of identity. For the sense of identity may change across the four experiences depicted in figure 2.7. This identity, which seems to be the cornerstone of our personality, may be a more fragile construct than we generally realize. Before embarking on a fuller consideration of identity, however, we turn to the topic of memory. As already stated in Chapter 1, memory is absolutely central to the mind. It is memory that links all four experiences depicted in figure 2.7. Indeed, there is no area of our psychological life which could carry on in the absence of memory. Thoughts, emotions, dreams – all depend on some kind of continuity over time. And, as we shall discuss, without memory there could, in fact, be no sense of identity. Memory is the very taproot of mind.

3
Memory: The Taproot of Mind

NUTS, BOLTS AND MYSTERIES

The search for the mechanisms in the brain which form the basis for memory has proved much more difficult than early researchers imagined. In the 1920s Lashley set out to establish where memories were stored. After a long series of studies he concluded that the 'engram' (the physical representation of something learnt) could not be localized. No single brain site could be identified as the locus for a specific memory trace. Rather, as far as memory was concerned the whole cortex of the brain appeared to work together – *en masse*, as it were. These ideas of Lashley's find expression today in two differing approaches. The first attempts to hold on to the basic idea of localization whilst giving due emphasis to the distributed nature of memory by arguing for multiple systems of memory. Each system involves some localized elements, but any one item to be stored in memory may be multiply coded in the brain. The second approach looks to some paradigm other than the mechanical which may support the holism implied in Lashley's conclusion.

The multiple systems view suggests that what may appear to us as one element of meaning or memory is, in brain terms, a conglomerate of subsidiary aspects. These aspects are stored in the brain in diverse sites, each involving different codes or features of the memory. Thus, for example, my memory of what a dolphin is is not, in brain terms, a single memory but involves visual, semantic, perhaps even emotional, subsidiary systems. This view has most often been advanced in connection with studies of patients with brain damage. McCarthy and Warrington describe a patient who has a selective impairment in the ability to define animals when presented with their names verbally. By contrast, he is able to define these animals when they are depicted in pictures, and is able to define inanimate objects when asked to do so verbally. Thus, when asked to define 'dolphin', he said, 'a fish or a bird'; when shown a picture, he said, 'Dolphin lives in water. . . they are trained to jump up and come out. . . . In America during the war years they started to get this particular animal to go through to look into ships.' Asked to define 'lighthouse' (verbal, no picture), he said, 'Round the coast, built up, tall building, lights revolve to warn ships.' There is, then, in this patient evidence for a remarkable degree of specificity in his deficit. As the authors put it, this pattern of observations 'not only refutes the notion of an "all-purpose" meaning store, but also provides positive evidence for multiple meaning representations'.[1]

The favoured analogy employed by those wishing to stress the fundamental holism of memory is that of holography. For Pribram,[2] the major figure articulating this view, it is not merely analogy. The principles by which holography operates are the principles operating in the brain. Storage of information becomes a function of the interference patterns between waves of neuronal activity, implying that memories are stored throughout the brain in a holistic fashion. Just as damage to a holographic plate does not destroy specific detail but rather leads to an overall loss of resolution, so too damage to the brain never dislodges specific memories but leads to more general lowering of memory abilities. The fact that a patient with localized brain damage may experience some selective and specific loss of ability does not necessarily imply that the storage element itself was localized. It could be that the input–output mechanism has been disturbed. Thus, in the example cited above, the brain damage has selectively interfered with the patient's ability to access the appropriate memories through verbally presented animal names. The memories themselves may be intact, and merely inaccessible through that route.

Bergland argues that the brain is primarily a hormonal system and that its functions are best explained by focusing our approach at the level of molecules and their interactions. Memory has a 'pattern-dependent molecular structure', and as such may only be understood when physics and chemistry further understand the basic forces of molecular interactions. He draws a parallel between memory and gravity. Gravity has proved something of an enigma in physicists' attempts to relate it to the other three basic forces of nature. It has been argued that a full understanding of these forces will only be achieved with the discovery of a fifth, unifying, force. So too with memory, argues Bergland; it will only be with the discovery of some such 'unifying' force that its mysteries will be unlocked. Perhaps more revolutionary still is his view that memory may be a function not only of the brain but of the body as a whole. This argument hinges on the fact that all brain molecules are found in various sites in bodily organs as well: 'If memory is dependent on hormones and if memory is holographic, finding the hormones of memory in many sites outside the brain moves the "engram for memory" that Lashley was searching for outside the brain.'[3]

The holistic views considered thus far suggest that information storage is focused in the brain (Pribram)[4] or the whole body (Bergland). A third possibility holds that neither of these is the site of storage. Information may be stored in non-physical fields of some kind. According to this third view, the brain itself is merely an input–output device but not the organ of information storage. As Sheldrake, who is a recent proponent of this view, puts it, 'It is not necessary for the fields to leave traces in the brain, any more than the programs to which a radio set is tuned leave traces in the set.'[5] If this were the case, then, obviously, memories themselves would not be lost through brain damage; it would be only the access to memories, dependent on brain activity, which was compromised. Access to memories, according to Sheldrake, is brought about by *morphic resonance*, a principle whereby one structure influences another in situations where there is similarity of form between the two structures. According to Sheldrake, then, a given brain state resonates with those memory fields which relate to the brain state present when the memory was established in the first place.

It is practically impossible at the present time to produce evidence that unequivocally supports one or other of these views of memory. Thus, for example, when a claim is made that specific, localized memories have been found in the brain, it could always be countered along the lines already discussed – that what was found constituted only a specific input–output mechanism, and not memory itself. A major proponent of the mechanistic, localizational view, Thompson, has recently made just such a claim, following his studies of a simple reflex, the

eye-blink reflex in rabbits.[6] When a rabbit is conditioned to blink
to a tone (by repeated pairings of the tone with the normal trigger
for the blink, a puff of air), it appears that the memory is 'held'
in a particular part of the rabbit's cerebellum. The evidence for
this claim is essentially twofold. First, when the site was lesioned
the conditioned response disappeared. Second, electrical recording
from key cells in the cerebellum showed responses time-locked to
the conditioned response.

As I have said, the kind of evidence that Thompson and others of
his persuasion employ does not necessarily contradict holographic
or field theories. For Thompson, the memory is embodied by
particular connections between nerves. For Sheldrake, those
same connections between the nerves operate the interface with
the non-physical memory fields. The problem in distinguishing
the two approaches is none other than the *mind–brain problem*
itself. The question we would ask Thompson is, how could
a particular nerve group in and of itself be the memory of,
say, a red rose? Nerves are one thing, but the experience
of the memory's richness seems to be another. The difficulty
with Sheldrake's position is that of specifying exactly what the
memory fields are, and how resonance transcends space and time
as he proposes.

There is undoubtedly a mystery about memory, and we arrive
at something of an impasse in attempting to support one view over
another. It is very much a continuation of the 'question of scale'
that we encountered in Chapter 1. The field theory would seem to
fit very well into the notion of a higher order, the implicate order
discussed there. In an earlier formulation of such a large-scale vista,
Bergson described memory as a manifestation of 'spirit'. When we
remember something, according to Bergson, the brain is involved
only in prolonging, or holding on to, the memory; the moment
of remembering itself does not involve the brain: 'The state of the
brain continues the remembrance; it gives it a hold on the present
by the materiality which it confers upon it: but pure memory is a
spiritual manifestation. With memory we are in very truth in the
domain of spirit.'[7]

Be they emphasizing 'spirit' or 'fields', non-mechanistic views
of memory invariably go beyond the personal to a collective level.
Yeats is perhaps one of the most articulate proponents of such
a view. He held nature herself to embody a 'great memory' of
which all our memories are but a part. The great memory is
reached through symbols, and, 'Whatever the passions of man

have gathered about, becomes a symbol in the great memory.'[8] Similarly, the collective unconscious, as postulated by Jung in his theory of the psyche, is essentially a memory system whereby the archetypes assert an influence over the activation of images in personal memory.

Ultimately, our response to these ideas owes more to personal experience and general attitudes than to scientific fact. To many, the appeal of a richer dimension to things than the purely individual strikes a meaningful chord, but, like all ideas based in a mystical perception of reality, these various holistic theories of memory await definitive substantiation. I would say that their strength lies primarily in their relationship to the broad sweep of human thought in areas of literature, religion and philosophy as well as science.

Despite the lack of precise formulation of the nature of the fields involved, there is considerable evidence to support many features of the view of memory advanced by Sheldrake. The place of 'resonance' in establishing connections is, for example, supported by recent studies of the responses of cells in the visual cortex of the brain.[9] These cells display a rhythmicity in their responses. Cells which were responding to stimuli of the same orientation responded with oscillations in phase with each other. More surprising was the observation that, when cells quite far apart in the visual region were stimulated by a long bar of light covering both receptive fields, their responses were in phase. When, however, they were stimulated by two shorter bars, one falling in one region and one in the other, both of the same orientation, their responses were no longer in phase. But how could the two cells 'know' that the first situation was different from the second? Presumably a 'higher' neurone or group of neurones has detected the fact that the first situation involves one whole bar *and signals this information by means of phase synchrony in 'lower' neurones*. Whatever the detail, some form of resonance is playing a crucial role here. I, for one, would be not at all surprised if some form of resonance is not a major feature of communication between neurones throughout the brain. Perhaps there is a whole brain 'language' yet to be discovered. . . .

It is also quite evident that memory is considerably more all-pervasive than is generally recognized. In a study by Raikov,[10] deeply hypnotized subjects were regressed to infancy. In addition to behavioural manifestations of infancy, the subjects displayed brainwave patterns characteristic of the infant age range. Such patterns could not be generated by any subjects attempting to act as if they were infants without hypnosis. Raikov interprets these striking results as a kind of unlocking of infantile memory patterns. It seems that the whole array of infant activity, including such things as crying without tears and eyes 'swimming' (neither of which could be simulated outside hypnosis), as well as distinctive patterns of brain activity, are reactivated in these circumstances. The question whether the medium for such memories is the brain itself (as Raikov assumes) or some extra-cerebral field (Sheldrake) is, of course, unresolved.

It may well be that memory is not only all-pervasive but all-inclusive as well. According to Cohen, Diderot, writing in the eighteenth century, was the first to state this explicitly:

> I am led to believe that everything we have seen, known, perceived, heard – even the trees of a deep forest – nay, even the disposition of the branches, the form of the leaves and the variety of the colours, the green tints and the light; the look of grains of sand at the edge of the sea, the unevenness of the crests of waves, whether agitated by a light breeze, or churned to foam by a storm; the multitude of human voices, of animal cries, and physical sounds, the melody and harmony of all songs, of all pieces of music, of all the concerts we have listened to, *all of it, unknown to us*, exists within us.[11]

Cohen quite rightly says that this theory of all-inclusiveness can be neither proved nor disproved. There seems little doubt, however, that memory is at least considerably richer than conscious recall suggests. The major question is why hypnosis, as in the Raikov study, releases these memories. This is an issue to be addressed later in the present chapter, and one to which we shall return in Chapter 7.

We are unable for the present to state unequivocally where and in what form memory exists. Our interest in the rest of this chapter focuses on the operation of memory and its relation to our sense of identity, the 'I' within. Let us finally cite Cohen again, for he surely captures the true essence of memory when he states that a facility for 'blending, fusing, annexing, linking, and adjoining is the principal power and property of memory'. He says: 'The mind is, as it were, forever gliding over its past and, in a different way, over its "future", juxtaposing, reshuffling, scattering, highlighting and coalescing traces originating at very different times and places, and under very different conditions.'[12]

THE GLORY OF KINGS

We have learned, 'The glory of God is to conceal a word.' (*Proverbs* 25:2) What is a 'word'? That of which it is written, 'The beginning of your word is truth,' (*Psalm* 119:160) and 'The glory of kings is to probe a word' (*Proverbs* 25:2). What is a 'word'? That of which it is written, 'A word fitly [Hebrew: *afenav*] spoken' (*Proverbs* 25:11). Do not read 'fitly' [*afenav*] but 'its wheel' [*ofenav*].

The *Bahir*[13]

This passage is very difficult to render into English. Not only does it draw on the similarity in Hebrew between the words for 'fitly' and 'wheel', it also plays with the dual meaning of the Hebrew *davar*, meaning a word or a thing (or matter). If the passage is read again with that in mind, the intention may become clearer.

In our day we are somewhat accustomed to the power of the written word. In the twelfth century, the effort involved in writing and copying manuscripts was considerable; consequently, authors chose their words with much more care than we do today. Nowhere was this more so than in mystical literature. The genius of a work such as the *Bahir* is that it not only describes mystical ideas, but also engages the reader in the exploration of such ideas. The quoted passage offers some rich insights into memory, both in a mundane and in a more metaphysical sense, if we can but enter into the spirit of exploration which it calls for.

So what is a 'word'? Underlying the quoted passage is the mystical idea that the word is an agent of creation (cf. John 1:1). Not only is God's word pulsing with the power of creation, but human words also, in mythical literature and superstition, possess mysterious power, as in naming ceremonies and magic incantations. In the symbolic imagery of religion, the word becomes the point of contact between the individual and the divine. Humankind, in the image of God, is unique amongst all creatures in using words. More than this, language points to the hidden processes whereby ideas are clothed in outer form.

It is on account of the special status of language that Jewish mysticism includes many strands of meditation which use letters and their permutations as the means whereby individuals may draw themselves closer to the divine realm. The foremost example is that of the thirteenth-century Abraham Abulafia. Abulafia reasoned that, in order for the soul to ascend beyond the prison of sensory and emotional forms, it must meditate on the letters of the Hebrew alphabet. The logic of this assertion, involving the kabbalistic notion that all combinations of these letters cohere ultimately in the Name of God, need not concern us here. What is of interest to psychology is the 'science of combinations' itself. As Scholem puts it:

> In fact this is nothing else than a very remarkable method of using associations as a way of meditation. It is not wholly the 'free play of association' as known to psychoanalysis; rather it is the way of passing from one association to another determined by certain rules which are, however, sufficiently lax. Every 'jump' opens a new sphere, defined by certain formal, *not* material, characteristics. Within this sphere the mind may freely associate. The 'jumping' unites, therefore, elements of free and guided association and is said to assure quite extraordinary results as far as the 'widening of the consciousness' of the initiate is concerned. The 'jumping' brings to light hidden processes of the mind, 'it liberates us from the prison of the natural sphere and leads us to the boundaries of the divine sphere'.[14]

The passage from the *Bahir* cited at the beginning of this section is more cryptic. It draws a parallel between the role of God and that of the mystic (a 'king' in the text) with regard to words. God conceals; the mystic peers through the veil. But it would be a mistake to think of this as some arcane game, as if a mischievous God were deliberately hiding things to make matters hard for us! The message of the *Bahir* is that there are two necessary poles to the process of creation. One, from above down, entails clothing the infinite (or, in the more scientific terms introduced in Chapter 1, establishing the explicate, from the implicate order). This is 'concealing a word'. The other, 'probing a word', becomes a means of freeing the sparks of that infinite realm concealed within the words. The movement between these two poles, that of God 'concealing' and the mystic 'probing', epitomizes the dynamic of creation. It is as if creation were akin to the breath cycle. The outbreath is the creative impulse from God which is returned, via the intermediary of human consciousness, to become the inbreath of God.

Psychologically, a word is a focus of meaning. A given word not only conveys its direct referential meaning, but also acts as a focus for a whole complex of interconnected concepts or images. In Chapter 2 I discussed the way in which incoming signals are matched against stored representations, or schemata, in arriving at the final percept. It seems reasonable to assume that these schemata are related to the linguistic repertoire available. Thus a schema activated when my eye is directed at a chair, for example, is linked to the neural machinery engaged when I speak the word 'chair', and so on. In reality, we must have access to an incredibly rich network of interconnections whenever we perceive an object or, indeed, use a word. Just as the act of perception is one of limiting the possibilities triggered by the sensory analysis, so too the use of language limits the train of thought to the appropriate words. In speaking, we must assume that some kind of field of activation spreads through our memory system, being focused in turn from one word to the next. Just as in perception we are conscious only of the end result, so too in speaking. The real work of language is preconscious.

In attempting to relate concepts borrowed from mysticism to the sphere of human psychology, it is necessary to recognize that the interplay between preconscious and conscious processes becomes projected in mysticism outwards on to the framework of creation. The 'higher' processes which underlie the ebb and flow of events in the phenomenal, 'lower' world parallel the preconscious processes flowing under the surface of our conscious experience.

In Chapter 2 we saw how contemplation brings into consciousness the wider sphere ('wheel') of preconscious meaning inherent in some object or scene. The same is true for the author of the *Bahir* when it comes to words. By entering the world view of mysticism and allowing the potential of even a single word to unfold in that unique, trance-like state of meditation or contemplation, the mystic is delving into a world that is normally obscured in the preconscious realm of mind.

When we read that 'the beginning of [God's] word is truth' in the context of the cited passage, we are being informed that the 'truth' antecedes the mind's focusing on to even a single word. It is what lies behind the word that is of the essence. So too, of course, with language as a whole. An idea may be perfect, but that perfection is lost when it is necessarily limited by the words we use to form the idea. Bohm captures the point at issue here, in the context of examining the nature of science: 'First of all, whatever we say is words, and what we want to talk about is generally not words. Second, whatever we *mean* by what we say is not what the thing actually is, though it may be similar. For the thing is always *more* than what we mean and is never exhausted by our concepts.'[15]

It will be argued later that the movement of mental process from preconscious to conscious is the formative step in the generation of our sense of identity. Thus the 'truth' always hangs just beyond us, whilst we remain in the bounds of this identity. Conversely, when the bounds of identity are loosed, as in mystical contemplation, an individual may have the sense of witnessing some kind of 'truth' even though it cannot subsequently be put into words.

The problem here is that we tend to get caught worrying about the supposed absolute nature of truth. Whilst there may be theological arguments for absolute truth, my interest is in the psychological implications of the cited passage. The 'truth' hanging beyond us is that we are capable of a 'higher' knowledge than that to which the 'I' in us is privy. In a state of contemplation, perhaps 'probing the words' of some scriptural text, or in simple meditation, we may experience the flash of light associated with such knowledge. The 'truth' vouchsafed by such experience concerns the potential within us for higher integrations of meaning beyond those triggered automatically. The 'I', incapable of limiting these intimations of transcendent meaning, gropes its way with the only word it has at its disposal – truth. How else can you specify the ineffable? But such 'psychological truth' is, as I have implied, relative. We strive for ever higher (that is, more inclusive) levels of integration. The exploration of associations, be they triggered even by a single word or phrase, pushes at the door to such higher levels of integration.

The tradition of rabbinical commentary on the text of the Hebrew Bible is precisely one of 'probing words' in this associative sense. In addition to direct associations based on meaning and grammar, words are explored for their anagrammatic and numerical[16] ramifications, particularly in more mystically inclined commentaries. Initial letters of whole phrases may even be called upon to elucidate some point of interpretation. A somewhat elaborate example of such verbal exploration is given below. It is extracted from the commentary of the fourteenth century by Jacob ben Asher, otherwise known as *Ba'al ha Turim*, on the episode in Genesis 28:12 where Jacob dreams of a ladder extending between earth and heaven. The extract concerns the phrase, 'Behold, a ladder set up' and introduces a plethora of alternate words and phrases deemed to be connected to the biblical extract by gematria (numerical correspondence).

'Ladder': By gematria [the word ladder equates to] 'this is the throne of glory'. By gematria [the word ladder also equates to] 'voice', because the voice of the prayers of the righteous becomes a ladder for angels to ascend. . . . By gematria [the word ladder also equates to] 'riches' [and also to] 'poverty', for one is lowering and one is ascent. . . . By gematria [the word ladder also equates to] 'Sinai', because it establishes Mount Sinai [i.e. as a preliminary, small-scale version of the later, global linkage between heaven and earth in the divine revelation]. 'A ladder set up': By gematria [these words equate to] 'his chariot' [a vehicle for mystic exploration of heavenly realms]. . . . 'And behold a ladder': By gematria [these words equate to] 'and this is the altar of sacrifice'. . . .

The point of these mental gymnastics is to explore the ramifications of Jacob's dream with the ladder, not in some random sense, but in a form which consolidates our understanding of the episode. It is not my purpose here to delve into biblical exegesis for its own sake. But it is certainly apparent that bringing together the concept of Jacob's ladder with those of prayer, sacrifice, mystic 'journeying' and the events of Mount Sinai leads our understanding into the complex of ways in which the mundane, human world and the transcendent, divine world may be bridged.

Contemplating the 'wheel' of connected meanings to a particular word is, then, a means of peering behind the veil of duality to touch the connectedness of all things – for, as mentioned already in the context of perception, the associations flow one into another. Whatever the reality of the projected worlds in their religious guise, such preconscious exploration is spiritually uplifting inasmuch as the individual becomes aware of a wider scale of meaning than otherwise gained. As the associations merge, the central concept – which may itself be incapable of expression in a single word – comes into focus, as in the example of Jacob's ladder. The parallels drawn through gematria become the signposts for our intuitive grasp of the text's deeper meaning. In fact, it may be that the place of such endeavours, be they meditative as in Abulafia's system, or more discursive as with Jacob ben Asher, is to be found more in oiling the cogs of the intuitive process than in discovering particular meanings of words, letter combinations or whatever. The means is what is important, not the goal.

Intuition is at the heart of our creativity. The ability to go beyond the islands of given information into the sea of preconscious thought and return with knowledge that somehow enables new connections, or new insights, to be established, and perhaps to be communicated to others, is the essence of human potential. Whether in artistic endeavours, science or psychotherapy, intuition is our most valuable guide. Reason may sharpen our understanding of ideas, but intuition alone reaches to new knowledge.

ON KNOWING MORE THAN YOU THINK YOU KNOW

Take a brief look, no more than a second or so, over the page at figure 3.1. Now (after having read this paragraph) close your eyes and relax. Let images of a day trip to the country form in your mind's eye. (For those who haven't worked with imagery before, the main thing is not to force it. Relaxation can be encouraged by focusing on your breath; follow the air as it enters your nose, and be aware of it flowing down to your lungs; you may feel some warmth in the chest area. Let the idea of a trip to the country be like a seed dropped on to the screen of your mind. Let the scenes unfold and follow them as they clothe the idea with details of this trip; what the weather's like, what scenery surrounds you, what sounds you can hear. Spend about three minutes exploring these images and remember – they don't have to be logical, for there's no hold on bizarre events cropping up in your visualization.)

You have just re-enacted (after a fashion) an interesting study concerning subliminal perception.[17] In the original study one group of subjects was shown the figure you have just looked at, whilst the other group saw figure 3.2. Following presentation of the picture, subjects were instructed to 'sit back, relax, close your eyes and wait for an image of a nature scene to come to your mind's eye'. They were then required to draw their image. Results indicated that a significantly higher proportion of the first group included birds, water and other duck-related associations in their drawings. This difference between the two groups, we must infer, is attributable to the only difference between the two pictures – the presence of a concealed image of a duck in figure 3.1. You may perhaps have noticed it when you first looked at it, but in the original study the picture was exposed for only one second on each of three exposures and no subject spontaneously reported seeing the concealed duck.

This study demonstrates the nature of subliminal perception. An image – in this case the duck – of which subjects were not conscious affected subsequent imagery. Generally, we think of a subliminal stimulus as one that is presented too fast or too faintly

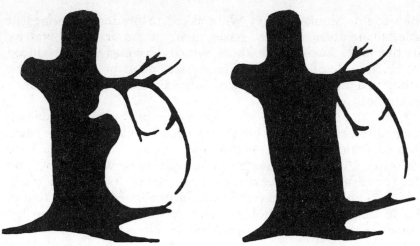

Figure 3.1   Figure 3.2

(Both figures reproduced by permission of the American Association for the Advancement of Science. From *Science*, 1966, *151*, 838. Copyright 1966 AAAS.)

for the subject to be conscious of it. However, there are stimuli around us all the time (especially in advertisements) which we may not notice. These may be classed with genuinely subliminal stimuli as influencing us unconsciously. Subliminal perception is a well-researched topic. It has repeatedly been demonstrated that words and images presented below the threshold for conscious registration may affect subsequent mental activity, for example, in the way we perceive or respond to other stimuli.

The notion that material not consciously noticed may influence imagery was first demonstrated by Poetzl in 1917. In his study pictures were briefly exposed (1/100 second) to subjects who were asked to state immediately what they had seen. The next day they described imagery that had occurred in their dreams. Results indicated that aspects of the pictures which had not been reported when first viewed, and were thus effectively subliminal, became incorporated into the dreams. Poetzl's basic paradigm has been replicated in more rigorous studies by Fisher and, more recently, using auditory subliminal material, by Kaser.[18]

In Kaser's study, key auditory phrases were speeded up to a rate at which conscious understanding was not possible. These were included on a tape with music playing at normal speed. Before and after listening to the tape, subjects were asked to allow an image to come into their minds and to draw it as best they could. Similarly, they were asked to produce drawings of subsequent dream images. Assessment of the drawings was by art therapists who did not know which drawings were produced at which stage of the study. Their assessments indicated that the subliminal phrases had influenced subjects' imagery and dreams to a significant degree.

Figure 3.3 reproduces one subject's drawing of the image which formed in her mind after having listened to the tape. There were four subliminal phrases on the tape: 'You are climbing a long staircase'; 'A piano is playing'; 'You wish to be with daddy'; and 'He is wearing a hat.' I leave it to the reader to discern the ways in which these messages have become incorporated in the drawing. To anyone alive to symbolism there can be little doubt about the impact of the subliminal material on this picture.

Figure 3.3: Picture drawn by a subject depicting imagery generated following subliminal stimuli. (From Kaser (1986). Reproduced with permission of Williams and Wilkins. From *Journal of Nervous and Mental Disease*, 1986, *174*, 403. Copyright Williams and Wilkins 1986.)

In interpreting these subliminal phenomena we return to the model developed in Chapter 2. It will be recalled that the first stage of the perceptual process involves analysis of incoming signals prior to the subsequent matching of the input model with stored schemata. It was stated there that perception – that is, conscious recognition – depends on the latter, matching stage. In the case of subliminal perception, the kinds of effects discussed above indicate that input analysis and memory search are occurring largely as they would in the case of normal perception. It is only the final matching stage which fails.

An instructive parallel may be drawn here with so-called awareness under anaesthesia. It has repeatedly been demonstrated that patients undergoing surgery with appropriate levels of anaesthetic may nevertheless be influenced by auditory input at the time of the operation.

In the first study of this kind, Levinson arranged for the anaesthetist to say, in some alarm, that the patient was turning blue and required more oxygen. Ten patients were included in the study. When the patients were subsequently hypnotized and regressed to the time of the operation, four recalled the words accurately and a further four showed signs of anxiety at the appropriate time. Only two out of the ten patients appeared to have been unaffected by the manœuvre. In a similar study, using deeper anaesthesia in major surgery, Blacher reports that, when later hypnotized, patients recalled 'in exact detail' what was said.[19]

The effect has been demonstrated in a more positive fashion (and without hypnotic intervention) by presenting encouraging words to patients during their operations. In a well-controlled study by Evans and Richardson,[20] patients were played a tape whilst undergoing hysterectomy. Obviously normal anaesthesia was maintained, and none of the patients was conscious of the tape contents, as revealed by later questioning.

The tape contents differed between two groups of patients. One group (control group) received a blank tape; the other (suggestion group), a tape with positive information and suggestions on it. These included phrases such as 'How quickly you recover from your operation depends upon you – the more you relax, the more comfortable you will be;' and 'The operation seems to be going very well and the patient is fine.' Post-operative assessments of the patients by nurses unaware of which group the patients were in revealed the following. Sixteen out of nineteen patients in the suggestion group were described as showing *better than average* recovery, whereas fourteen out of twenty in the control group showed recovery *as, or poorer than, expected*. A further interesting statistic indicated a significantly shorter post-operative stay in hospital for the suggestion group by comparison with the control group.

There can be little doubt, then, that auditory material is analysed to a high level (in other words, to a level at which verbal meaning is extracted) whilst the patient is unconscious. So much so that the *Lancet* warns in an editorial that patients should be guarded from the possibly irreverent conversations around them in the operating theatre.[21]

The nature of brain activity during anaesthesia has been assessed by observing the evoked responses to auditory input. As mentioned in Chapter 2, these responses give an indication of the brain's involvement in the different stages of perception. Studies have demonstrated that the portions of these electrical responses corresponding to analysis of the input in the auditory cortex are not abolished with levels of anaesthetic even higher than those required for surgery. It is only the late components of these electrical responses, assumed to correspond to the matching stage discussed above, which are blocked by the anaesthetic.[22]

A reasonable interpretation of these data would suggest that, when the subliminal input (or input during anaesthesia) has been analysed through cortical feature detectors, it activates associated memory schemata. Although the final matching stage does not take place, and we are, therefore, not conscious of sensory input, the activated schemata may nevertheless have a crucial influence on subsequent brain activity. They may critically influence subsequent imagery, for example, and, in the case of surgery, may affect subsequent recovery.

These ideas are depicted in figure 3.4, which hypothetically considers the consequences of viewing figure 3.1 with its concealed duck. It is envisaged that a rich network of associated schemata becomes activated through the memory search which follows on the heels of a simple form analysis of the visual input. This network is depicted in verbal form in the figure, although it would presumably be largely preverbal in reality. Whilst the tree is the only aspect of the scene reaching the final matching stage, all the activated schemata may be more readily incorporated in the subject's imagery than other, non-activated ones. In effect, these activated schemata are presumed to generate a framework

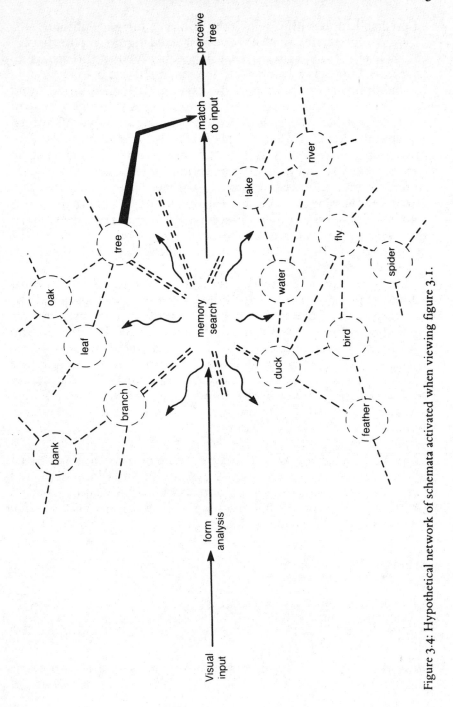

Figure 3.4: Hypothetical network of schemata activated when viewing figure 3.1.

of predisposition within which the subject's imagery unfolds.[23]

We could equally well have constructed figure 3.4 to display the 'wheel' of associations that Jacob ben Asher directs us to in connection with Jacob's ladder, as discussed earlier. As in the subliminal examples, it is the contemplative, intuitive mind that comes to the fore. An intuitive grasp brings forward material that had previously been preconscious only. A rational viewpoint would probably reject ben Asher's commentary as empty speculation. On this point it is worth noting that, in experiments on subliminal perception, effects are more pronounced with intuitive, relaxed awareness than with focused, attentive awareness. Murch, for example, notes that in his own studies on subliminal perception, subjects' responses which they felt to be 'completely intuitive' more often reflected the subliminal effect than did responses which they characterized as 'premeditated'.[24]

The implication from the wealth of studies on subliminal effects in psychology is that underlying the conscious mind the reverberations of barely noticed events must be ever-present. We undoubtedly know more than we think we know all the time. And it is this ever-active flow of preconscious material that shapes the island we call 'I'. After all, I have the sense that the image conjured up in my mind's eye is 'my' creation. Yet, according to the studies reviewed here, the key determining aspects of the stimulus may actually be beyond 'I' – subliminal. Evidently we have a problem with the word 'my' in this context.

The issue is really one of *control*. There is something in the individual which needs to believe that it controls the mind; that it conjures up the imagery in the kinds of situations discussed here. Indeed, it believes that it controls the very dynamic of mind processes – thought. That something is 'I'. But it may not be such a king as it would have us believe!

MEMORY AND IDENTITY

We have, each of us, a life-story, an inner narrative – whose continuity, whose sense, *is* our lives. It might be said that each of us constructs and lives, a 'narrative', and that this narrative *is* us, our identities.[25]

Whatever 'I' is, it is nothing without memory. For continuity is the hallmark of our sense of identity. Whenever I am aware of myself, there must be an implicit train of recollections of myself as agent in the world. If I have no past, what kind of present can I inhabit? Without memory there could only be a nebulous feeling of being a real person. But it would be a person without 'I', without a history.

In the passage cited above, Sacks writes in the context of describing patients who have sustained brain damage giving rise to impairments of memory. Writing about one patient in particular, a Mr Thompson, he graphically describes the impact of his devastating amnesia on the sense of identity: '. . .it is not just a faculty, or some faculties, which are damaged, but the very citadel, the self, the soul itself'.

So what is left in a patient such as Mr Thompson? In Chapter 2 we saw that underlying our perception of the world is the *quest for meaning*. Amnesia does not directly affect perception, because this quest is still intact. More fundamentally, it is not only the quest to perceive meaning, but the quest to construct a centre to that meaning which remains. This centre is our very identity. A patient such as Mr Thompson, despite having lost the continuity of identity which is its very core, still quests for a sense of identity with every moment.

Sacks describes how Mr Thompson constantly invents himself in relation to the circumstances around him in an attempt to compensate for his memory loss:

> Abysses of amnesia continually opened up beneath him, but he would bridge them, nimbly, by fluent confabulations and fictions of all kinds. For him they were not fictions, but how he suddenly saw, or interpreted, the world. . . . Such a patient *must literally make himself (and his world) up every moment*.

Thus Mr Thompson is variously a shop owner, a clergyman; greeting the doctor as a customer, an old friend, the butcher next door. . . .

We all construct our identities in response to the insistent quest for meaning. The 'common-sense' notion that there is something substantial and never-changing about identity is simply not sustained by psychological study, as will be explored further in Chapter 4. As Sacks eloquently puts it, identity is a narrative. And, as with literary narrative, it is a means to the end of establishing continuity. So, the 'I' is not the *conductor* of the quest for meaning, but is actually part of the mind's *solution* to that quest. By giving the individual the sense of something solid and unchanging within, the 'I' conveys permanence on what would otherwise be shifting sands of both our internal and external worlds. 'I' gives us a secure foundation. It underscores our sense of the reality of time and engenders existential meaning. But it is a construct. The difference, then, between ourselves and patients suffering from severe amnesia is simply that our construction of identity is not compromised by a lack of continuity. We have a coherence which, barring unforeseen trauma or mystical experience, is unshakeable.

We generally consider that the effects of amnesia on identity, as in the case of Mr Thompson, are secondary to the memory loss which lies at the heart of the disorder. The patient has lost the ability to store and/or retrieve information of whatever kind. It is only as a consequence of this loss that there is any confusion over identity. However, if you reflect on the situation you will realize that it could, in fact, be the other way round. There may be no loss of memory as such, but an inability to cement successive constructions of identity into a continuous stream. The amnesia evident in the typical responses of not recognizing objects, people or scenes perceived previously would then be attributable not to a failure of storage but to the fact that the 'I' currently attempting to recall the object is not the same 'I' that made the initial connection with the object.

Such a distinction between two different ways of conceptualizing the problems of amnesia may seem somewhat hair-splitting. It is, however, crucial to a deeper understanding of memory and identity. Let us first turn to some studies that support the view of amnesia being proposed here, before reassessing the relationship between memory and identity.

The relevant studies are those that have indicated that a distinction should be drawn between *implicit* and *explicit* memory. There are hundreds of studies which demonstrate that amnesic patients, unable to recall information at will, are nevertheless often able to perform in a manner that would be impossible were there literally no memory of the information. Thus, although patients are amnesic when explicit recall is required, they may implicitly access relevant, intact memories.[26] In a sense, the many 'regular' abilities of these patients testify to implicit memory. After all, the ability to talk, dress oneself, play an instrument and so on implicitly depend on working memory systems. The crucial psychological observations, however, concern the dissociation between intentional and non-intentional recollection of material presented after the onset of amnesia.

Consider the following study.[27] Amnesic patients were given lists of words to learn. Subsequent testing revealed the classic symptoms of amnesia – patients' abilities to recall or recognize any words were seriously impaired. This study is interesting, however, for the results obtained when patients were given cues to help them. The cues consisted of the three first letters from words in the lists. Patients were required to complete this stem to form the word in the original lists. In separate experiments patients were given differing instructions and their performance was compared with appropriate control groups. In one study patients were instructed to use the stems to help them *remember* the words ('Try to think of a word from the [lists] with the same beginning letters'). In another study, patients were required to look at the stem and write down the *'first word that comes to mind'*. Patients in the first study performed poorly compared to the controls; those in the second study, on a par with the controls.

A second example may be drawn from the work of de Haan, Young and Newcombe on a patient suffering from *prosopagnosia*, the loss of ability to recognize faces as discussed in Chapter 2. Their patient, referred to as P.H., was unable to name faces which he would be expected to know (famous sportsmen, politicians and personalities), nor could he even recognize that they were familiar. However, when tested for covert (implicit) recognition his performance was analogous to that of normal subjects. One test, for example, investigated the interference due to face recognition on reaction times in a name categorization task. If a normal subject is asked to decide whether a name (for instance, 'Mick Jagger') belongs in the category of pop star or politician, his or her performance is impaired if a photo of a politician is presented simultaneously. This is an interference effect which obviously depends on face recognition. The point here is that P.H. also showed such interference, even though there was no overt – that is conscious – recognition of the faces. As the authors put it, 'P.H.'s problem is not that he does not recognize faces; it is that he is unaware of the recognition that has taken place.'[28]

This kind of covert recognition of faces in prosopagnosic patients has been further substantiated by examining physiological indices of the brain's processing of faces.[29] In one of these studies, it was demonstrated that patients produced more frequent and higher-amplitude electrodermal responses when viewing familiar faces (those, say, of relatives and friends), by comparison with

unfamiliar ones. The electrodermal response is a response recorded from the skin, generally on the fingers, and reflects
the activity of our autonomic nervous system. It is thus a
general indicator of the impact that stimuli have on us whether
or not these are perceived consciously. Being prosopagnosic,
the patients were unable to recognize the familiar faces: they
experienced no sense of familiarity and were unable to provide
any verbal evidence of recognition by naming them. Despite
this, the differential electrodermal responses obtained with these
prosopagnosic patients were analogous to what we find in normal
subjects and imply that, despite the lack of overt recognition,
the patients' brains were assessing the faces appropriately at
some level prior to conscious recognition. A similar conclusion
emerges from a second study which analysed the event-related
potentials (ERPs) recorded from a patient's scalp. As discussed
in Chapter 2, these ERPs reflect the brain's processing of
stimuli. As in the first study, the point of interest concerned
responses to familiar and unfamiliar faces. The patient was, of
course, unable overtly to differentiate these categories. However,
both the amplitude and latency of key components of the
ERP varied in ways which suggested that the brain was
indeed sensitive to the difference between the two categories.

It is not only with relatively simple material that these implicit
memory phenomena have been demonstrated. Glisky, Schacter
and Tulving[30] attempted to train a densely amnesic patient
to use a microcomputer. Over many training sessions they
met with reasonable success: the patient learnt to write and
edit programs, and to use disks for storage and retrieval of
information. And yet the patient remembered *nothing* about
the computer explicitly, even denying at the beginning of
each session that he had ever worked on a computer before.

It appears from these and similar studies that amnesia consists of
a *dissociation of knowledge from identity or self*. 'The amnesic patient
without conscious memories does not know where he is, when
he is, "who" he is.'[31] However, in circumstances requiring no
reference to self, he does *know*. In other words, the abilities
demonstrated in these studies – implicit memory abilities – differ
from normal memory functions only in that the patient's 'I' does
not control them.

In extrapolating from these studies of amnesic patients to normal
individuals, it should be borne in mind that similar, although
not so striking, dissociations have been demonstrated in normal

subjects with no brain damage. The phenomenon of post-hypnotic suggestion is further evidence that the situation we have described in amnesic patients may be generalized to the normal population. In this context the crucial point is that subjects, even though no longer hypnotized, have no memory for the tasks they have been instructed to perform, yet perform them apparently without intention. Thus, for example, if a subject had been instructed under hypnosis to touch their nose at some cue subsequent to emerging from the hypnotic trance, it would be done right on cue but apparently inadvertently. If asked why they did this, they would typically reply in a rather nonchalant fashion, saying, for example, that their nose itched.

Perhaps something similar accounts for the observations of Raikov noted earlier. He observed striking activation of infantile memory, including characteristic brainwave patterns, during hypnotic age regression. It may be that these 'memory feats' are possible due to the attenuation of the subject's sense of 'I' under control from the hypnotist. In other words, infantile memories may be extensive within us but we cannot access them because they were laid down before the 'I' formed. As adults, under normal circumstances we can only recall that to which our current 'I' has connection. There is plenty of material from psychoanalysis and allied disciplines which would support this contention.[32]

It should be quite clear that there are useful parallels which may be drawn between implicit memory and the phenomena associated with subliminal perception and awareness under anaesthesia described earlier. At the end of the previous section I stated that the issue was really one of control; so too with these cases of implicit memory. The relevant memories have not been lost; it is the patient's control over them that has suffered.

Now the significance of this fact is considerable for our understanding of mind. In Chapter 1 I stated that mind emerges when Being encounters a storage medium; memory is the *sine qua non* of mind. These patients have not lost mind; simply a particular form of access to memory.

Let us formulate the nature of access to memory more fully and in terms consistent with the observations described in this chapter. I propose that when an event is experienced, its representation in memory includes a reference to the 'I' which actually experienced the event; let us call it an 'I-tag'. Subsequent voluntary recall consists of effecting connection to the appropriate 'I-tag'.[33] There is no effort to be expended in 'finding the memory'. In my view, memory is present and effective whenever current patterns of activity bear resemblance to past patterns of activity. In this I agree with Sheldrake's concept of the resonance of similar forms. Memory is, then, all-pervasive. However, as discussed briefly above and more fully in Chapter 4, 'I' is not a fixed entity. Therefore, a currently constellated 'I' may not always relate to the 'I-tag' connected to some specific memory. Under such circumstances we cannot consciously, or voluntarily, recall that memory. The memory is still present and effective – simply not accessible through the conscious route.

Now, the phenomena described in this chapter may be understood in the light of this proposal in the following ways (figure 3.5). In the case of subliminal perception or awareness under anaesthesia, the subject's 'I' makes no connection to the stimulus material presented. Indeed, this is precisely what is meant in operational terms when we say that the subject was not conscious of the material. There can therefore be no 'I-tag' in the memory for that material and, accordingly, no conscious recollection of it.

In the case of amnesia, whilst there was an 'I' connection to the stimuli in the first place, at the time of attempting recall the patient's current 'I' can no longer effect connection to it. The continuity between present and past identity has been lost. *The problem, then, is one of identity, not of memory.* The case of P. H., for example, would be explained by saying that his brain damage specifically disrupts the consolidation of the 'I' that accompanies the perception of faces. The linchpin to this argument is the concept of the multiplicity of 'I' to be addressed in Chapter 4.

There are evidently two ways in which memory becomes actualized – in other words, two forms of *thinking*. One, evidenced in explicit memory, is intentional recognition or recall. In this case, the current 'I' connects with the appropriate 'I-tag', as described above. Such activity is, necessarily, under the control of 'I' and therefore reflects rational needs ('I wish to write, therefore I must remember where I left my pen'). The other form of thinking is outside of 'I'; it is the *pure memory process* which I conceive to be a ceaseless resonance between structures or fields based on similarity.

Figure 3.5: A model of memory/identity relations. Figure 3.5a represents the nature of subliminal effects; figure 3.5b represents a patient with amnesia for faces who displays implicit memory ability. In the figures three separate phases are indicated. (i) Initial perception of key stimulus. P1 to P4 represent four from the large set of ongoing perceptions. Each connects to the subject's identity, giving

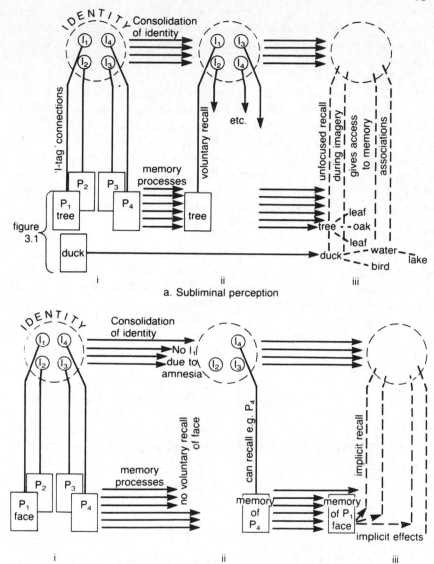

a. Subliminal perception

b. Amnesia for faces

four 'I-tags' (I1 to I4). (ii) Subsequent test of voluntary recall. The subliminal stimulus (concealed duck) cannot be recalled since its memory image lacks an 'I-tag'. The amnesic patient cannot recall the face since the key 'I-tag' can no longer be accessed. (iii) Imagery or implicit recall condition. In both conditions the key memory images are still present, only inaccessible by normal, voluntary means. Imagery/implicit recall enables features directly or indirectly associated with the key stimulus to influence present mental activity.

This pure memory process is not motivated by personal goals but will, nevertheless, impact upon current intentional activity. Hence it may give rise to the effects observed in the studies described in this chapter.[34]

In the second section of this chapter we saw that a kind of 'free-wheeling' examination of associations to a concept, idea or object may yield an intuitive grasp of the concept's 'true' nature; a grasp that cannot be conveyed adequately by words on account of the words' limitations. Such activity strikes the balance between the two forms of thought described here. For it brings the fruits of the pure memory process within the orbit of intentional thinking. And in so doing, it necessarily extends the sphere of 'I'.

We have come full circle to our discussion of contemplation in Chapter 2. Any divisions we erect between memory, thought and perception are conceptual only; they cannot be real. As we have seen, memory underlies perception, and thought is simply the actualization of memory structures or fields. Whether we focus our study on perception or on memory we arrive at the same conclusion: underlying the processes which relate the world to our sense of identity is a veritable sea of activity, the pure memory process. As discussed in Chapter 1, we conventionally ascribe consciousness to identity, and the pure process is therefore not conscious. But the paradox is that in the rich moment when we may actually be open to that sea of pure activity – that is, when we give up personal control of memory – we actually feel *more* conscious. We must be guided here by experience. Terminology should be a servant, not a master. So let us simply accept, for the time being, the relativity of consciousness:

> To be conscious is not to be in time.
> But only in time can the moment in the rose-garden,
> The moment in the arbour where the rain beat,
> The moment in the draughty church at smokefall
> Be remembered. . . .
> T. S. Eliot, *Four Quartets*, Burnt Norton

4

Identity and Beyond

*The human being is an open possibility, incomplete and incompletable.
Hence he is always more and other than what he has brought to realisation
in himself.*[1]

ON BECOMING

What is 'I'? These three simple words penetrate right to the heart
as far as human psychology is concerned. But it is a question which
goes beyond psychology into the realm of spiritual traditions, for
the great explorers of the nature of self have been the mystics
of the world's religions. Whatever the final goals of mysticism,
knowledge of self seems to have been the ubiquitous key to their
realization. Our interest lies, then, in drawing together the insights
to be gleaned from both sides of this divide, from the psychological
and from the mystical traditions.

In the Hebrew Bible, God's nature as manifested at different
times is expressed by specific names. These names are not merely
labels of convenience, but are viewed as capturing the essence of
the particular divine face. The 'highest' name of God thus revealed
translates as 'I will be that which I will be' (Exodus 3:14). The verb
'to be' is in the imperfect tense, which normally implies the future
in Hebrew. However, the imperfect more generally indicates an
incomplete action (and therefore the King James translation, 'I am
that I am', misses an important emphasis). And here we find a
crucial point with regard to 'I' at the human level as well: that it
is never complete – nor, therefore, whole. At the root of 'I' is a
process rather than a structure; a process of becoming.

A second idea conveyed by 'I will be that which I will be'

concerns the mirroring process implied by the repetition of the verb, as if the Creator's essential Being consists in a desire to know Himself. As the *Zohar* puts it in describing the first stirrings of creation, 'Before there was balance, countenance beheld not countenance.'[2] And, in this view, which also comes across in the philosophy of Bergson, the whole purpose of creation is for these two divine 'countenances' to be reconciled, to be reunited in a perfect mirror – the mirror of consciousness. In this way humankind is the essential partner to God in the unfolding process of creation.

Jung captures this idea of partnership when he writes of 'the service which man can render to God' as being one of bringing the contents of the unconscious into consciousness. This is done in order 'that light may emerge from the darkness, that the Creator may become conscious of His creation, and man conscious of himself'. As he boldly puts it, 'If the Creator were conscious of Himself, He would not need conscious creatures. . . .'[3] Searching for a 'myth of our own', he writes: 'Now I knew what it was, and knew even more: that man is indispensable for the completion of creation; that, in fact, he himself is the second creator of the world. . . . Human consciousness created objective existence and meaning, and man found his indispensable place in the great process of being.'

A cornerstone of the kabbalistic viewpoint is that 'above' and 'below' are related through correspondence. Thus we may infer that the mirroring process at the heart of the divine 'identity' is recapitulated in a parallel in human identity, for the human is the microcosm of the divine. The mirroring process in ourselves concerns the power to reflect on self. It is this which underlies our sense of identity, and, as with the name discussed above, it is a process that can never be complete. Identity is a striving to be that which we hold as an ideal.

But, so the spiritual traditions insist, individuals may play their part in the cosmic process, in the Creator's quest for reunification, only when the mirror of their personal consciousness is cleansed. This requires awareness of the simple process of becoming which underlies 'I', uncluttered by the accretions which 'I' makes in its desire for security. This alone, the deepest knowledge of self, is the precondition for restoring balance on the cosmic, as well the personal, scale. 'Can you polish your mysterious mirror,' asks Lao Tzu, 'and leave no blemish?'[4]

Returning to the name of God, 'I' as subject of the verb is

conveyed by the Hebrew letter *alef*. Indeed, the first person imperfect is always thus formed with the prefix of an *alef*. As noted in Chapter 1, *alef*, the first letter of the alphabet, is characterized by silence. Moreover, 'It looks like the brain,' says the *Bahir*, and symbolizes the continuity between human thought and 'God's thought': '[Human] thought has no end, for as a man thinks he descends to the end of the world.' The *alef* implies 'following thought to ultimate infinity'.[5] In other words, the substantiality of 'I' is illusory (*alef* has no sound), and as we explore the real nature of self (*alef* as image of brain) we become aware of the spiritual quality inherent in the source of our Being (relationship between human thought and 'God's thought').

The ultimate closeness to God is achieved when the individual becomes united with the divine, the *unio mystica*. According to Idel, the quest for such union seems to have been particularly central in the mysticism of Abulafia and his followers. The significance of the name we have been considering, 'I will be that which I will be', is highlighted in a text by Abulafia or one of his colleagues which considers the doubling of the word 'I' involved in this name and in such biblical phrases as 'I-I the Lord' Isaiah (43:11). This doubling of 'I' is viewed as an expression of the union between the 'supernal divine power' and the 'human power'. In this sense, there is an intense intimacy between divine and human identity, and, as Idel argues, '. . . it seems that the phrase: "I–I" is an exclamation by a mystic, indicating his awareness of becoming divine'.[6]

The modern Hindu sage, Sri Ramana Maharshi, seems to be exploring the same point:

> By inquiring into the nature of the I, the I perishes. With it you and he [objects] also perish. The resultant state, which shines as Absolute Being, is one's own natural state, the Self. . . . The only inquiry leading to Self-realization is seeking the source of the 'I' with in-turned mind and without uttering the word 'I'. . . . If one inquires 'Who am I?' within the mind, the individual 'I' falls down abashed. . . and immediately Reality manifests itself spontaneously as 'I–I'.[7]

Ramana identifies this 'I–I' with the Infinite, and his words may be construed as an ideal psychological commentary to the name of God with which we opened this section.

THE IDENTITY PLANE

The model of perception advanced in Chapter 2 specifies three key operations. These are:

1. *Analysis*. Neural systems respond to the presence in the sensory input of discrete features and the neuronal input model is thereby generated.
2. *Search*. There follows a search through the memory system for schemata resembling the input model.
3. *Match*. A comparison is effected between the results of operations 1 and 2. Should the input model and accessed schemata match, the process ends. The subject perceives the model. If there is no direct match, the analysis is modified until a match is achieved.

Now, it should be apparent from what we have said about memory that the second operation is hardly a 'search' at all. As the neuronal input model is generated, the pure memory process comes into operation. Any memory schemata which bear resemblance to the input model will be activated automatically by resonance. This is not a directed operation, as the word 'search' implies, but an inevitable consequence of the nature of memory. Of course, some schemata will be more strongly activated than others, depending on the extent of resemblance, and we may assume that the most strongly activated schema will 'win out' when it comes to the matching stage.

With the foregoing framework in mind we may begin our analysis of the nature of identity. As far as perception is concerned, it seems that the sense of 'I' arises as memory images are matched to the neuronal input models. The crucial point is that unless and until such a match occurs there is no 'I'. Now, of course, unless we are asleep or in a coma, these memory-input matches take place all the time. By definition, to perceive is to have an identity (otherwise we would be talking of sensation and not perception). Even when an individual is responding to subliminal inputs – in which case no match occurs and therefore there is no 'I' to perceive that input – other concurrent material is being perceived and an overall sense of identity is not lost.

Two points which arise from the foregoing should be stressed.

First, it is apparent that identity is not some kind of unchanging inner person, passively awaiting incoming information. 'I', according to this model, is generated anew in every moment. Second, the model implies that identity is not unitary. 'I' must be a composite, a shifting amalgam connecting the whole array of current inputs to our prior experiences with those, or similar, inputs stored in memory. Without memory there can, therefore, be no sense of identity. On the other hand, 'I' is not a fixed structure in memory. It arises through our interactions with the world around us.

As discussed in Chapter 3, memory images, or schemata, come complete with their 'I-tags'. These are the basic data from which our sense of identity is constructed. In any given moment, a number of such 'I-tags' are presumably activated as sensory systems interact with memory in the ways set out in the model of perception. Thus I may be holding a pen which triggers one 'I-tag', sitting by a familiar plant, another 'I-tag', listening to a favourite piece of music, a third 'I-tag' – and so on. Each 'I-tag' embodies my past identity state when the given entity was experienced previously. We can envisage these many 'I-tags' as constituting a plane of the mind, which I shall call the *identity plane*. I use the term 'plane' here in a metaphorical sense only. The mind cannot be described literally in geometrical terms since it has no literal spatial attributes. Neither is the identity plane to be construed as tied to a particular plane or level within the brain. It is merely a convenient label for the sense of identity as it is generated through the processes I have discussed.

Now it is quite clear that we do not experience ourselves as being fragmented in the way that the foregoing discussion might imply. Our sense of identity is that of a single, unified and continuous 'I'. However, it should become clear through the material to be examined later in this chapter that there is something of an illusion here. The unified 'I' is an entity constructed from the fragmented identity plane to make *retrospective sense of mental events*. But this is an issue to be examined more fully in the next section. Here I wish to focus on the nature of the identity plane.

The identity plane comprises an endless flux of 'I-tags' from which 'I' is continually constructed. Furthermore, the current 'I' in any given moment becomes the 'I-tag' attached to new memories of the present scene. Again, the point is that 'I' never remains the same. This is a highly dynamic process whereby 'I-tags' are continually being drawn from memory, and, as the present scene itself enters memory, updated in memory. In this flux of 'I', the 'I-tags' predominating in any given situation will be those attached to memories having the highest density of associations to the present situation. In effect, the updating of 'I-tags' constitutes the personal evolution of 'I'. Figure 4.1 attempts to illustrate the

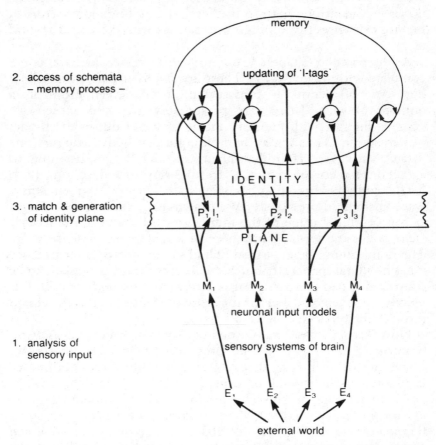

Figure 4.1: Generation of the identity plane. Events in the external world (e.g. E1 pen, E2 plant, E3 music, E4 subliminal event) are perceived via the matching process described earlier (P1 etc.). Each match incorporates the appropriate 'I-tag' (I1 etc.), embodying the subject's prior contact with the event. 'I-tags' are updated as the current 'I' in turn is consolidated in memory. Note: Events are not as isolated as this diagram may imply. They are connected both to preceding events and to contemporary events. The flux of perception comes about as the memory process models external reality largely on the basis of these connections between events.

point but is inevitably limited to a static representation. Again, what characterizes 'I' in this model is the cumulative state of flux that supports it.

Of course, 'I' is generated by internal inputs as well as external ones. In other words, 'I' think as well as perceive. Thinking is not so very different from perceiving, as Helmholtz pointed out last century. Both involve logical deductions on the basis of given data. In the terms employed here, thinking is the psychological process of activating memory images and manipulating them one to another. Perception involves exactly the same process but takes place in relation to sensory data.

If we follow the argument further, it is not actually the case that 'I' think. Rather, each memory image that is activated during thought contributes its 'I-tag' to the ongoing construction of 'I'. 'I' is actually a product of thought, not the master of it. Interestingly enough, it further follows that if thinking were genuinely to create new connections and new forms, there would necessarily be an attenuation of 'I'. 'I-tags' embody my connection to *past* images, but a *new* image has no 'I-tag'. Therefore, for the time that a new image engages the mind, there can be no 'I'. This is indeed the case in true creativity. As reported by those who have attempted to reflect on their own creativity, the creative moments seem to come in some twilight zone of preconsciousness: 'Unless preconscious processes can flow freely there can be no true creativity,' writes Kubie.[8] But this point is best left to the artists themselves. In answering a question concerning the creativity in her own poetry, Amy Lowell writes

> It makes not the slightest difference that the question as asked me refers solely to my own poems, for I know as little of how they are made as I do of anyone else's. What I do know about them is only a millionth part of what there must be to know. I meet them where they touch consciousness, and that is already a considerable distance along the road of evolution.[9]

It may be argued that this moment of creative inspiration is the only time when we truly exist in the present, when we are not simply rehashing the past. In other words, whenever 'I' am, past associations are necessarily clouding the present moment. Of course, as soon as the poet reflects upon the primary intuition, 'I' is reconstituted and can begin to work on forming the poem. (In the exceptional case of Coleridge's 'Kubla Khan', it would seem that this latter stage was bypassed altogether.)

As we will discuss in the final section of this chapter, it is possible to transcend the identity plane, which will engender a new psychological state (an 'altered state of consciousness'). As we have seen, the moment of creativity is just such a moment of transcendence. Generally speaking, it is the fragmentation of the identity plane which constitutes the major block to realization of our highest potential, as in creativity. On account of the identity plane being an amalgam of 'I-tags', it is essentially conservative; it always seeks to relate to the present in terms of past identities. Memory is indeed the master here and consequently, whenever 'I' am, I am actually in the past. Transcendence of the identity plane is achieved through awareness of the present moment, and that means awareness of becoming.

The reader may object that this model seems divorced from experience. We experience ourselves as a single self, continuous and whole, and memory is our servant, not a master. However, we must be careful to distinguish the personality characteristics of 'I' from the *feeling* of 'I'. We do have an enduring feeling of selfhood, a point to be explored in Chapter 5. That is not in question. But the substance of 'I' is open to doubt.

The reader may like to consider this point in the form of an experiential exercise. Consider the nature of your 'self'. As you attempt to specify its nature, you will, no doubt, bring various aspects to mind. The exercise is one of detaching from each of these aspects in turn. What remains as you strip them away? Is there some core you can experience beyond the various aspects you have specified? You may consider relationships, for example. Thus you probably define yourself in part as so-and-so's son, brother, sister, wife, husband and so on. Is it possible to be yourself irrespective of those relationships? What about career, status, possessions and so on? More fundamentally, what about dispositions and personal skills? Can you be the same 'I' stripped of those qualities of which you are proud. . . ?

This is an exercise in imagination, but that does not make it any less important in psychological terms. The aim of the exercise is really that of a meditative contemplation of self. Indeed, experience of meditation is probably necessary for the reader to gain the insight into self at issue here.

It *is* possible to strip away all the aspects (and more) mentioned above. Eventually you will be left with the feeling of 'I'. Not this or that aspect, just a feeling which cannot be put into words. And then. . . awareness. Simple Being.

THE MULTIPLICITY OF 'I'

The notion that 'I' is a multiple entity and that our sense of being a single, unitary self is illusory could be described as an idea whose time has come. The publication of articles and books from biologists, psychologists and philosophers arguing the point has recently developed avalanche proportions.[10] The idea itself is not new, having a strong tradition in Buddhism and Western mysticism,[11] and surfacing in psychiatry through the work of Binet and Janet in particular, at the end of the last century.[12] However, the recent flowering of interest is attributable largely to the scientific input from research on split-brain patients, and the phenomenon of *blindsight* to be discussed below.

There are essentially two points that need to be emphasized as we introduce the concept of multiplicity of 'I', both of which we have already met earlier in this book. First, there is the issue of *control*. Although 'I' has the impression that it is in control, it is evident from studies reviewed in Chapter 3 and those to be discussed here that this is often not the case. Actions are planned and executed from outside of 'I', but nevertheless 'I' deems itself in control; it interprets events accordingly and thereby furthers its *raison d'être*.

The second point concerns *consciousness*. Many authors describe brain or mind processes outside of 'I', *even be they inaccessible to 'I'*, as being conscious. Thus, for example, Beahrs states that '. . .all mental activity is really conscious and that when we talk of the (or an) unconscious we must be referring to something conscious at another level'.[13] In this sense, the multiplicity of 'I' is identified with multiplicity of consciousness.

I have already confronted the problem of terminology underlying this issue in Chapter 1. I am of the opinion that to talk of multiple consciousness is to misuse the term. By 'conscious' either we mean 'accessible', or we mean the basic quality of mind, identified in Chapter 1 as 'Being'. Either way, I do not think it can be divided or multiple. In terms of the model developed here, the identity plane is *one* plane of mind which accounts for the unified nature of our experience of self, the stream of consciousness. However, this plane is constellated as a shifting amalgam of 'I-tags' and, therefore, its contents are not unified and are only a sub-set of mental activity ongoing at any one time. It is 'I' that is multiple and partial, not consciousness or Being.

The psychological study of split-brain patients has given rise to several competing views of the nature of self and consciousness, often focused in the question as to whether consciousness is divided by the operation. It follows from what I have already said that I disagree that consciousness is divided at all. What is apparent from the many studies of split-brain patients, especially those conducted by Gazzaniga and his colleagues, is that mental processes are *modular* in format. Gazzaniga further argues that the patient's sense of self is most firmly bound up with one particular module, a language-based *interpreter* situated in the left hemisphere. This interpreter continually assesses the causes and meaning of events it witnesses *in terms consistent to itself*. For Gazzaniga, consciousness is the output of this interpreter.[14] The point is that the split-brain operation does not divide consciousness, but merely affects the extent to which brain/mind processes are accessible to 'I'. In this way the operation only exaggerates a split which is inherent in our normal state anyway.

There are many studies on which these conclusions are based and they have been extensively reviewed.[15] A few examples only need be presented here to convey the major arguments. The studies indicate the way in which activity controlled from the patient's disconnected right hemisphere is explained (or even explained away) by the speaking left hemisphere.

In one study, two pictures were flashed to the patient such that one would be relayed to the left, and the other to the right, hemisphere. In front of the patient was a set of different pictures. The patient's task was to point to those pictures from the array which related to the original pictures flashed on the screen. The patient used both hands to point and therefore, since each hemisphere controls the opposite hand, the left hand would point to the picture related to that flashed to the right hemisphere, whilst the right hand would point to an association with the picture flashed to the left hemisphere. The fact that the hemispheres have been surgically severed means, of course, that the left hemisphere cannot directly influence the left hand, nor the right hemisphere the right hand.

When the two pictures were a chicken claw flashed to the left hemisphere and a snow scene flashed to the right, the patient pointed to a chicken with his right hand and a shovel with his left hand. These were obviously the 'correct' answers. The interesting point is the reason given by the patient for these choices. When asked, he said: 'Oh, that's simple. The chicken claw goes with

the chicken, and you need a shovel to clean out the chicken shed.'
Now this is clearly an interpretation by the left hemisphere of
the information available to it. This hemisphere knew it saw the
chicken claw and that the left hand pointed to the shovel (since
it could 'see' that hand even though it did not control it). What
it did not know, on account of the cross hemisphere pathway,
the corpus callosum, having been cut, is that a snow scene was
flashed to its partner. Thus it appears that the left brain has
interpreted the situation in terms consistent with the information
available to it. We know that it has given this interpretation to the
experimenter. It seems reasonable to assume, moreover, that this
is its interpretation for the patient himself. The patient is not only
saying that he pointed to the shovel because you need it to clean out
the chicken shed; this is what he believes to be the interpretation
of his own actions. In other words, the patient's 'I' – that is, the
point from which he observes his own actions – is constructed
by this interpreter.

In another example, the word 'walk' was flashed to the patient's
right hemisphere. He obeyed the command, standing up and
beginning to leave the testing area. When asked where he was
going, the answer came: 'I'm going into the house to get a Coke.'
Again, this was a rationalization by the left hemisphere to bring the
cause of action under its control, as if to say, 'I'm going because I
have freely decided to. . . .'

A third example concerns a rather gruesome film shown only to
the right hemisphere, depicting a person throwing another into a
fire. The patient commented: 'I don't really know what I saw; I
think just a white flash. Maybe some trees, red trees like in the fall.
I don't know why but I feel kind of scared. I feel jumpy. I don't
like this room, or maybe it's you getting me nervous.' Gazzaniga
comments that she then made an aside to a colleague out of his
hearing, 'I know I like Dr Gazzaniga, but right now I'm scared of
him for some reason.'

The explanation for this third example is, presumably, that the
emotional impact of the film crossed from the right to the left brain
side via the still intact subcortical pathways. The substantive, or
conceptual, content of the film is, however, locked up in the
right hemisphere. The left brain interpreter therefore rationalizes
the feelings of fear in the best way it can, projecting them on to
some externalized source. In this case, it seems that the unfortunate
experimenter was the target for projection! In fact this particular
study is relevant to emotion in general. How often do individuals,

and especially groups, project feelings which are perhaps unclearly perceived by themselves, outwards on to some target – perhaps an ostracized individual or racial group. Here is the basis of what MacLean has aptly termed the 'paranoid streak in man'.

The split-brain studies reviewed here seem to be suggesting that the left hemisphere is continually interpreting what it is able to glean of activity determined by the right hemisphere. Further studies that Gazzaniga has conducted suggest that the situation is, in fact, more complicated than this. The brain is not only divided into two functionally discrete regions, the left and right hemispheres. Rather, the whole brain is made up of functional modules, with the interpreter being just one of the left hemisphere's modules. The situation is more complex than might be implied by supposing that sometimes the left does not know what the right is doing. The brain is more like a society, and, as we all know, in any society many subsidiary groupings can develop degrees of relative autonomy and be happily oblivious of other groupings. In summary, Gazzaniga believes that

> . . . human brain architecture is organized in terms of functional modules capable of working both co-operatively and independently. These modules can carry out their functions in parallel and outside of the realm of conscious experience. . . . Monitoring all of this is a left-brain based system called the interpreter. The interpreter considers all the outputs of the functional modules as soon as they are made and immediately constructs a hypothesis as to why particular actions occurred.[16]

What we experience is the output of the interpreter. We do not experience events as they happen; we experience events for their meaning to us. This is the consequence of the quest for meaning introduced earlier. In our daily, mundane interactions with the world around us, it is the interpreter which fulfils this quest. It does this not merely by explaining events, but by generating that within us which becomes the focus of such explanations, namely 'I'. Indeed, the explanations and 'I' are one and the same thing.

In relation to the model of mind being developed over these pages, I see the role of the interpreter as follows. The output of each brain module includes the various 'I-tags' generated through that module's involvement with memory. Each individual 'I-tag' is the basis of meaning since it embodies the individual's involvement with some specific object or event in the past. If I am looking at my pen, the 'I-tag' gives the connection I have with it, its meaning to me. But this is not enough to satisfy the quest for meaning, since such experience would be fragmentary. At any one time there must be hundreds of 'I-tags' activated by my present situation, and from one moment to the next this array would continually change. Continuity would be absent from my experience. It is the interpreter that overcomes this problem. In generating a hypothesis, as Gazzaniga suggests, as to why particular actions occurred, it synthesizes a single 'I' from this array of 'I-tags'. The hypothesis *is* 'I', a kind of final common path in the identity plane which is the centre of immediate experience. The continuity of 'I' is, then, a product of the interpreter. The interpreter functions to place events, and ultimately our lives, in context, and this demands both continuity in time and a sense of control. 'I' gives us both, and thereby satisfies the quest for meaning.

LANGUAGE AND IDENTITY

Being localized within the brain's left hemisphere, the interpreter would seem to be intimately bound up with language. Indeed, language is our most powerful tool for explanation and explanation is the major concern of the interpreter. However, in making this identification between the brain's machinery for language and the interpreter, we need to distinguish the deeper from the more superficial aspects of language. For example, in split-brain patients we sometimes find superficial language skills present in the right hemisphere, but the interpreter is nevertheless restricted to the left side. These superficial skills include naming and understanding simple sentences, but where the right hemisphere seems to be deficient is in the use of the rules of syntax. Thus, for example, it could not understand the difference between phrases such as 'the flying planes' and 'flying the planes'.[17] Here we encounter the deeper aspects of language which concern applying quite complex rules of organization to the generation (speaking) and reception (listening) of sound sequences.

The idea that the specialization of the left hemisphere goes deeper than speech itself receives support from another line of evidence – the study of the brain organization underlying sign language in the deaf. American sign language (ASL), which has been most fully investigated, includes a rich base of syntactical elements which are, of course, conveyed by the use of gestures in space. Now, this raises an interesting question. Given that, in the majority of individuals, visual perception of spatial relations is a major specialization of the right hemisphere, which hemisphere would control ASL? The question has been answered through assessing the impact of localized brain damage in deaf signers. The answer is unequivocal: damage to the left hemisphere interferes with ASL, whilst damage to the right hemisphere has minimal effects in this regard. Furthermore, as in non-deaf patients, damage to the right hemisphere in these deaf signers interferes with general spatial abilities, implying that the right hemisphere in non-brain-damaged deaf signers is still specialized for spatial abilities. Despite this specialization, there must be a more fundamental reason for the left hemisphere's involvement in ASL. It is surely that only the left hemisphere is able to handle the kind of transformations involved in syntax.

Bellugi, Poizner and Klima confirmed this by means of some interesting observations of signers' use of space in their hand movements. In ASL, space may be used in two ways. One is to depict the spatial layout of objects being described, for instance the arrangement of furniture in a room. The other use of space concerns the syntax of the language itself. They studied the ways in which such use of space was affected by brain damage in deaf signers. It was apparent that these two ways were differentiated along hemispheric lines: 'Even within signing, the use of space to represent *syntactic* relations and the use of space to represent *spatial* relations may be differentially affected by brain damage, with the syntactic relations disrupted by left hemisphere damage and the spatial relations disrupted by right hemisphere damage.'[18]

Language, as they make clear, involves two structural levels: one comprises the word, or gesture, lexicon, and the second consists of the grammatical scaffolding underlying sentences. It is the second for which the left hemisphere alone is specialized. And, I would argue, the transformations involved in applying this grammatical scaffolding are the same transformations as those involved in constructing the sense of 'I', discussed in relation to the work of the interpreter in the previous section. 'I' can only exist when the mind establishes a separation between subject and object, which is an essentially grammatical problem. Thus language and identity are fundamentally intertwined.

The distinction between different levels of language is central to the discussion, for we need to be quite clear that the interpreter is not simply a speech device. Indeed, it seems most likely that speech, as a means of communication, arose as a secondary benefit to the primary evolutionary advance that the interpreter brought about – the creation of an egocentric, and therefore controllable, world view.

The distinction is well brought out by Whorf in his hypothesis of *linguistic determinism*:

> We are inclined to think of language simply as a technique of expression, and not to realize that language first of all is a classification and arrangement of the stream of sensory experience which results in a certain world-order, a certain segment of the world that is easily expressible by the type of symbolic means that language employs.[19]

Language, in this view, is not simply the words we use, but a means for interpreting the world, whether or not that interpretation is formed into outward speech. As Jerison puts it, language 'evolved as a unique adaptation to contribute to the construction of "reality". Thus, '. . .when we talk we share realities' '.[20]

In my view, the construction of reality may not be separated from the construction of 'I'; both are brought about by the work of the interpreter. As has been argued already, 'I' is not some detached observer, simply peering at the world. Rather, the quest for meaning is met by the operation of the interpreter which generates a unified vision of the world through its systematization of 'I-tags'. It would be quite untenable, however, to propose that our construction of reality is a responsibility of the left hemisphere's interpreter alone. The isolated right hemisphere perceives and manipulates objects and, as we have seen, draws inferences. It is not devoid of reality orientation. However, its reality may not be identified with that which we communicate to others. In other words, we live in two 'realities'. One is experienced by 'I'; as such it is determined by the will to control and is a product of the interpreter. The other embodies a fully organized, but non-egocentric, view of the world. It follows that the skills at which the right hemisphere excels are those which are best performed from the reality of 'non-I'. These include listening to music, where the will to control and interpret would be counter-productive.

Language is very much concerned with the will to control. It is not only that we may control others through cunning use of language, but that grammar itself enables the world to be organized in terms consistent with 'I'. And, as we have seen, 'I', as the unified focus of the identity plane, exists specifically to give a sense of control in the individual's construction of reality.

'I', then, does not exist in a vacuum. It is the complementary dimension to the construction of reality by the interpreter.

These are perhaps difficult concepts to digest, mainly because they do not immediately accord with personal experience. 'I' seems quite substantial and separate from outer reality, which in turn seems quite objective. The notion that these cherished 'truths' are, in fact, illusory is suggested from several quarters. The world's mystics have been practically unanimous in asserting it. The psychological and neuropsychological studies discussed above (and more studies to be examined throughout the book) are impossible to explain within the framework of those cherished 'truths'. A third line of evidence for the model being developed here comes from an understanding of the nature of childhood autism.

The autistic child presents a somewhat puzzling array of symptoms. First, there are problems of communication. Second, the autistic child displays a restricted use of imagination, for example in play. Third, the child may become unduly fixated on some particular object or scene – a spinning top, for example. Psychologists have attempted to understand what the various symptoms may have in common and to offer an explanation for the condition which would 'explain' the wide range of symptoms. It is generally recognized today that such an explanation involves those fundamental processes whereby the child begins to understand what it means to 'have a mind'. The problem is one of language, not only in the superficial sense of communication but in the deeper sense of establishing the reality of self, upon which any meaningful communication is contingent. Without 'I' there can be no coherent reality to an individual's world. An examination of the nature of the central disorder in autism lends further support for the role of the interpreter as discussed in this chapter, for it presents itself, I believe, as the clearest explanation of the problem.

The autistic child has difficulty in establishing normal social relationships and in using language. It has generally been established, however, that these are outward symptoms of a more fundamental deficit. Hermelin[21] concluded from a series of studies that the fundamental deficit in autism concerns the ability to integrate current sensory input with stored representations of previous experience. The autistic child therefore lacks mental mobility, being unable to detach from the impact of the immediate sensory situation. For example, if asked to recall a list of words an autistic child is likely to repeat, in somewhat rote fashion, the last words heard with no regard to meaning. A non-autistic child of comparable ability will take meaning into account, remembering words that perhaps went together to form a sentence or phrase. Similar observations have been made with non-verbal material, for example pictures or toys. The autistic child seems to lack the ability to generalize on the basis of experience, whatever the specific modality involved. As discussed in Chapter 2, normally the perceptual process is geared to the generation of meaning. The individual's previous experience with objects and contexts becomes an integral part of the perceptual process through the matching of input to schemata. It is this matching process that Hermelin specifically targets as the primary disturbance in autistic children.

I have argued above that this matching process generates the identity plane. The meaning inherent in a given situation is inseparably bound up with the identity of the individual perceiving it. Thus, if this is indeed the general area of disturbance in autism, it is as much a disorder of identity formation as it is a disorder of perceiving the meaning of external objects and people.

Recently, Leslie[22] has argued that the problem lies in the autistic child's development of a *theory of mind*. A theory of mind, he suggests, is implicitly required for understanding behaviour. Children need to relate what can be observed in the behaviour of others to those mental states within themselves which relate to such behaviour. In effect, what is being said here is that we can only know others through knowing ourselves, and that the seeds of such insight are sown in childhood. For example, the child may need to take into account another's beliefs or expectations rather than rely solely on overt behavioural manifestations. On this view, games of pretend are important in developing the child's theory of mind since they enable rehearsal of new mental states to take place. It is essentially a question of building up internal representations of the ways in which people's mental states relate to their outward behaviour.

Not only is impairment in pretend play a specific feature of autism but, according to research conducted by Leslie and colleagues, it appears that these children are specifically impaired in their theory of mind. They perform particularly poorly in 'games' involving understanding the mental states – that is, beliefs and knowledge – of characters other than themselves. In one study, for example, two experimenters were involved.

A coin was hidden in a simple hiding place in the child's view. One experimenter then went out of the room; whilst she was out, the second experimenter moved the coin to another hiding place. Again, this was in full view of the child. The question under examination here was whether the child would be able to see the situation from the first experimenter's point of view (for instance, when she comes back into the room, where will she start looking for the coin?). Could the child understand the mental state of the first experimenter? Autistic children had great difficulty in these kinds of studies. Their performance was poor not only compared to normal children, but also in comparison to Down's Syndrome children and to children with specific language impairment. This latter comparison is particularly important since it demonstrates clearly that the difficulty in comprehending others' mental states is not a consequence of language difficulties *per se*. The autistic children, claims Leslie, have problems specifically in their theory of mind.

It seems to me that we need to consider a little more deeply what underlies this idea of a 'theory of mind'. Certainly games of pretence are important in building up the range of scenarios that children may incorporate in their theory of mind. But surely there is a crucial prerequisite to this process. Children must be able to *observe their own mental processes*. Albeit in only a rudimentary way at first, such an observation would form the basis of the comparisons with others' behaviour which underscores the embryonic theory of mind. The ability to observe one's own mental processes could only become possible as the child's sense of 'I' begins to form. 'I' becomes an observation point on the mind. It is the means by which the developing mind begins to know itself. The normal child, then, has the major task, starting before the age of two, of building up the sense of 'I' in order to facilitate observation of the state *in their own mind* relating to pretence, beliefs and the like. In this way the seeds of the child's theory of mind are sown. Returning now to autism, we may propose that the essential deficit is precisely in this early development of 'I'. The autistic child is impoverished in their theory of mind because the interpreter fails to assume its role; the child lives in a world lacking any point of reference from which to construct a coherent sense of the meaning of things. The problem would seem to be in the area of language, not in the superficial sense of communication (although this is secondarily affected) but in the essential aspect of interpretation and classification mentioned earlier.

I will have more to say about the role of language in relation to the identity plane when I consider the phenomenon of *blindsight* below. For now, let me summarize the arguments. The identity plane is conceived of as a shifting array of 'I-tags', each of which embodies one's past personal connection to present impressions. From these, the sense of a single 'I' is generated through the work of the interpreter. Present impressions (which include feelings as well as sensations and thoughts) are interpreted as emanating from a single locus of control – 'I'. Although this 'I' is constructed anew each moment, the impetus of the interpreter is necessarily towards continuity. That is to say, the *raison d'être* of the interpreter is to generate consistent explanations of events and, complementarily, a consistent focus for those explanations – 'I'. Therefore the interpreter generates a bridge between successive constructions of 'I'. The explanations of the interpreter are set in terms of the laws of causation, which bring about the experience of time as we know it and the experience of the 'stream of consciousness'.

We may assume that 'I-tags' themselves are constellated into groupings, giving rise to what have been called 'subpersonalities'. Thus, although 'I' is constructed anew each moment, it tends to fall back on familiar ground by embodying one or another predominant image we have of ourselves. Rowan defines a subpersonality as 'a semi-permanent and semi-autonomous region of the personality capable of acting as a person', and suggests that an average person displays between four and nine such subpersonalities. [23]

We may become aware of the multiplicity of 'I's through the internal dialogue by which they communicate and by means of which they are maintained. Thus, in general, we may find that the inner commentary that seems to be with us most of the time can be related to different characters, one perhaps a parental authority figure, one a hedonist, another a priestly figure and so on. Each delivers its lines to one of its colleagues in an attempt to assert its will. It can be useful to get to know these foci of inner dialogue in order to achieve greater integration of self, but there is some danger of perpetuating personal myths and of confusing levels of meaning, an issue to be addressed in the next section.

Our internal dialogue is, I believe, the surface structure of the process being performed by the interpreter all the time we are conscious. Hence my comment in the last paragraph concerning the maintenance of our multiplicity of 'I's. By 'surface structure' I mean superficial communication: as one 'I' chatters to another on the surface, on a deeper level it consolidates its status as an organ of power and focus of our subjective reality.

In this notion of internal dialogue we arrive at the same conclusion as that drawn by Weiskrantz from his influential studies of blindsight, to which we now turn. He concludes that questions such as 'What do you see?'

> refer not only to the result or outcome of a process, but also to a 'commentary' upon it. . . . We have suggested that the commentary system is activated when we characteristically are able to carry out cognitive operations upon current or stored events, that is, to classify, to order, to rehearse, to imagine, to provide a 'schema' within which behaviour is initiated and directed, and to communicate.[24]

To translate this into the terms I am employing, I would say that the commentary system constitutes a surface to the interpreter's deeper 'cognitive operations'.

The term 'blindsight' was coined by Weiskrantz to refer to residual visual capacities in apparently blind areas of a patient's visual field. It has been found that certain details of visual stimuli, of which the patient reports no awareness, can nevertheless be reported quite accurately when the patient is encouraged to guess. More specifically, such a patient has damage in the area of their visual cortex at the rear of the brain, and consequently a blind portion of the visual field corresponding to the damaged brain region. Despite this 'blindness', the first such patient studied by Weiskrantz was able to reach for visual stimuli with 'considerable accuracy'; differentiate the orientation of a vertical line from a horizontal or a diagonal; and differentiate the letters 'X' and 'O'. All these abilities were demonstrated with stimuli inside the 'blind' field.[25]

Further studies have confirmed the observations on other patients and even demonstrated somewhat higher levels of processing for stimuli in the blind part of the visual field. For example, patients were able to discriminate between the two images in figure 4.2 even though the crucial section, the lower right circle with cut-out, was presented in the 'blind' field. Their ability to say whether or not a triangle was present testifies to the presence of residual capacity in the field, even though they claimed not to 'see' the crucial section. Marcel[26] reports further that patients have knowledge of the shape of objects in the 'blind' field. This was demonstrated by observing the adjustments in wrist and finger positions made as patients reached for objects only visible through the 'blind' field. The adjustments were appropriate to the shapes of the objects, implying that even in the absence of conscious seeing the patients have knowledge of the shapes. Marcel also demonstrated that a word presented in the 'blind' field (for example, 'river') can influence the way in which the patient interprets an ambiguous word presented auditorily (for example, 'bank'). Evidently, the processing of visual information in the 'blind' field proceeds at least to indicate the shape of the letters, so that linguistic processes can come into operation.

In all these cases the crucial point is that patients report no awareness of the key stimuli; they respond at the automatic level or by guessing. In physiological terms we may attribute their abilities to undamaged regions of the brain, either in the cortex itself or in other regions lower down in the midbrain which have visual functions. Psychologically, these studies clearly relate to the cases reviewed in the last chapter. Whatever visual knowledge is present in these patients, it is not accessible to 'I'; it gains no access to the commentary system. Indeed, Weiskrantz reports that it is sometimes difficult to engage patients in the required 'guessing game'; they cannot 'see' and so will not 'lie' by pretending that they can.

Finally, this raises an interesting parallel to the situation discussed earlier with regard to autistic children. As we saw,

Figure 4.2: (a) 'Regular' and (b) 'Irregular' Kaniza triangles. The subject is asked to state whether the figure is a triangle or not. The critical portion, the lower right circle with cut-out, is presented in the 'blind' field. (From Weiskrantz, *Blindsight: A Case Study and Implications*. Copyright L. Weiskrantz 1986. Reproduced by permission of Oxford University Press.)

these children are unable to play the pretend games which are viewed as important in establishing a theory of mind. I have already said that underlying this process in the normal child is the work of the interpreter in separating 'I' as an observation station on the mind. Establishing the primitive 'I' is for the child necessary but, perhaps, painful. For as soon as there is 'I' there is, necessarily, 'not-I', and the wholeness of mind is broken. Games of pretend extend 'I' into the area which had previously belonged to 'not-I', and thus the child grows psychologically. But for an adult to accept that 'not-I' may possess knowledge not available to 'I' is hard, and undoubtedly underlies the resistance encountered in blindsight patients. This is the resistance we must all overcome if we would embrace the challenge of our own potential and seek to move beyond the 'I' that the child grew into. This resistance intimates the *shadow* as formulated in Jung's scheme; it is our natural response to the fiery breath of those dragons awaiting us in *terra incognita*. It is the resistance to any kind of exploration of our inner world. Opposed to this resistance is the dim recollection of something valuable which lies awaiting us where the battlements of 'I' end.

To my mind no one has understood these matters as far as children are concerned better than the child psychologist Frances Wickes, and I leave the last word here to her:

> Experiences of timeless realities may come to a very young child. . . .
> As the child grows older, problems of the outer world press upon him. His ego must grow to meet the demands of greater consciousness and numinous experience may appear to be forgotten by the ego, but it is remembered by the self – that sage who from the beginning lives in the psyche of the child and speaks the defining word in times of peril. . . . Thus the self gives testimony to the Great Realities of the Soul.[27]

BEYOND THE IDENTITY PLANE

In his commentary on the mystical philosophy of Gurdjieff, Nicoll emphasizes a number of points which bear close comparison with those we have distilled through our consideration of neuropsychology. A cornerstone of his thinking is that we are an amalgam of different 'I's, each clamouring for pre-eminence. These 'I's are 'people who are not me but whom I take, without question, as myself. . . . So we have only *Imaginary "I"* – that is, we imagine we have a real, permanent, unchanging I. But we have not.' This state of delusion is maintained through the kind of inner commentary described earlier:

> Have you ever listened to your 'I's talking in you? Often 'I's carry on a long conversation, but you do not observe it. You think it is you talking to yourself. Because of the illusion that you have only one 'you', you cannot do anything about this inner situation to separate from it. To think it is always 'you' talking to yourself is to put the feeling of I into what is an 'I' in you, to identify with each of the 'I's that are talking in you.

This somewhat grim state of affairs may be overcome, according to Nicoll, by the process of self-observation and by withdrawing the feeling of 'I' from these 'people' inside us. As we observe ourselves and see these 'I's for what they are, we begin to change, perhaps even glimpsing the 'Real I in the far distance': 'Self-observation is the knife that begins to separate, to remove, what you take as *you*, from what is real. Everything real leads to Real I: everything false leads to False Personality.' Here the mysticism shines through, for Real I is of a completely different order from the multiplicity of 'I's and 'behind Real I lies God'.[28]

Convoluted as the thinking may appear, the whole of the preceding paragraph up until the last, more 'mystical', point holds up in the light of the neuroscientific material we have been considering. The notion of a multiplicity of 'I's seems to be the consequence of the modular organization of the brain, with the illusion of a unified 'I' being attributable to the left hemisphere's interpreter. Further, the 'conversation' between 'I's may be identified with the commentary system that Weiskrantz is led to posit through his studies of blindsight.

The role of observation in Nicoll's scheme is particularly interesting. What exactly is being observed and what does the observing? The answer to the first part of the question is straight-forward: the various 'I's should be observed, with a view to noticing their conditional nature. Such observation is the preliminary to self-change, whereby the individual detaches from superficial and neurotic aspects of personality. But what is doing the observing? It could be argued that a parallel 'I' observes, 'I_1' observing 'I_2' etc. But this is neither the flavour of Nicoll's approach nor the feeling of what is actually happening as expressed by those who have followed the discipline. Rather, it would appear that in order to observe the coming and going of 'I's, the individual begins to operate from a qualitatively different region of their mind. This shift within the individual is itself part of the desired self-change. In other words, the importance of self-observation in this scheme is not only to gain information about what may be observed, but also to change the centre of gravity of consciousness. Self-knowledge, beloved of the ancients, is not simply a question of one from the multiplicity of 'I's gaining greater understanding of its fellow actors. It is a state of being which, by comparison, is all-knowing; the view as given from the top of the mountain.

The multiplicity of 'I's is founded in what I have called the identity plane. In view of the foregoing, it seems that there is a second plane of mind from which we can, as it were, look down on the ebb and flow of 'I's in the identity plane. I shall call this second one the *higher plane*. My hypothesis of a higher plane is not only advanced to accommodate some interesting aspects of mystical philosophy – after all, these may be misleading. The higher plane is entertained as a meaningful approach to brain function because it presents itself as a logical extension to the model of mind advanced so far.

We have seen that sensory brain processes constitute a matrix of preconscious activity involving interactions with the pure memory process. The 'I-tags' emerging from memory constitute the identity plane and the whole matrix is limited when the interpreter introduces the coherence of a single, apparently causative, element, 'I', into the picture. Now, I conceive the higher plane as being *devoid of 'I-tags'*. It is the immediate interface with the pure memory process prior to the activation of 'I-tags'. If, for example, I am looking at my pen, the higher plane witnesses only its 'pure pen-ness', without personal reference. Occasionally, perhaps when tired, such experiences occur to all of us. The object we are looking at loses its meaning. Similarly, if a word or phrase is repeated over and over it may become meaningless to us. In effect, we slip out of the identity plane at such moments. The point is, the higher plane is not only some mystical, transcendent goal, but is a part of brain processes involved in perception (and thinking and emotion) all the time.

Since the higher plane is devoid of 'I-tags', it is inaccessible to 'I'. 'I' cannot decide suddenly to experience the higher plane; there is no handle for 'I' to hold on to. However, it does have the quality of observation about it. Or rather, it observes. Furthermore, it has 'knowledge', as in the case of blindsight patients. This is knowledge outside the sphere of 'I'.

To the extent that it observes and knows, the higher plane is more than just a fragmentary step in brain processing. In fact, as we will discuss in Chapter 7, it is very much the true person, the inner essence which transcends the ebb and flow of 'I-tags'. Again, it is mystical literature which captures this notion of an inner essence emerging when identity is attentuated. As Stace says, using the terms 'empirical ego' and 'pure ego' for my 'identity plane' and 'higher plane' respectively: 'One may . . . say that the mystic gets rid of the empirical ego whereupon the pure ego, normally hidden, emerges into the light. The empirical ego is the stream of consciousness. The pure ego is the unity which holds the manifold of the stream together.'[29]

If we conceptualize each 'I-tag' as a strand of the mind, 'I' becomes a bundle of these strands. It is a bundle constantly being loosed and rebound as the constitution of 'I' changes from moment to moment. Such is the activity that the interpreter performs in the identity plane. We can envisage the potential for ever more inclusive bundles. The more we 'know ourselves', the more inclusive 'I' becomes. But the paradox is that the ultimate inclusiveness, 'the unity which holds the manifold together', is without 'I', as we have defined the higher plane. It is as if each 'I-tag' has its particular colour of light of such a kind that, were the whole array to be present together, the light would be colourless. So, whether the output of the pure memory process is with or without 'I-tags', the result is the same. We may thus conceive the higher plane, as Jung does the self, as a kind of total 'I': it is 'our life's goal, for it is the completest expression of that fateful combination we call individuality'.[30] Alternatively, we may conceive the higher plane as no-self, as does Buddhism, for it is devoid of 'I'. For Buddhism, the sense of an 'I in itself' is an illusion and the cause of all suffering.[31]

The fluidity inherent in this view of the mind suggests that any one 'state of consciousness' may rapidly change into another. There would seem to be three qualitatively different ways in which the individual may experience an alteration in their consciousness. The first involves what we may call a horizontal shift. The 'I' which is the output from the interpreter is toppled and another grouping of 'I-tags', again constelled by the interpreter, takes its place. Most daydreams involve shifts of this kind, as do many drug effects. Second, there is the sudden 'vertical' shift, in which the operation of the interpreter is temporarily attenuated. The individual experiences the higher plane in such a moment as an intimation of self. Both of these kinds of experience may be accompanied by emotional changes, giving the experience a striking quality, as of intense joy, or, indeed, intense fear. These emotional effects can be understood in relation to activity of the brain's limbic system as we will see in Chapter 5.

Both of these shifts in consciousness are to be distinguished from the third, which is a more controlled and longer-term shift in consciousness towards the higher plane. This shift is the goal of mysticism and transpersonal psychotherapies. The shift comes about through what amounts to a two-pronged attack on the identity plane. First, there are various techniques practised with the aim of stopping the commentary and the process of identification which maintain the identity plane. Second, the individual works with symbolic material in order to establish a new rapport with the sea of preconscious material out of which the identity plane emerged in the first place. The latter process depends upon the creative imagination, or active imagination as Jung called it.

The first of these two attacks on the identity plane limits the tendency to identify mind processes with 'I'. Many mystical and psychological practices have been developed to achieve this aim. Such practices are well exemplified by the Buddhist concept of *mindfulness*. In the words of the Buddha: 'In what is seen there must be only the seen; in what is heard there must be only the heard; in what is sensed (as smell, taste or touch) there must be only what is sensed; in what is thought there must be only what is thought.'

Perception, or indeed thought, of any kind necessarily involves the pure memory process specified earlier; otherwise there could be no meaning at all. What the practice of mindfulness demands is that we stop the process there, that the 'I-tags' which feed the interpreter's will to be the centre of its world be attenuated: 'In employing the methods of Bare Attention,' says Nyanaponika, the mind 'goes back to the seed state of things. . . . Observation reverts to the very first phase of the process of perception when mind is in a purely receptive state, and when attention is restricted to a bare noticing of the object.'[32]

The second aspect of our journey towards the higher plane, active imagination, is very much the partner to the first. As we cease identifying with 'I', so we begin to become aware of what had previously been preconscious material. Active imagination is specifically a technique for working with preconscious material, in particular to enable the individual to relate to transpersonal features

– symbols and archetypes. It involves the controlled exploration of imagery and associations, as described in Chapters 2 and 3. Mavromatis describes the state to be cultivated as follows:

> [It is endowed with] the character of preconsciousness: that is, of sensitivity and openness both to external and internal stimuli that may lie beyond the normal reach of consciousness. It lifts the filters imposed on the mind by the consciousness and logic of the waking state. This permits the emergence of material and frames of reference from deeper layers of the mind. [33]

For Jung, active imagination is a process whereby unconscious material, including archetypal images, is integrated within consciousness. It is a necessary part of what he termed the individuation process whereby we reach our full potential in the self. Active imagination is 'the art of letting things happen, action in non-action, letting go of oneself'. [34] Images should be allowed to appear and unfold, as it were, of their own accord. In reality, active imagination is simply a matter of objective observation; it is the discipline of watching, whilst not consciously limiting, the spontaneous image-generating nature of the unconscious. Thus, active imagination and the process with which I started this section, self-observation, are essentially the same. The various 'I's that may be observed to float in and out of the mind's centre stage themselves arise through the image-generating propensity of the mind. Each 'I' is a product of imagination, an image generated to meet that moment's need.

Imagination thus lies right at the heart of the nature of mind. It will be recalled that the means by which the child's theory of mind is established in the early years of infancy is, according to Leslie, pretence, itself an embryonic flexing of imagination. And now we have seen that imagination is a key factor in the drive to transcend the limitations of identity. In a very real sense we create ourselves in the first place. And we recreate ourselves in chasing our highest potential. I think Coleridge well captured the centrality of imagination when he called it 'a repetition in the finite mind of the eternal act of creation in the infinite I AM'. [35]

5

The Archaeology of Self

THE FEELING OF 'I' (REVISITED)

As I got to my feet it hit me. The stench, the lights flashing frantically, the terror. But this time it was worse than ever – the smell overpowering, the panic unbearable. I had to get out, get away. But how? . . . Then my thought processes started to splinter. . . . The terror grew and the flashing of the light became blinding. I had to escape.

Lurching blindly against desks I crashed my way out of the room. And then it happened: there was a sudden explosion of happiness and significance. Suddenly – at last – all the conflicting pieces of the pattern seemed to fuse for a dazzling second. It was an unimaginable world of pure joy, complete fulfilment; peace and a vision of perfection that shot the world through with a final significance. It was God. It lasted for a second – for less than a second – before I heard myself screaming with the pain of its loss and blackness blotted everything out.[1]

The above passage is a description by Karen Armstrong of an epileptic attack that she suffered. I think we would look long and hard to find a more dramatic description of a personal 'heaven and hell'. Not for nothing was epilepsy dubbed the sacred disease by the early Greeks and Romans!

The experience, so vividly depicted in Armstrong's words, exemplifies the vertical shift in consciousness I introduced at the end of Chapter 4. There are clear alterations in the content of consciousness, particularly in the area of emotion, prior to the patient blacking out. The extremes of emotion are very often triggered in such epileptic episodes, many attacks inducing panic and terror. Occasionally, as in Armstrong's case, the pendulum swings to the side of ecstasy; in Dostoevsky's phrase, the 'brain seemed to catch fire at brief moments'. Other distinctive alterations in consciousness include depersonalization and the experience of *déjà vu* or *jamais vu* (an intense feeling of the 'strangeness' of things which are actually familiar). Depersonalization refers to a disturbance in the patient's sense of self. Often the onset of the attack brings a sense of unreality about the patient's self, as if it is somehow detached from the world or from their own body. A patient cited by Critchley, for example, states that 'My head does not seem to be on my body any more, and the right side of my head is not there. The feeling is as if I were in the air, seeing my body lying on the bed. . . .'[2]

The specific kind of epilepsy we are dealing with here is *temporal lobe epilepsy*, and the alterations of consciousness would seem to be due to abnormal activity in the brain's *limbic system*. This system, depicted in figure 5.1, is known to be concerned with emotion and the co-ordination of memory. Mandell suggests that the euphoric states associated with temporal lobe epilepsy, sexual activity and such drugs as amphetamine, cocaine and LSD may be attributed to slow synchronous electrical activity in the hippocampal–septal region of the limbic system. This leads to his view that here also is the brain region which underlies transcendent experience, the site of 'God in the brain', as he puts it.[3]

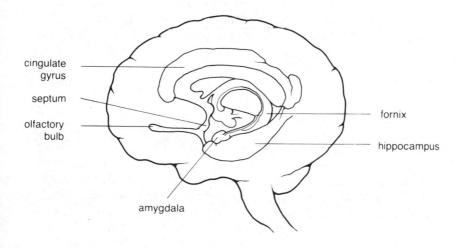

cingulate gyrus

septum

olfactory bulb

fornix

hippocampus

amygdala

Figure 5.1: Major Structures of the Limbic System.

The question raised here concerns the limits of reductionism: is transcendent experience nothing more than the subjective dimension to certain 'twitchings' amongst specific brain cells – perhaps abnormal 'twitchings' at that? The first point to make in this context is that apparently 'mystical' experience of the kind generated in temporal lobe epilepsy is not necessarily relevant to the goals of mysticism. As Stace notes, the hyperemotionalism of some mystics is not 'part of the universal core of mysticism'.[4] Indeed, experiences of an emotional nature occurring during traditional forms of meditation, even when accompanied by an apparently transcendent aspect, may be treated quite dismissively by a knowing teacher. One of the foremost writers on mysticism in the twentieth century, Evelyn Underhill, has this to say:

> All who are or may be concerned with the spiritual training, help, and counselling of others ought clearly to recognize that there are elements in religious experience which represent, not a true sublimation, but either disguised primitive cravings and ideas, or uprushes from lower instinctive levels: for these experiences have their special dangers. . . . As a matter of fact, a good deal of religious emotion is of this kind.[5]

We must be careful not to confuse a temporary, pathological disturbance of the sense of self, which may occasion glimpses of the higher plane as discussed in Chapter 4, with the controlled shift in consciousness involved in transcendence. The latter may involve no extremes of emotion – simply an enlargement of one's vision and a sense of connection to an ultimate unity.

Indeed, the distinction between pathological and mystical experience may perhaps only be upheld when we make reference to a non-physical dimension which underlies this sense of union. At a purely psychological level the distinction is blurred. William James is perhaps our best guide here. In his conclusion to *The Varieties of Religious Experience* he distils the essence of all meaningful religious experience by simply positing that the individual makes contact with 'more'. The first aspect of this 'more' we may understand as what we have specified as the higher plane, that matrix of preconscious processes described earlier: 'Let me then propose, as an hypothesis, that whatever it may be on its *farther* side, the "more" with which in religious experience we feel ourselves connected is on its *hither* side the subconscious continuation of our conscious life.'

In itself, as I have implied, this remains inadequate to the distinction between the pathological and the sublime. But, as James continues, 'The further limits of our Being plunge, it seems to me, into an altogether other dimension of existence from the sensible and merely "understandable" world.' Further, this other dimension 'is not merely ideal, for it produces effects in this world'.[6]

Whether pathological brain activity such as that in temporal lobe epilepsy gives any kind of short cut to this 'unseen region' I rather doubt. What the experiential phenomena associated with temporal lobe epilepsy do reveal are, first, the intimate relation between emotion and the sense of self, and, second, the fragility of self. In the earlier discussion of the sense of 'I' (page 82), the feeling of 'I' was emphasized. We established in Chapter 4 that the left hemisphere's interpreter is responsible for the commentary that links successive 'I's into an apparently unbroken chain. Now we must consider the cerebral basis of the feeling of 'I'. The feeling of 'I' underlies the continuity of 'I'; without it the commentary system would have no core around which to form its own continuity.

Let me suggest an analogy. Consider listening to a radio station. The continuity of the programme is determined by factors operating at different levels. On the surface it is dependent on the spoken content, with the announcer occasionally reminding us of the station's identity. But in a more fundamental sense, the continuity is a function of the integrity of the transmission. If there were disturbance of the 'air waves' we would pick up, at best, disjointed fragments of the station. So too with our sense of self. The feeling of 'I' parallels the integrity of the transmission. The interpreter supplies the content. The experiences of temporal lobe epileptic patients testify to the disjointed sense of self when the region of the brain concerned with feeling, the limbic system, is disturbed. As Kissin points out, Descartes' maxim, 'I think therefore I am', should perhaps be replaced with the more accurate, 'I feel therefore I am.'[7]

The feeling of 'I' would appear to be dependent on the limbic system. This is not to imply that the limbic system is only self-directed. Our feeling of 'I' is also bound up with the feeling tone occurring in response to our perception of objects and people around us. MacLean, who coined the term 'limbic system' in the first place and has amassed much evidence to support its role in relation to feeling, sums up its role as playing 'the central role in generating affective feelings, including those important for a sense of reality of oneself and the environment and a conviction of what is true and important'.[8]

Our awareness of any object is lacking unless the emotional quality it evokes is present. This may be difficult to realize since we tend to think of meaning in intellectual terms. But, as considered reflection should confirm, emotion is the seal of meaning. The evolutionarily most recent region of the brain, the neocortex with its twin cerebral hemispheres, may be indispensable to the analysis of an object's form, but my relationship to that object is cemented in the limbic system. If, to take an example, I look at a rose, it may be that the analysis of its colour and texture, which is carried out in the neocortex, conveys its objective reality. But it is emotion which brings the experience to life, establishing the real meaning to me. Similarly with the sense of 'I'. The interpreter may convey the logic of control, how 'I' choose a particular picture (split-brain studies) or what 'I' saw on the screen (blindsight); but it is the limbic system which gives 'I' meaning.

The anatomical connections of the limbic system can give us an insight into its role. It has downward connections, in particular, to the hypothalamus and related 'core-brain' structures which are concerned with drive states and the primitive dimension of pleasure–pain. Its upward connections are to the neocortex, where sensory and association areas are concerned with analysis of the outside world. Thus the limbic system may be conceived of as mediating between these two regions. That is to say that the primitive positive–negative (pleasure–pain) evaluation becomes refined into the range of feelings, or affects, that outside stimuli arouse in us. At the same time, those stimuli become meaningful to us through their evocation of affects. To consider the rose mentioned above, the analyses flooding down from the neocortex interact in the limbic system with the – presumably positive (unless I had just pricked my thumb on the rose's thorns) – evaluation from core-brain structures, giving rise to a complex of feelings which merge with the feeling of 'I' in my awareness of the rose.

All this leaves out a crucial aspect of our responses to objects around us – the involvement of memory. Access to memory constitutes the second major function of the limbic system. The amnesic patients discussed in Chapter 3 all have damage to some part of this brain system. Furthermore, from experiments on animals there is extensive evidence pointing to the central role played by limbic structures, in particular the hippocampus, in co-ordinating the access of memories.

The juxtaposition of structures concerned with emotion and those involved with memory should not surprise us. Memories invariably have a feeling tone to them which is perhaps the key to their retrieval. An event that leaves us unmoved is not one that is particularly memorable. In a review of the limbic system, Mueller summarizes these inter-relationships:

> It appears that sensory experience achieves meaning or attains permanence in memory only to the extent that it is paired, however indirectly, with the experience of pleasure or pain at a core-brain or 'visceral' level. Those structures that have been implicated in the pathology of memory . . . are also part of the brain's emotional circuitry.[9]

Let us return to Oliver Sacks's patient, Mr Thompson, whom we met in Chapter 3. Mr Thompson has a severe memory loss and consequent problems of identity. As remarked before, Mr Thompson constantly confabulates an identity for himself. But the feature that Sacks emphasizes as striking anyone who has been in contact with Mr Thompson for a period of time is a 'strange loss of feeling'. And Sacks clearly conveys the point that I considered above, the way in which a sense of the reality of things (and of ourselves) is bound up with feeling:

> . . . under his fluency, even his frenzy, is a strange loss of feeling – that feeling, or judgement, which distinguishes between 'real' and 'unreal', 'true' and 'untrue' . . . , important and trivial, relevant or irrelevant. What comes out, torrentially, in his ceaseless confabulation, has, finally, a peculiar quality of indifference . . .; as if nothing really mattered any more.[10]

Furthermore, the limbic system incorporates those structures which in lower mammals constitute the 'smell brain', and in ourselves continue to play a role in smell as well as their roles in memory and emotion. The olfactory references in phrases such as 'feeling the atmosphere' or 'smelling something wrong' seem to support the apparent cerebral basis to the juxtaposition of feeling and smell. The writer Proust brilliantly evokes the threefold interaction between smell or taste, emotion and memory in his novel *Remembrance of Things Past*:

> But when from a long-distant past nothing subsists, after the people are dead, after the things are broken and scattered, still, alone, more

fragile, but with more vitality, more unsubstantial, more persistent, more faithful, the smell and taste of things remain poised a long time, like souls, ready to remind us, waiting and hoping for their moment, amid the ruins of the rest; and bear unfaltering, in the tiny and almost impalpable drop of their essence, the vast structure of recollection.[11]

As we shall explore more fully in Chapter 7, Proust regards this poignant triggering of memories as revealing the deepest nature of self. As we struggle to make conscious the fragments of memory evoked within us, so we unlock the various emotional knots intertwined with those memories. Indeed, the relationship between memory and emotion is a central concern for all forms of therapy and spiritual development.

The point here can be well illustrated by the following incident recounted by someone whom we shall call Jim, a member of a group concerned with meditation and self-awareness. Jim was strolling with his son-in-law along a country lane when he found himself being carried back to his childhood by a particular, poignant smell. On the surface he was carrying on a conversation about politics, but he was aware of something deeper stirring inside. Just then they came to a gate beside a field in which were two horses. Jim realized that the smell had been that of the horses. The son-in-law called to the horses, but Jim, who had been afraid of horses since one kicked him in his army days, was wary. Since that accident, Jim had not been able to go near horses. But something was different this time. He began consciously to 'centre himself', entering a meditative state of mind focused in an awareness of the heart. The horse turned to Jim and started nudging him – his fear had disappeared.

Whilst recounting this episode, Jim found himself relaxing – feeling, as he put it, like a child in the relaxed security of home. Quite unexpectedly, and seemingly ushered in by the relaxed state, the missing piece of the puzzle suddenly fell into place. He recalled himself as a child in the company of 'old man Benson', the local carter. Jim spent many pleasant hours around the Shire horses in Benson's yard. And, if he was lucky, the old man would even put him up on one of them for a ride. As the memories flooded back to Jim, so a feeling of being more complete, more at home, permeated his consciousness.

With hindsight we can understand how the smell of horses in the country lane triggered the whole episode, for it took Jim back to his childhood. The positive emotions bound up with his childhood experience of horses had become locked away – repressed, in Freudian terms – on account of the fear triggered by the later accident. But a high price was being paid in maintaining this amnesic barrier to his childhood experiences with horses. It was not just a specific set of memories that were sealed away, but an entire swathe of childhood emotions. If Jim is to realize some of his potential, he has to penetrate this barrier and make contact with that child in 'old man Benson's yard'. Fear is thus a valuable emotion, for it often intimates where we should begin digging to contact some of that 'more' in the words of William James earlier.

We are now in a position to understand further the amnesia discussed in Chapter 3. I suggested there (page 68/ff) that the problem in these amnesic patients is not a loss of memory as such but a disturbance in the mechanisms concerned with identity, giving rise to problems in access to memory. It seems that these patients can no longer cement the successive constructions of 'I' into a continual stream. As mentioned above, these patients all have damage to one or another region of the limbic system. We must infer that it is the integrative role of the limbic system which has been lost. Different sites of damage give rise to different features of the syndrome, but, in general, the patient retains the moment-to-moment feeling of 'I'. That is, there is no evidence of depersonalization. Similarly, the left hemisphere's interpreter continues to function normally and attempts to rationalize or even covers up the discontinuity in 'I'. But the discontinuity is, nevertheless, the central problem for these patients; and it follows that the limbic system not only generates the feeling of 'I' but normally also lends that quality of meaning to 'I' which comes with continuity over time. It is the latter, integrative, function which seems to be lost in amnesia. Again, Sacks sums up the point with literary force when he writes of Mr Thompson that he had lost 'that unfathomable, mysterious, myriad-levelled depth which somehow defines identity'.[12]

In summary, then, we may conclude that the role played by the limbic system in our awareness of self is twofold. First, it generates the moment-to-moment feeling of 'I' – an intangible quality difficult to express in words but evidenced by its loss in many cases of temporal lobe epilepsy. Second, it appears to have an integrative role in giving 'I' meaning by establishing temporal continuity. This second function is obviously bound up with its known involvement in memory, and is again supported by the experience of pathological cases – this time cases of amnesia attributable to brain damage. In the normal individual these two roles are indistinguishable. The hallmark of the feeling of 'I' is precisely its enduring quality. It does not come and go, but pervades our life. It is the emotional scaffolding which supports the interpreter's *conceptual* continuity of 'I'.

A HARMONY OF THE HEMISPHERES?

Over recent years many words have been written concerning the cerebral basis of consciousness and the self. Every author seems to have his or her favoured region of the brain, some stressing the role of the cerebral hemispheres, others arguing that the primitive brainstem is most important, and so on. I have entitled this chapter 'The Archaeology of Self' to reflect my view that the self is not one thing, to be located in a specific brain region, but a quality that emerges from the sum of human brain activity. Differing regions of the brain contribute differing aspects of the self. Just as the brain is a hierarchically organized structure, with more advanced regions superimposed on more primitive ones, so too the self reveals its own archaeology. Some aspects of self are primitive and shared with other animals; others are more advanced and uniquely human. Indeed, the worth of viewing the self through this lens of brain science lies precisely in guiding our own personal insight by highlighting differing features of self.

MacLean, whose thoughts on the role of the limbic system we have already encountered, has proposed an influential theory suggesting that the human brain comprises three, evolutionarily distinct, levels (figure 5.2). Each level functions in a qualitatively distinct fashion, and the harmonious interaction of these levels underscores the ideal state of human consciousness:

> . . . in its evolution, the human brain expands in a hierarchic fashion along the lines of three basic patterns . . . characterized as reptilian, paleomammalian, and neomammalian. It deserves reemphasis that the three formations are markedly different in chemistry and structure and in an evolutionary sense eons apart. Extensively interconnected, the three basic formations represent an amalgamation of three-brains-in-one, or what may appropriately be called a *triune* brain.[13]

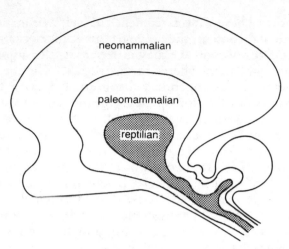

Figure 5.2: The triune brain as conceived by McLean. The oldest brain region, corresponding roughly to the brainstem, is a heritage from the reptilian phase of evolution; the paleomammalian brain, corresponding to the limbic system, derives from structures that evolved with early mammals; and the neomammalian, including the cerebral hemispheres, has progressively expanded during the development of higher mammals.

Each of these three brain levels is considered to have 'its own special intelligence, its own subjectivity, its own sense of time and space, and its own memory, motor, and other functions'.

MacLean's approach considers the kinds of functions that each level of the brain performs, and the shortcomings of human nature when an evolutionary higher level is swamped by a lower level. My interest is more in the self and how these three levels contribute to that complex. MacLean's framework is useful since it clearly demarcates those brain structures included in each archaeological stratum. So far we have seen that the limbic system, which corresponds to the paleomammalian level in MacLean's framework, contributes the feeling of 'I' and sense of reality to self. In the next section we will examine the role of the brainstem and associated structures, corresponding roughly to the reptilian brain, in generating the basic sense of separateness from the environment which underscores 'I'. In this section we will examine further the role of the two hemispheres of the neocortex – the neomammalian brain in MacLean's scheme.

The neocortex includes all the neural machinery responsible for detailed analysis and manipulation of the external world. As such, it generates those aspects of self contingent on our interaction

with the world. These aspects cement the self within its social
and environmental context; they give us our reality orientation.

As we have already seen, we may differentiate the involvement
of the left and right hemispheres in this regard. The interpreter,
in the left hemisphere, engenders the unified 'I' as a focus of
control and is responsible for our self-commentary. In this way,
it generates the immediate aspects of self that we all experience.
But, as I have implied, there is more to the self if we can delve
beneath the surface. Thus the reality of the right hemisphere is no
less a component of self, but constitutes a non-egocentric view of
the world. For the right hemisphere there is no drive to integrate
the 'I-tags' into an intellectually consistent commentary. The self
as experienced in its right hemispheric incarnation is unified, not
through an interpretive commentary, but only through the unified
feeling tone engendered by the limbic system.

The literature on differences between the two hemispheres
relevant to our understanding of self is extensive. Many authors
have chronicled the relative strengths of the two hemispheres,
the left being dominant in analytical states, the right in more
holistic states. One study in particular encapsulates the issues under
discussion here. Gott, Hughes and Whipple studied a woman who
had the distinctive ability to switch, at will, between two different
mental states. The two states appeared to be differentiated along
the lines of known specializations of the two hemispheres. State one
was best suited to her verbal and generally manipulative activities;
state two was associated with relaxed moods, playing music and
drawing. In state one she identified herself as a businesswoman;
in state two as a gardener. More details of her characterization of
these states appear in figure 5.3.

By monitoring the EEG whilst she was in each of the two states,
the researchers established that these two states did indeed relate
to the left and right hemispheres respectively. When she was
in state one, analysis of the alpha component of the EEG indicated relative activation of the left hemisphere, and when in
state two relative activation of the right hemisphere. Furthermore, performance of verbal tasks was facilitated in state one,
whilst performance of visual spatial tasks was higher when in state
two.

Evidence was thus obtained to support an objective description
in terms of brain activity of these two subjective states. We may
not all display such vividly demarcated states as these, but, as
the authors speculate, her 'voluntary control of hemispheric

Area of interest	State 1	State 2
Identity:	me business woman	it gardner
Activities:	planning, writing, arithmetic, chess, reading for information, reading music	spatial tasks, drawing, design, sports, playing music, reading for pleasure
Emotions:	new situations, meeting people, confrontations, angry moods, logical discussions, sense of time	with friends, openness, sexual moods, relaxation, when tired

Figure 5.3 Characterization of the two conscious states in the subject studied by Gott *et al.* (1984). State 1 was associated with predominant left hemisphere activation; state 2 with predominant right hemisphere activation. (Adapted from the original by permission of Pergamon Press. From *Neuropsychologia*, 1984, 22, 66.)

dominance patterns may be a latent human potential. . .'.[14] Particularly relevant to the dimensions of self under discussion here is the woman's designation of state one as 'me' and state two as 'it'. This would seem to be a clear subjective correlate of the difference in self according to whether or not the left hemisphere's interpreter ruled the state. The personal stamp is intrinsic to the self only when the interpreter gives it the controlling quality discussed earlier. It is perhaps paradoxical, but I think true, that an awareness of self is achieved without this personal stamp during moments of intense activity which causes our self-commentary to cease. This kind of awareness of self is a direct, and not a reflective, experience.

Such experiences, in which the sense of 'I' and internal commentary are attenuated, have been characterized by Csikszentmihalyi[15] as *flow experiences*. As a rock climber reported to him, 'One tends to get . . . so involved he might lose the consciousness of his own identity.' Or another:

You aren't really the master, but are moving with something else. That's part of where the really good feeling comes from. You are moving in harmony with something else, the piece of rock as well

as the weather and scenery. You're part of it and thus lose some of
the feeling of individual separation.

Similar experiences were recounted by, amongst others, dancers,
musicians describing the act of composition, and high-level chess
players reflecting on their games. The kinds of skills involved
here undoubtedly demand intense neocortical activity. Evidently,
however, the interpreter has been silenced, giving the experiences
their special character. 'The moment awareness is split so as to
perceive the activity from "outside", the flow is interrupted.'
    It seems to me that the flowing quality of these experiences is the
product of the limbic feeling tone together with the predominant
right hemisphere involvement. The latter gives the experience its
distinctively outward-directed, or reality-oriented, quality. This
may be contrasted with certain more 'primitive' experiences where
the individual experiences flow but reality-orientation is lost, as in
trance states and certain drug states. We may suggest that these
latter states are ruled more from limbic and even 'reptilian' brain
regions. The flow experiences of rock climbers, chess players and
the like are, I believe, experiences of self depending on significant
neocortical integration, but stripped of the 'self-commentary' of
the left hemisphere's interpreter.[16]
    All this is not to imply that the right hemisphere gets all the
stars for 'higher' states. It is the interpreter, and concomitant
self-commentary, that seem to inhibit the fullest realization of
our potential. But the interpreter is only one aspect of the left
hemisphere's functioning. Indeed, it has been suggested that
full human potential is realized by making maximum use of
the strengths of each hemisphere, thereby bringing them into
harmonious relationship. Bogen and Bogen,[17] for example, argued
that creativity depends on such an integration of hemispheric
function, with the right hemisphere generating intuitive leaps or
flashes of insight, and the left formulating the insights and perhaps
subjecting them to analytical scrutiny. In a similar vein, it has been
suggested that meditation may bring about a richer integration of
hemispheric functioning, by bringing the self-commentary under
some form of higher discipline. On the last point, however, the
extensive literature on the physiological effects of meditation is
somewhat equivocal and does not allow any firm conclusions to
be drawn. It may well be that, in both creativity and meditation,
hemispheric effects represent the tip of the iceberg, with more
substantial changes occurring in subcortical brain areas. Taub, for

example, notes that meditation is accompanied by a suppression of electrical activity in the cortical hemispheres of the brain.[18] He argues that the primitive brainstem and, in particular, the reticular formation which occupies much of this lowest stratum of the brain, are central to our experience of self. We turn now, therefore, to an examination of the brainstem and its possible role in our awareness of self.

THE SEED OF SELF

In the first section of this chapter I used the analogy of a radio transmission to convey various dimensions of the unity of self. The coherence of the content of the transmission is analogous to the coherence in the self-commentary generated by the interpreter, whilst the integrity of the transmission depends more fundamentally on the transmitter and radio waves. The latter corresponds, in our analogy, to the feeling of self generated in the limbic system. The analogy is useful further in conceptualizing a third aspect of self. More fundamental than both features mentioned before is the power that makes the whole system work; without power there could be no transmission.

The parallel to this third aspect of the analogy lies in a consideration of the role of the brainstem region. Damage in the region of the upper brainstem and thalamus causes the condition of *akinetic mutism*, a form of coma in which the patient lies motionless with no sign of consciousness. Only occasional, almost machine-like, opening and movement of the eyes indicate any vestige of awareness. In such a patient we could well envisage that the 'power' has been turned off. It has long been known that the brainstem region houses a diffuse system of neurones, the reticular formation, which projects upwards to 'activate' the cortex. This arousal system is distinguished by having non-specific inputs – that is, individual neurones within the system may have inputs from several senses and not from just one specific sense. It is generally argued that the reticular formation, being non-specific in this way, could not perform complex analysis of detailed sensory input. Rather, it is conceived of as simply detecting novelty and change, and functioning to alert the cortex which consequently attends in detail to the appropriate specific signals. As a frequently used analogy puts it, the reticular formation turns on the searchlight to illumine a particular area of detail. Small wonder, then, that neurological impairment at its upper end, where it interconnects with thalamic systems *en route* to its widespread impact on the whole brain, gives rise to coma.

Here, then, is the first point to make about the contribution of the most primitive brain region, the brainstem. It is somehow responsible for the raw energy of awareness. We said in Chapter 1 that Being is a universal property and that awareness is directed Being, a product of nervous systems. We may further speculate here that the brainstem region is the particular site in the human brain devoted to this function of generating awareness. It is the powerhouse of the brain.

As a general rule power is only known by its effects. So too in this analogy with the brain. It is in its interactions with other regions that the importance of the brainstem can be discerned. Thus, in interaction with higher brain regions the brainstem reticular formation maintains the state of arousal. It also underscores selective awareness and, according to Scheibel, our ability to 'know that we know'.[19] But can we be more specific in relation to the involvement of this brainstem region in self-awareness? To begin answering this question I will draw on experiential evidence from meditation and trance states.

In Chapter 4, I defended the notion of a feeling of 'I' by reference to a meditative exercise: stripping away the various concepts of 'I' until only the feeling is left. But one can take it further. When one continues, stripping away even the feeling of 'I', one arrives at what I choose to call the *seed of self*. There is still awareness, and there *is* a sense of self. But this may be misleading. This awareness of self is more of a bodily sense than anything else. One may be focused in one's heart or even in the rhythm of the breath. Or one may be aware of self only as of a space. And it is from this awareness of self that one is most acutely aware of one's connection to the 'other dimension of existence' of which James spoke.

The hallmark of this state is *balance*. Meditative postures invariably stress bodily balance, and experientially the 'space' of self in a deep meditative state is in perfect balance. It seems reasonable to stress the role of brainstem structures in this context: not only does the reticular formation have a special role in relation to awareness, but also the centres concerned with balance and control of breathing and heart function are to be found in this brain region. Indeed, the process of 'centring oneself', which is a ubiquitous preliminary to meditation and/or serious spiritual work, specifically involves awareness of bodily processes. Stripped of the spiritual dimension, the same emphasis may be seen in, for example, progressive relaxation techniques. Awareness is focused into the physical body by tensing and relaxing groups of muscles systematically from the toes upwards. The effectiveness of this technique may be improved by having the individual focus on their breathing, so that they tense with the inbreath and 'breathe out all the tension' in a controlled outbreath. I find it also effective to direct the individual's awareness to the heart: 'warmth begins to spread from the centre of your chest . . . warmth gradually bathing the whole chest area' and so on.

The physical body itself is defined by its outer boundary, dividing 'self' from 'nonself'. Internally, the integrity of this self–nonself divide is maintained by the immune system, which has the ability to distinguish material intrinsic to the body (self) from foreign material (nonself). This recognition of self is an essential prerequisite for the immune system's ability to destroy foreign agents such as viruses. It is one of the greatest challenges within medical science today to understand how the immune system arbitrates the self–nonself distinction. But arbitrate it must, otherwise it would attack not only invading bodies but also the individual's own cells. This is, of course, the central problem in autoimmune diseases such as rheumatoid arthritis.

The seed of self is the psychological parallel to this basic differentiation achieved by the immune system. It is the primitive awareness of one's being an integrity and distinct from anything else. It is the awareness of 'self' as distinct from 'other'. In the meditative or relaxation states mentioned above, there may be no awareness of any specifics of self, no sense of identity nor feeling of 'I', but this basic psychic integrity is still present.

As far as the seed of self is concerned, the bodily and psychological dimensions are integral to each other. The 'knowledge' of self inherent in the operation of the immune system is the same knowledge which gives the meditator a sense of his own integrity. Mind and body are one. This holism underlies the psychological dimension to healing, as evidenced, for example, in the placebo effect and the influence of imagery on the immune system.

With the involvement of brain regions evolutionarily more advanced than the brainstem, this mind–body holism becomes somewhat obscured beneath the complexity of those aspects of self which I have already considered. Nevertheless, the bodily dimension to our sense of self is of immense importance. Not only do our bodies become the conveyers of our self to others through the way we dress, and so on, they also become reflections of our own psychology of self to ourselves. We carry an image of our bodies which is the physical concomitant to the sense of 'I'.

A great deal has been written about this body image and especially about the ways in which it may become disturbed. Damage to any of several brain regions can lead to bizarre disturbances of this image: for example, a patient's paralysed limb can be seen by them as belonging to someone else. More than once a patient has toppled out of bed after discovering a 'strange' leg in bed with them. They attempt to throw this leg out, ending up on the floor because it is actually their own leg!

The body image is not simply a mechanical view of our own bodies. It is an image constructed by the brain, which is as much a psychological, as it is a purely physical, image. Thus, for example, the way we view our own bodies may be decidedly different from the way in which others see us. Of course, this is particularly true during the years of adolescence, when we have to cope with a changing physical body as well as a change in the importance we attach to presentation of self.

The argument that the body image is constructed in the brain, and is not simply a transcription of bodily signals, is well supported by the appearance of 'phantom limbs' following amputations. When such a phenomenon occurs, the patient may experience the limb in great detail – even feeling, for example, a ring on the finger of an absent arm, or a bunion they used to have on the foot of a now absent leg. Furthermore, these phantom limbs are undoubtedly very real to the patients concerned and are not simply vague recollections of the absent limbs. Finally, it is important to note that the experience of the phantom limb cannot be attributed solely to the activity of the cut nerves in the stump of the limb. For all these reasons, it is quite clear that the phantom is a very real image of the absent limb, more or less as the patient had been used to perceiving it. In other words, the patient's body image has not 'caught up' with the changed physical situation. Evidently, the phantom arises through the activity of brain systems which themselves generate our bodily image of self. Normally, nerve inputs from the entire body feed into this image, but they do not on their own create it. 'We don't need a body to feel a body,' writes Melzack.[20] 'The experience of the body is produced by networks in the brain, which are normally triggered or modulated by inputs from the body.'

The most basic awareness that an organism can have of its own body – that associated with the seed of self, as discussed above – I consider to be generated by activity in the brainstem region. But the richness of the body image as a whole undoubtedly draws on widespread brain regions. In the terms that Melzack employs, a 'signature of self' is generated in widespread brain regions. This signature is 'transduced' into awareness by a 'sentient neural hub' located in the core of the brainstem.

Amputation, then, produces a disturbance in the co-ordination between mental and bodily space. Such a disturbance is also apparent when this delicate balance is attacked from the other side of the equation – that is, from the mental side. There are countless instances of, for example, drugs or hypnosis generating a sense of self disjointed from bodily space. An often quoted experience is that of 'floating off' and looking down on one's body, a so-called out-of-body experience. Distinct from this are cases of boundary loss, where the sense of self begins to merge with the surrounding space. Lilly notes that such a loss of the boundaries of self can occur within the kinds of experience that individuals encounter during sensory deprivation in the water tank as described in Chapter 2:

> There can be a beginning fusion between Self and one's surrounds. The surrounds can become liquid, and flow in a myriad of colors. At this point the distinctions between Self and the surrounds begin to be lost. One no longer has boundaries, one spreads out and becomes some of the flowing materials, the flowing energies. There is a loss of the boundaries and the distinctions between Self and the surroundings.[20]

Such an experience takes us beyond even the seed of self as the self–nonself distinction becomes blurred. Similar effects are often reported as a patient is just 'going under' a general anaesthetic and when coming round. Clearly hallucinatory, these phenomena may nevertheless point to an undercurrent of mental activity devoid of self. Perhaps in these cases the brainstem, unchecked by higher brain levels, loses its crucial role in maintaining the primitive seed of self. It is as if the individual is 'at sea' with a rudder unable to hold the course. Disturbing as such a state sounds, it evidently has its attractions. Lilly, for example, reports no shortage of volunteers for his sensory deprivation work. And a state similarly devoid of self, one of undifferentiated awareness, has been the perennial goal of the world's mystics. Why?

BLACK FIRE AND WHITE FIRE

> Even darkness will not cause darkness around you and night will shine like the day; the darkness is as the light.
>
> Psalm 139:12

> Black does not cease to be black, nor white, white. But black is white and white is black. The opposites coincide without ceasing to be what they are in themselves.

The above words concerning black and white were written by the theologian Rudolph Otto. They are quoted by Stace in his discussion of what he regards as one of the universal characteristics of mysticism – paradox. For Stace, the paradoxical nature of mystical experience is the reason for its ineffability. We have no concepts or schematic structures that can adequately cope with the absence of logic in the mystical experience, so how can we put the experience into words? Only, argues Stace, by using paradox in the language we choose: 'The language is only paradoxical because the experience is paradoxical.'[22]

Interestingly enough, it appears that our words themselves convey the place of paradox in human experience. According to Sagan,[23] the word, 'black' derives from the Anglo-Saxon 'blaece'. He points to the relationship between this root and the Anglo-Saxon 'blac' which evidently connoted white, as found in the modern English 'bleach' or 'blanch' and the French 'blanc'. This etymological relationship between black and white intimates a poignant psycholinguistic parallel to Otto's statement above.

There is a rich psychological vein to be tapped in analysing relationships between words and their derivations. Just as Freud realized that the way in which the individual uses words, especially in dreams and free association, may reveal insights into the structure of their mind, so too analysis of the language itself can reveal deeper understandings of the concepts involved, as it were, in the collective mind. An interesting example is the word 'atonement'. Evidently, it is only through elevation to a state of 'at-one-ment' that personal errors or 'sins' can be overcome. One has to go to the source of those patterns of behaviour which underscore the particular 'sins', and endeavour to recreate oneself in a new mould.

The notion that etymology may be employed as a means of

exploring features of the human mind is put eloquently by Thass-Thienemann: 'Language reveals not the prehistory of material things, but the prehistory of the human mind.'[24] And further:

> Language materializes the collective quality of man which is operative in every individual. This growth of language permits speaking about the 'wisdom of language'. This wisdom, the deposit of common experiences through the millennia, is the knowledge of the 'collective' and unconscious motives of man.

Thass-Thienemann goes on to discuss this paradoxical etymological link between black and white, pointing, for example, to the English 'blank', 'bleach' and 'blink', which originally referred to 'shining'. He traces this paradox to the duality inherent in our perception of fire: 'One moment shining, glowing black, the next moment coal-black and sooty.' But is this concrete allusion really an adequate explanation for the most fundamental fusion of opposites represented in this paradoxical relationship between black and white? The union of opposites has been recognized by Jung and others as the quintessential symbol of the processes of psychological growth and creativity. Thus, for example, when we consider the rabbinical dictum that the Torah, the heart of the Hebrew Bible, was written before the creation of the world with 'black fire on white fire', the place to look for understanding is not specifically in our perception of fire, but in our experience of creativity and consciousness, of which fire is the archetypal symbol.

Jewish mysticism is very much a mysticism of language. Like many religious cultures, Judaism holds its language to be a holy tongue. The Hebrew letters are said to be the agents of creation and they, and the language as a whole, comprise a repository of spiritual insights. Thus the *Sefer Yezirah*, the oldest systematization of Jewish mystical thinking, conceives of creation as a process whereby letters are rotated in a cosmic sphere: the Creator permutes the letters to give form to every created thing. The *Sefer Yezirah* gives the example of the two Hebrew words which transliterate as *oneg* and *nega*, meaning 'joy' and 'plague'. The same three Hebrew characters form both words, but they differ as to whether the Creator assembles them 'for good' or 'for bad'.[25]

I have mentioned already, in Chapter 3, that mystical insights into the nature of creation may be considered as projections of our own creativity. There we discussed the contemplative examination of the 'wheel' of a word – its associations. Here, we are concerned with a state in which a word could just as easily fuse into its opposite – black into white, joy into plague. This fusion between opposites is a product of the undifferentiated state beyond the seed of self, where self fuses with nonself. And it is the mystic's encounter with this state that underscores the paradoxicality in mysticism. As Stace says, 'You cannot have a concept of anything *within* the undifferentiated unity because there are no separate items to be conceptualized.'[26]

It is interesting to note in this context that Rothenberg sees creativity as characterized by what he calls *Janusian thinking*. When asked to come up with word associations, for example, creative individuals more often rapidly generated opposites than did less creative types. Rothenberg hypothesizes that, just as the Roman god Janus had faces pointing both ways at the same time, so the creative individual has ready access to this Janusian process, 'the simultaneous conceptualization of opposites'.[27] Rothenberg points out that Janus was the god of 'beginnings', presiding over daybreak, and was considered to be the promoter of all initiative. The name of the month 'January' as the beginning of the year is a relic of this god's status. I would suggest that it is the fluidity of movement between the undifferentiated state where opposites unite and the normal conscious state that is the hallmark of creativity. In Yeats's words, 'The nobleness of the arts is in the mingling of contraries.'[28]

Our greatest challenge lies not only in the creation of works of art but, more fundamentally, in the *recreation of ourselves*. This is what the quest for self-realization effectively amounts to. Whether we see this quest in terms of connecting to some kind of 'Real I', as Nicoll put it, or of finding our complete self unfettered from neurotic restrictions, as a more psychological viewpoint may have it, the endeavour is essentially creative. Certainly Yeats grasped this, and his creative work with the pen was very much the means to, and manifestation of, his struggle to a higher, or fuller, consciousness. His approach stressed again the mingling of opposites in the quest for full consciousness. But in this case it is the ultimate opposition, that between self and anti-self, as he called it, which has to be confronted and resolved:

> *Ille*:   By the help of an image
> I call to my own opposite, summon all
> That I have handled least, least looked upon.
> *Hic*:   And I would find myself and not an image.
>   W. B. Yeats, *Ego Dominus Tuus*

The literary and magical basis to Yeats's aspirations find their psychological counterpart in Jung's depiction of the shadow and in his view of the process of individuation as the unification of opposites. Such individuation must involve, at some point, contact with the fluid, undifferentiated state we have referred to, the *prima materia* of the alchemists.

This undifferentiated state is aptly symbolized as darkness, for nothing can be distinguished in the deepest night. But, as Jung says, 'It is a curious paradox that the approach to a region which seems to us the way into utter darkness should yield the light of illumination as its fruit.'[29] In Psalm 139, quoted at the head of this section, the paradox is confronted. In verse 11 we read, 'Even the night shall be light about me.' The Hebrew translated here as 'about me' (*ba'adeni*) is a curious form which the *Midrash*[30] picks up as a pun on the Hebrew for 'Eden'. The phrase then literally means, 'Even the night shall be light *in my Eden.*'

I have already examined, in Chapter 1, the meaning of Adam's eating of the fruit in relation to the symbolism of light and the change of psychological state. At first he lived in an undifferentiated state, whereas afterwards he entered a state where there was knowledge of difference. Now we must consider the return journey. This is the mystic's quest – to regain the light that shines in darkness. In biblical symbolism it is the passage from slavery to freedom, from a land of affliction to a promised land. We can discern in the phrase 'milk and honey' the twofold symbolism of light and the primordial union of mother and child which underscores the psychological impact of the all-providing garden. Milk is white, and honey embodies the golden light. Further, as Thass-Thienemann illustrates, many languages and folk traditions maintain the link between bees and the womb.[31] Indeed, the Psalm we are considering goes on, immediately after equating darkness and light, to refer to the prebirth state ('Thou hast covered me in my mother's womb'). A talmudic[32] comment holds that the embryo in the womb has the benefit of a glowing light on its head which enables it to see from 'one end of the world to the other'. Whilst the embryo in the womb is the immediate subject in this allusion, the deeper connotation surely relates to light in the context of the transcendent function and the spiritual rebirth of the individual. That this may involve, in psychological terms, establishing a clear connection to the child within is an insight which is to be found in most schools of transpersonal psychotherapy.

A further intimation of the 'light out of darkness' comes in the tractate of the Talmud devoted to the details of the Passover festival, in which the journey of return and birth of the Jewish nation is re-enacted. The tractate opens with a subtle discussion of the interplay between light and dark. The opening word is the Hebrew *aur*, usually meaning 'light', which prefixes a consideration of the preliminaries to the festival. There follows a prolonged discussion as to whether the meaning of *aur* here is 'day' or 'night'. Perhaps paradoxically, the conclusion is that it refers to night! The meaning of this passage concerns the relationship between the exoteric and esoteric aspects of the festival. Outwardly, the preliminaries begin at night; inwardly, it is for the individual to penetrate to the light that shines in that darkness.

As I have said, the ultimate in human potential is to recreate ourselves. Mystics may not set out so to do, believing that union with God, or escape from the wheel of life, is their aim. Be that as it may, recreation of self *is* the invariable consequence of intense mystical experience and/or mystical exercises. Traditionally, this has been expressed in terms of the symbolism of death and rebirth. One dies to the old in order that the new may take root. In the religious sphere, the profound personality changes accompanying conversion experiences have been well documented. James writes at length about such experiences, citing Starbuck's conclusion that they give rise to 'a changed attitude towards life, which is fairly constant and permanent'.[33]

We recreate ourselves through contact with the undifferentiated source of our Being. This is the journey into the darkness. In Chapter 4 I said that there are two aspects to our search for the highest within us. These are, first, mindfulness or ceasing from the automatic identification with 'I', and, second, active imagination. The practice of active imagination may lead on from simple associative imagery to encounters with images or symbols that well up from the undifferentiated state we have been considering. Similar encounters may emerge through meditation. These are the encounters that shape the self we must recreate.

Of course, this process of recreation is not unlimited. 'Rebirth' cannot change the essence we are born with. But we can establish conscious connection with that essence. That is the significance of recreation of self. It is like the play of the master's chisel uncovering a form already gleaned in the eye of the true artist.

Sometimes, a similar deep change is effected in the individual, which actually has nothing to do with their essence. Another person establishes a power of persuasion over the individual, effecting change in that individual's whole orientation and belief system. Such is the process we call 'brainwashing'. There are in fact significant similarities between the self-imposed conditions of the mystic and those confronting a prisoner undergoing brainwashing (or indeed the novice entering a cult). The kinds of sensory restriction and asceticism found in mysticism have their parallels in isolation, prolonged blindfolding and brutalization in the case of the prisoner. Regarding terrorists' hostages, it has been noted how frequently they may 'convert' to identification with their captors and their cause. This phenomenon is referred to as the 'Stockholm syndrome' after an incident in Stockholm in which hostages were held in bank vaults by robbers for several days. When police finally stormed the vaults, they were surprised at the extent of sympathy the hostages had developed towards their captors. One hostage, for example, shouted, 'I won't let you hurt him', referring to one of the robbers. Furthermore, the hostages expressed great attachment to the robbers afterwards, even refusing to testify against them. McKenzie[34] argues that these conversion phenomena may be traced to the similarities between the hostage's situation and that met with in brainwashing, including such features as fear, disorientation and sensory deprivation (such as being blindfolded and having restricted movement).

Another parallel between mysticism and more mundane 'conversion' may be found in the case of the Chinese 'thought reform' under Mao Tse-tung. Lifton illustrates how, through intense processes of self-scrutiny, experience of guilt, self-surrender and confession, the recipient of such thought reform passed through a rebirth experience: 'The break with his family and his past is his symbolic death – the mystical union with The Government and The People, his rebirth.'[35] The parallels, particularly with the asceticism and intense examination of guilt developed by Christian mystics such as St Theresa and St John of the Cross, are striking.

These diverse kinds of psychological manipulations point to a common conclusion: to effect real change in the person, the deepest part of them must be touched. It is not the rational mind, where the 'I' holds court, which determines our allegiances and personality. It is rather the primitive seed of self, emerging from the bedrock undifferentiated state, which shapes our nature. It seems likely that those psychological manipulations which most effectively change the individual work primarily at the brainstem level, and secondarily via the limbic system. Only then is the more advanced cortex changed in its outlook. If you wish to open someone to your influence (be it for good or bad), the last thing you should do is appeal to their intellect, as the testimony of history most forcefully demonstrates. Indeed, the great tyrannical movements of history have been viewed convincingly by Koestler and MacLean as substituting in the mass population the driving force of primitive brain regions for the more reality-oriented cortical regions.[36]

In physiological terms sensory deprivation, for example, has been viewed as effectively turning down the cortex and turning up the brainstem level of activity. Hypnosis may provide a second example in which the balance of brain activity seems to become redistributed towards limbic and brainstem regions as the individual enters a more malleable state. A central feature of hypnotic induction procedures is their emphasis on rhythm, which is thought to have particular impact on the old brain structures. At the same time, the use of techniques to restrict the focus of attention may lead to a lowering of cortical activity. A typical procedure may, for example, insist that the subject see only a single light or mark on the wall. The suggestions of the hypnotist, as well as encouraging the subject to relinquish control, generally include paradoxical elements and we may further speculate that this itself encourages movement towards the undifferentiated state discussed above.

A fruitful comparison may be drawn between the imagery-rich hypnotic state and that of dreaming, for, as will be discussed in Chapter 6, the physiological control of the dream state has been thoroughly researched and is known to centre on the brainstem. Hobson observes that: 'The fact that induction of both hypnotic and sleep states involves rhythmic stimulation and eye fixation may not be a coincidence. Both procedures may help to gain access to and control over the brain-stem centers that appear to be fundamental to conscious-state regulation.'[37]

Recreation of self can, then, be for good or for evil. We may usefully distinguish different classes of phenomena, all of which bring about the kinds of changes under consideration here. It is perhaps useful to conceive of them as lying on a continuum in which the locus of control varies. At one end of the continuum the individual is forced to change against their will. At the other end, the individual attempts to effect change within by their own will. At the former end we would include brainwashing; at the latter, mysticism. Between these two extremes lie the various forms of psychotherapy. Different schools of psychotherapy clearly differ considerably in their means, but the end of effecting change places them on the same continuum as that on which we can realistically equate mysticism and brainwashing.

The paramount point of differentiation between these various forms of psychological manipulation concerns what it is that guides the person's 'rebirth'. In all cases, there is some image or ideal implanted within for their reborn personality to cohere around. In the Chinese 'thought reform' it was an image of the State or the Party; in many a cult it is the image of the guru; in psychotherapy, it is ideally an image of the person's whole personality unfettered by restrictive accretions; for the mystic, perhaps an image of God. This last is, however, somewhat ambivalent, for an image of God is hardly something with definition. Ultimately, the mystic is directed towards an image of nothingness, if one can talk of such a thing. The ideal of the mystic differs from the others in that it promotes simplicity and the emptying of self.

THE FLAWED DIAMOND

In a biological sense, survival is a question of maintaining the self–nonself divide. The membrane between an organism and its environment is necessarily permeable to enable the exchange of materials, but it is also a barrier – the source of the divide in the first place. This is as true of ourselves as it is of an amoeba. Even though we are covered with skin and hair, the inside of our body is still in interaction with our environment via crucial membranes – those in the lungs and in the digestive system for example, as well as the skin itself. The principle remains the same. The maintenance of the self–nonself divide is the primary biological imperative. When the integrity of the divide is lost, the matter which had been constellated in that living organism will rejoin the common pool; the organism must die.

In this chapter we have been considering various aspects of our sense of self, summarized in figure 5.4. Each is a stage in the complexity accruing around the above simple biological imperative. The seed of self, which I identify with the most primitive brain regions, is an awareness of self as distinct from nonself. More primitive still is the undifferentiated state discussed in the last section. Both of these, the undifferentiated state and the seed of self, are experienced directly only when more complex expressions of self are silenced in meditation or allied states. But they are ever-present during more mundane states, albeit beneath the surface. The more complex expressions of self themselves are contingent upon the seed of self. Without the fundamental self–nonself differentiation there would be no feeling of 'I'; no 'I' as generated by the interpreter. In other words we have, in the aspects of self considered in this chapter, a hierarchy. And, as in any hierarchy, a flaw in the foundations will manifest throughout the whole system.

It is with this perspective in mind that I return now to the question of autism. In Chapter 4 I considered the autistic child's difficulties as a failure to establish an adequate theory of mind, in turn attributable to a failure of the interpreter. In this section, the nature of the neurological impairments which may underlie this failure will be addressed.[38]

There have been some suggestions of a disturbance in the relationship between the two hemispheres in the brains of autistic children, with possible brain damage in the left hemisphere. Such a pattern of brain disturbance would certainly support the suggested impairment in the functioning of the left hemisphere's

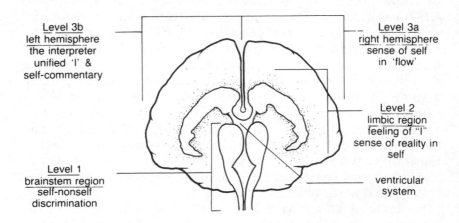

Figure 5.4: The Archaeology of Self

interpreter. However, the evidence is somewhat equivocal; whilst it is possible that some autistic children have such brain damage, it seems highly unlikely that it is a condition universal in autism.

In fact, it is unlikely that there is one single cause of the autistic syndrome. Damage in any one of several brain regions and neurochemical systems may underlie the disorder.[39] Such a conclusion is consistent with the view advanced here that the self comprises a hierarchy of aspects. If the deficit in autistic children lies, as suggested, in their theory of mind and the role of the interpreter, we might expect to find problems associated with neurological impairment at any stage of the hierarchy. Thus, we find good evidence in autistic children for abnormal functions associated with any one or more of the reticular formation, limbic structures and, as already mentioned, hemispheric lateralization.

Ornitz[40] argues for the importance of the brainstem, with pathology in this region being a significant cause of autism. In particular, he considers that such damage interferes with the normal modulation of sensory and motor systems that takes place in the brainstem. Such modulation effects a kind of fine tuning of the signals, which is essential to normal perception and attention. One of the symptoms of autism involves either a lack of responsiveness, or exaggerated reactions, to sensory input. These are just the kinds of reactions we might expect if the brainstem modulation of signals was abnormal. A more specific example is that of habituation, the process whereby we normally cease responding to a repeated stimulus. Such habituation is controlled from the brainstem and involves modulation of the input. The proposal that abnormalities of the brainstem may be a factor in autism is suggested by studies which have shown that autistic children have abnormally slow rates of habituation.[41] As far as motor behaviour is concerned, autistic children engage in highly repetitive, often ritualized, activities. The parallel between poor habituation to sensory stimuli and perseverance of motor behaviour points to a common cause in faulty modulation of signals; in both cases there is an inappropriate prolonging of activity.

Within the brainstem region, the vestibular nuclei and their relation to pathways in the reticular formation are of particular interest. These systems are concerned with our sense of balance. Several studies have implicated vestibular abnormalities in autistic children. Ornitz's work involves controlled angular acceleration of children in a revolving chair. Under these conditions, normal vestibular mechanisms generate a characteristic pattern of jumping eye movements called nystagmus. In Ornitz's studies the autistic children's nystagmus was impaired by comparison with normal children. Drawing on this and other physiological work, Ornitz concludes that autism is associated with dysfunction in a neuronal network in the brainstem reticular formation which is integrated with vestibular function. This conclusion is supported by a study which examined the size of brain ventricles (fluid-filled spaces in the brain) in autistic and other children. Using a brain imaging technique, the fourth ventricle was found to be enlarged in the autistic group compared to the control group. This enlargement may be attributable to abnormalities in the brainstem tissue which borders the ventricle, thus supporting the case for pathology of the brainstem as a factor in autism. [42]

Autistic children are renowned for their abnormal responses in the area of balance, engaging in prolonged spontaneous bursts of whirling or rocking. It may be that these children are attempting to compensate for inadequate vestibular stimulation. Such abnormalities are also apparent with regard to stimuli outside themselves. There are many reports of prolonged fascination with spinning objects such as tops. That all these responses are characteristic, in lesser amounts, of normal children suggests that they are part of the developmental process. By whirling, the child is perhaps exploring the limits of sensation associated with the body self.

There is undoubtedly a complex relationship between our sense of balance and our perception of space and of objects in that space around us. In Chapter 2 I described the effects of wearing prisms that distort the image on the retina. More dramatic studies have employed special glasses designed to turn everything upside-down. When such glasses are worn, the effect is to distort our own body awareness; rather than simply seeing an upside-down world, we may feel our body to be upside-down. Thus, perception of objects around us is very directly related to the way in which signals concerning balance are interpreted in the brain. These and other studies make it clear that our sense of balance is not only a device for keeping the body upright. In the complex interactions of sensory data within the process of perception, our sense of balance becomes a yardstick for the evaluation of the world around us. We perceive objects in relation to ourselves. How far away is the stick? What modifications to my posture must I make to keep my balance if I reach for the stick? Will the weight of the stick overbalance me? These are the kinds of questions inherent in all perception. The young child has to work up laboriously to the automatic inclusion of these kinds of questions in everyday interactions with the world. Small wonder, then, that where there is damage or difficulty in the vestibular area the child withdraws from the world.

The flaw here, then, concerns the seed of self – the relationship between the child's body and objects external to it. All the apparently higher-level problems in autism – problems of language, cognition and social relating – may be ramifications of this fundamental problem. As Ornitz suggests, higher brain regions may themselves be secondarily influenced by dysfunction in the brainstem. Thus, when language does develop in the autistic child, the notable absence of the pronoun 'I' in the child's conversation may be a reflection of a problem with the seed of self at the brainstem level. Despert summed up the situation in terms very similar to those employed here, by saying that 'the "I not I" distinction is not established in the autistic child'.[43]

There are no final conclusions to be drawn yet with regard to the biological cause(s) of autism. As mentioned earlier, different cases may be attributable to differing pathology. I have focused on the possible involvement of the brainstem because it is particularly revealing with regard to the hierarchical view of self developed in this chapter.

The self is perhaps best conveyed by the analogy of a building with foundations and storeys fulfilling differing roles. The case of autism illustrates the problems of establishing the foundations in the first place. With uncertain foundations the whole building can, sadly, never be set on a completely even keel.

In the last section it was concluded, from a consideration of the concept of recreating the self, that to achieve real self-change we must consciously encounter our primitive foundations of self. Understanding the nature of autism can give us some insight into the way in which those foundations are laid in the first place. The normal child goes through the same kinds of stages we see exaggerated in the autistic child. The distinction is, of course, that the normal child rapidly passes beyond these stages. If, as adults, we would travel on a path of self-change, be it through therapy or mysticism, we must loosen the bonds of those early stages. In this sense we become similar to the autistic child in struggling with the primitive foundations of self. It is certainly relevant to point out the striking parallels between the struggles of the autistic child and those encountered on the age-old ascetic path to human potential – a life of ritual and withdrawal from the world. There is an awesome symmetry here. The autistic child struggles to discover their separateness from others and from the world; the ascetic struggles to realize their union with the world and with the Other.

The whirling dance of the Dervishes, a mystical Islamic sect, is undertaken to realign the individual's foundations of self. It well illustrates the parallel between certain aspects of the autistic child's struggle and that of the mystic. For the autistic, prolonged spinning presumably helps stimulate an impoverished vestibular system. As a mystical practice it exemplifies the kind of psychological growth attained through controlled observation during a trance-like state. At the outset, as the novice's eye sweeps around the spinning circle, there is a feeling of sickness and a desire to grasp on to objects visually. With practice, one develops the skill of seeing objects despite their endless motion, and the sickness subsides. Then, if the effort is right, the moment-to-moment grasping of objects fades and the whole circle is impressed on the mind in a single moment, centre and circumference in union. 'At the still point of the turning world' one is simply, as the traditional accompanying gesture indicates, the axis whereby the Creator gives to His creation. Right hand cupped to receive from above and left hand directing the flow downwards, the dancer takes his place in the mystery of creation.

6

Dreaming and the Brain

THE BIOLOGY OF DREAMING

In calling this section 'the biology of dreaming' I deliberately
confront an issue which has been under the surface of much of
the material we have been considering. Biology is a science and
is, accordingly, concerned with the world of observable, objective
phenomena. Dreaming, on the other hand, refers to a private,
subjective experience. The biologist is necessarily on the outside
looking in; the dreamer is on the inside. Stated more generally,
the issue here is the mind–brain relationship. The brain, as a bodily
organ, is approachable via all the various physical techniques that
are available to science. The mind may only be approached either
introspectively in oneself, or, possibly, through inference in others
from their behaviour and self-reports. The explosion of interest in
the biology of dreaming, since the pioneering discovery of *rapid eye
movements* (REMs) and their relationship to the dream state,[1] carries
the undoubted fascination of attempting to bridge this great divide.

REMs occur during a specific stage of sleep (REM sleep) and
seem to indicate that the sleeper is dreaming. Individuals woken
up during REM sleep are more likely to report that they were
experiencing a dream than is the case when they are woken up
from a stage of sleep without REMs (non-REM sleep).

The subject of dreaming is particularly poignant with regard to
the nature of explanation and meaning. What causes us to dream,
and what do the images experienced in dreams mean? These are
the questions that have preoccupied humankind over the ages;
and, of course, they continue to fascinate us today. As we shall

see, great progress has been made in specifying the activity of the brain associated with REM sleep. But such understanding of mechanism does not of itself fully answer the above questions. It would be as if we attempted to 'explain' a Picasso by specifying the mechanisms of light absorption and reflection in the pigments of the paint used.

Just as we would approach the painting in relation to higher-order considerations, such as feeling-tone or symbolism, so we must recognize the reality of similarly higher-order dimensions within our dream lives. As befits a book focusing on our understanding of the brain, we wish to examine the biological evidence. But, in interpreting the evidence, let us also keep one eye open to the psychological and spiritual dimensions to dreaming. Each of these three hierarchical spheres – the biological, the psychological and the spiritual – bears meaning in its own terms. Whilst they are undoubtedly interdependent, each may be said to constitute a separate 'world' which comprises properties irreducible to the world below it. Thus, whilst dreaming is undoubtedly an experience associated with a specific brain state, even a full description of that state does not delimit the psychological, let alone the spiritual, meaning of the dream. At the same time, a knowledge of the biology of dreaming should offer a foundation from which to approach certainly the psychological world and possibly also the spiritual world. As with this book as a whole, what we are seeking is a framework from the biological evidence which will allow us to approach the deeper issues of mind.

The biological material is essentially twofold. First, we have material concerning the activity of the brain and nervous system as a whole during REM sleep. Second, we have comparative data concerning the relative amounts of REM and non-REM sleep in different species and at different stages of development.

To return to the mind–brain relationship, it is apparent that the changes in the nervous system associated with REM sleep certainly support our experience of dreams. Quite generally, REM sleep is a period of very high brain activity, a biological state which parallels the experience of intense activity characteristic of dreaming. More specifically, we can describe the REM state biologically as one in which the brain stimulates its own sensory systems and generates motor command signals. The latter are not actually executed by the bodily muscles, since another part of the brain renders those muscles non-functional during the REM state. Such a system clearly parallels the experienced reality of dreams, in which our senses are fully active and in which we appear to move, speak and act in as rich a fashion as we do when awake.

The various changes in nervous system activity are co-ordinated from several centres in the brainstem region. The sensory activation begins in a brainstem region called the *pons* and spreads to the adjacent vestibular region and to the *thalamus*, a kind of central switchboard from where signals are relayed to all the sensory areas of the brain. It is known that auditory and tactile senses are stimulated during REM sleep in this way. More active than these, however, is the visual pathway from the pons to the visual cortex. Bursts of electrical activity called *PGO waves* are co-ordinated with the rapid eye movements themselves. Moreover, these bursts are similar in kind to bursts recorded in the visual cortex during the waking state. The generally agreed dominance of vision in dreams supports the conclusion that this endogenous (that is, from within) sensory activity is responsible for the hallucinatory nature of dreams.

As for the motor aspect of dreams, activity has been recorded during REM sleep in the motor cortex and other brain regions involved with the control of movement during our waking lives. Indeed, the output neurones from the motor cortex are as active during REM sleep as they are when conveying movement commands during wakefulness. At the same time, a region in the pons generates a massive inhibition on the motor neurones of the spinal cord, giving rise to a kind of paralysis called *atonia*. Thus, the neurophysiological evidence again appears to explain the experience in dreaming. When I am aware of running furiously to escape some bug-eyed monster in my dream, it may be envisaged that all the appropriate command signals are being generated by the brain. The presumed equivalence between such command signals during REM sleep and in the waking state surely underlies the power and sense of reality associated with the experience. Of course, I do not really move because the atonia has 'turned off' my spinal cord. It reminds me of practising an electric guitar with the amplifier unplugged. As we saw earlier in relation to the phantom limb experience, the subjective experience of one's own body and its activities does not entirely depend upon the feedback from the body itself. Just as a patient may be entirely convinced of the reality of their phantom limb, so there is generally no question as to the reality of our 'phantom body' during REM sleep. In a very real sense we live in a world of images.

Further neurophysiological characteristics of REM sleep tie in well with the experienced nature of dreaming. The upper end of the reticular formation activates the entire cortex, whilst slightly behind is a region which triggers a distinct wave pattern in the hippocampus, called *theta*. The cortical activation presumably gives rise to the cognitive, 'thinking' dimension in dreams, whilst the hippocampal theta may indicate attentional and memory mechanisms.[2] More will be said on these aspects when considering the functions of REM sleep later. Finally, the status of the REM stage of sleep as one in which the individual is 'locked into' their internal world is supported by studies indicating that peripheral senses are attenuated. For example, sensory nerves in the skin and muscles, which normally play a major role in bodily awareness, are inhibited during the REM state.

In conclusion, these six neurophysiological characteristics of the REM state, summarized in figure 6.1, combine to give a powerful picture of our condition when dreaming. In no other aspect of our psychology does the neurophysiological evidence seem to dovetail quite so well with the experiential dimension. The REM state is unequivocally a state which is discontinuous with both the waking, and the non-REM sleep, state.

When it comes to considering function the picture is not so clear, however. In the following sections I shall consider the functions of REM sleep in some detail. But a preliminary question should be asked. Does the progression of the brain into the stage of REM sleep actually cause the psychological experience of dreaming? This is the question that most poignantly crosses the brain–mind divide. The answer, perhaps predictably, is not clear-cut. Whilst the REM state certainly parallels the dream state, several studies have indicated that dream-like mentation may take place during non-REM sleep. Generally, such mentation is either not especially bizarre, which would seem to be an important characteristic of 'full-blown' dreams, or to be associated with abnormal behaviour. Examples of the latter include sleep-walking and night terrors. A tentative conclusion would be that dream-like experiences may be generated outside of the REM state, but that the REM state is the optimum physiological state for the protection of the dreamer whilst dreaming. Thus, for example, we do not sleep-walk during REM sleep. The most parsimonious view, I believe, is one which holds that the need to dream is a psychological need for which a conducive biological state (REM) has developed. The need may possibly be met outside of REM, but perhaps unsatisfactorily.

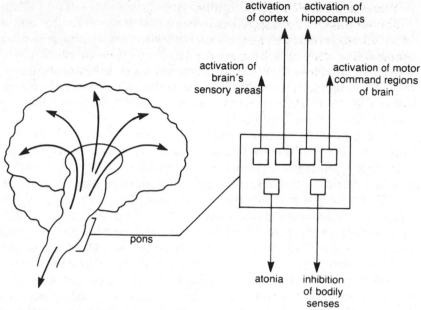

Figure 6.1: Neurophysiological Characteristics of REM Sleep.

Support for this view may be drawn from evidence which suggests that the association between the REM state and dreaming is loosened in schizophrenia. In his book on *Sleep and Dreaming* Cohen[3] cites three lines of evidence for this position. First, reports of dream-like fantasy were obtained with equal frequency in both REM and non-REM sleep in individuals who scored high on a test for schizophrenia. In 'normal' subjects there was a clear differentiation, with more fantasy material coming from REM sleep reports. The second kind of evidence concerns the *REM rebound* phenomenon. If normal individuals are prevented from entering the REM stage of sleep over a few nights (by waking them whenever they begin to enter it), when they are finally allowed to sleep without disturbance the amount of REM sleep rises compared to normal. This rebound parallels other biological effects: if, for example, someone were deprived of water for a period of time, we would find a similar 'rebound' when they were finally allowed to drink. Extra water would be consumed by comparison with a normal drink. The REM rebound effect implies that deprivation of REM sleep deprives the individual of a key function which must subsequently be made up. In the case of acute schizophrenics, there is little or no REM rebound following deprivation of REM sleep. This would seem to suggest that, whatever that key function might be, schizophrenics either manage without it or obtain it during non-REM sleep or whilst awake. The third line of evidence cited by Cohen concerns more direct observations of brain physiology. In some schizophrenics PGO-like activity was recorded during non-REM sleep. As discussed above, such activity is normally a characteristic of the REM state alone.

All these observations imply a blurring of the distinction between REM and non-REM sleep in schizophrenics. It may be that the key function mentioned above involves a need for fantasy in some form. In the schizophrenic, this need is met as much in non-REM sleep – and, of course, in waking life – as it is in REM sleep. In other words, the blurring of the boundary between REM and non-REM sleep in schizophrenics may parallel the blurring of the boundary between fantasy and reality which characterizes schizophrenia. The need to dream, then, is fundamental in all of us, but the symptoms of schizophrenia manifest when our dreaming is not limited to its protective biological state of REM sleep. To return to the question of causation, the evidence does not support a simple view that dreaming is directly caused by the brain entering the REM state. As I have argued, REM sleep may be considered a conducive state, but not a necessary state, for dreaming.

This raises the interesting question as to whether the normal individual may be able to meet the need for fantasy, which may be one aspect of the need to dream outside of sleep – for example through working with imagery. In the last section of this chapter I will examine another kind of 'dreaming' – visions associated with a self-induced trance state. It is worth noting here, in the context of my discussion of schizophrenia, that the need to hold on to one's sanity whilst embarking on such visionary trances is a central feature of the traditional training involved in these disciplines.

The second major input from biology to our understanding of REM sleep concerns phylogeny and ontogeny. Phylogeny deals with comparisons across species, and ontogeny refers to developmental considerations. Jouvet[4] argues that there is an inverse relationship between the maturity of a newborn animal's brain and the amount of REM sleep it naturally gets. The more mature its brain, the lower the proportion of REM sleep in its typical sleeping pattern. This particularly holds as far as maturity of the visual system is concerned. Thus newborn kittens, whose eyes are closed because of a relatively immature visual system, spend something like 98 per cent of their total sleep time in REM. Guinea pigs, on the other hand, whose brains are almost totally mature at birth, spend only around 6 per cent of sleep time in REM.

REM sleep is a characteristic of all species of mammals with the exception of an evolutionary old group called nontherians. Much interest has been focused on a small Australian hedgehog-like nontherian, the *echidna*. The echidna displays normal non-REM sleep, but a total absence of REM sleep. Although its brain as a whole is small, the echidna has a relatively enormous cortex. The proportion of its prefrontal cortex to overall brain size is higher than in any other mammal, including ourselves. As we shall see when considering the functions of REM sleep, it has been suggested that the echidna needs this huge cortex to perform functions which are carried out more efficiently in other mammals by REM sleep. The nature of this evolutionary fossil strongly supports the view that REM plays a crucial role in relation to learning and memory.

Developmentally, REM sleep is more prevalent in the young. We know from studies of premature infants, and even from studies of the foetus in the womb, that very large amounts of time are spent in REM sleep during the earliest months. It appears that REM sleep is in fact the primary state in the womb; non-REM sleep and wakefulness develop subsequently, as depicted in figure 6.2. If REM sleep relates to the experience of dreaming, this raises the intriguing question as to what the foetus is dreaming about. I cited earlier the talmudic statement that the foetus sees from one end of the world to the other. Perhaps it is the REM state that facilitates such a feat! More prosaically, this evidence supports the phylogenetic evidence in suggesting a role for REM sleep in the development of the brain.

THE FUNCTIONS OF DREAMING

In the last section, I introduced a framework incorporating three worlds of meaning: the biological, the psychological and the spiritual. In assessing the functions of dreaming I shall make use of this framework, for different theories may be seen to be focused in different regions of the framework. It is not my intention to review exhaustively the many theories of dreaming. Rather, I wish to convey the flavour of theories as they relate to this threefold framework. I consider that all the theories to be mentioned advance

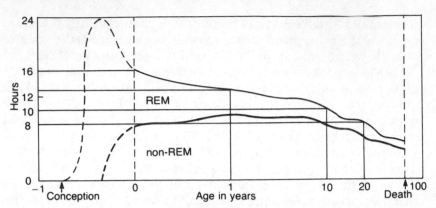

Figure 6.2. The Ontogeny of Sleep. The chart shows the proportions of each 24-hour day that are devoted to wakefulness, REM sleep, and non-REM sleep over our lifetime. The proportions before birth are estimates based on the patterns found in premature infants. (From SLEEP by J. Allan Hobson. Copyright © 1989 by J. Allan Hobson. Reproduced by permission of W. H. Freeman and Company.)

our understanding of dreaming to some extent. Where there are points of divergence between the approaches, more often than not they simply reflect different emphases. Thus, an author who stresses the biological function of dreams may consider that there is no psychological meaning to the dream images themselves; they are purely random. Such a theorist is a 'world apart' from the psychologist who encourages us to interpret our dream images. They speak a different language because their focus is different. My view holds each world to function not only by dependent interaction, but also through correspondence, with each other world. Understanding the biological role of REM sleep may therefore give us genuine insight into the psychological place of dreaming, and even into our spiritual nature. In synthesizing an understanding of the role of dreaming, I shall finally in the next section be relating REM sleep to the model of mind which has been developed over previous chapters.

In a recent review of REM sleep, Vertes suggests that it plays a 'sentinel' role. He argues that prolonged sleep can be harmful to the brain, leading to disruption of function or even damage to neurones. At the extreme, according to this hypothesis, death may ensue – as, for example, in the case of 'cot deaths' (sudden infant death syndrome), since the brain's control over vital bodily functions may be compromised. The periodic activation of the brain during REM sleep serves to protect against such harmful effects. As Vertes puts it, 'In effect, REM sleep is the brain's safeguard for preventing the temporary loss of consciousness during sleep from developing into permanent unconsciousness.'[5] This is a purely biological theory. The content of dream images is seemingly not important. The sentinel function is achieved simply by biological activation. Indeed, Vertes argues against a role for REM sleep in 'higher order functions' since brain activity during REM sleep is co-ordinated entirely from the primitive brainstem.

The phylogenetic and ontogenetic evidence summarized in the previous section assumes a great importance in the thinking of Jouvet. He argues that REM sleep seems to play a key role in the maturation of the brain. More specifically, he thinks that REM sleep provides a 'safe' period for the animal to activate inherited plans of behaviour. The argument here is that an inherited plan – involving, for example, predatory or mating behaviour – does not dictate exact muscle sequences. Rather it sets general goals. It is necessary, therefore, for the animal to integrate the plan with the precise muscle control routines by means of which the goal may be achieved in real life. Play during the waking hours is one way in which such integration may be achieved, but REM sleep allows for rehearsal with less constraint since there is no danger to the animal itself or its playmates. REM sleep represents rehearsal 'off-line', as it were. Evidence for this proposal comes from observing the kinds of behaviours seen when the 'off-line' status is interfered with. Experiments have been conducted in which the bodily muscle atonia is inhibited by lesioning the precise area of the brainstem which normally causes it. Animals treated in this way actually get up and engage in overt behaviour during REM sleep, apparently acting out their 'dreams'. According to Jouvet, the behaviour seen at such times appears highly stereotyped: the animals 'suddenly stand up, leap, and either display some aggressive behaviour or play with their front paws as they might play with a mouse, or they show a rage behaviour or a defense reaction against a large predator'.[6] That this state is genuinely REM sleep without atonia, and not simply wakefulness, is suggested by the presence of various REM sleep characteristics such as an active EEG, hippocampal theta, and rapid eye movements themselves.[7]

It is not only brain systems involved with motor behaviour that may be receiving their fine tuning during REM sleep. Kasamatsu and Pettigrew[8] have demonstrated that a family of neurotransmitters called *catecholamines* are crucially involved in enabling sensory feature-detecting neurones to be modified by experience. As we saw in Chapter 2, visual neurones, for example, do not simply 'see' the world as it is. They are crucially set to pick up aspects of the world relevant to the organism's model of external reality. There is a critical period during development when these neurones become aligned to the organism's environment. Thus, if an animal is raised in a 'world' dominated by vertical lines, later examination reveals a sensory system dominated by responses to verticals but with hardly any responses to horizontals. The interesting point with regard to REM sleep is that the brainstem regions responsible for the catecholamines' influence on the developing visual system are the same regions which trigger activity in the visual system during REM sleep. Pettigrew's work may therefore suggest that modifications to the sensory system are effected specifically during REM sleep. It is an intriguing idea that REM sleep may reflect the operation of some kind of executive system which somehow masterminds the direction in which the brain's plasticity should develop. Whilst this is most important during the early developmental period, REM sleep may continue to effect minor changes to brain systems throughout the lifespan.

Jouvet's theory is, again, essentially biological, pertaining as it does to the maturation of the brain in the early stages of development. The images that infants experience during their dreams – assuming, of course, that there is any such experience – presumably reflect the maturational changes being effected. When, for example, an infant displays sucking movements during REM sleep (as occurs both in the womb and after birth), we may envisage that primitive images of suckling are active. These could involve, for example, reaching towards the breast and sensing the texture of contact. These images would presumably involve a strong emotional component, and we can envisage REM sleep as effecting links between emotional and sensory-motor images. This is, of course, conjecture. Jouvet's theory does, however, give a foundation to such speculation and takes us closer to more overtly psychological theories. The essence of the theory holds that during REM sleep some kind of equilibration is effected between the brain's inherited goals and the available repertoire of interaction with the real world. It is but a short step from here to a more depth-psychological approach. Jung, for example, viewed the collective unconscious as 'the functioning of the inherited brain structure'.[9] In his view the archetypes, formative complexes in the collective unconscious, can play an organizing role in dreams. Is it possible to see a parallel here to Jouvet's theory – an archetype, as an inherited structure may need to be 'plugged in' to our everyday psychological life? Just as newborn infants may need REM sleep to key their images of suckling into the reality of interaction with their mother, so we may need REM sleep/dreams to perceive the power of, say, the *anima* or *animus* in some creative endeavour of ours.

Theories focused in the world of cognitive psychology have in common the idea that information in memory requires some kind of processing during REM sleep to enable optimal functioning of the individual. Theories leaning to the biological side generally regard endeavours to recall or interpret dreams as without benefit. Thus, Winson writes that 'it is a matter of chance, not related to their function, that we are aware of dreams at all'.[10] Crick and Mitchison[11] go a stage further in regarding the recall of dreams as actually counterproductive to the function of REM sleep. They view REM sleep as a period in which superfluous activity in the cortex is 'unlearned', jettisoned, in order that our memory should maintain its efficiency. Attempts to recall dreams are, accordingly, analogous to attempts to hold on to unnecessary garbage. Winson's view is that during REM sleep the residue from recent events is integrated with past associations and made accessible for guiding future behaviour. He argues that the enlarged cortex of the echidna is necessary to allow for learning in a mammal which does not have the advantage of this 'book-keeping' function in REM sleep. A greater storage space is required when the system lacks efficiency.

Many authors adopt positions basically similar to Winson's in stressing the integrating function of REM sleep, but hold a more central psychological viewpoint in considering the content of the dreams itself to be significant and worthy of reflection and interpretation. There is indeed, from work with both animals and humans, a wealth of evidence to connect REM sleep to the effective operation of memory.[12] Scrima, for example, studied the ability of a group of narcoleptics to recall anagrams. Narcolepsy is a condition where the patient has difficulty remaining awake for normal lengths of time. Moreover, the patient often goes directly into REM sleep on falling asleep. Scrima was therefore able to assess the effectiveness of recall when learning was immediately followed by a period of REM sleep. The results were quite clear-cut. Recall of the anagrams was better after a period of REM sleep than it was after a similar length of non-REM sleep. The recall following REM sleep was also superior to the subjects' recall in a third condition in which the learning period was followed by a period of wakefulness. In this third condition subjects performed a distracting task during the period of wakefulness. The results suggested that REM sleep seemed to be performing some function which facilitated subsequent recall of information. For Scrima, not only does REM sleep integrate and assimilate information in memory, but consciously working with the content of one's dreams can be beneficial:

> It may well be that if greater attention is given to one's own dreams, i.e., attempting to remember them upon waking and relating them to past experience and current concerns, one may discover that such introspection raises to consciousness adaptive new outlooks and possibilities in daily life.[13]

Of course, such advice has the added advantage of keeping armies of analysts and therapists in gainful employment! From the perspective of Crick and Mitchison's approach, the advice is simply wrong. Theirs is one of the few theories about REM sleep which positively discourages remembering, let alone interpreting, dream images. It has to be said that, whilst the evidence for the seminal role of REM sleep in relation to memory is strong, the issue of interpretation of dreams does not rest on a sure scientific foundation. This is inevitable as we move along the framework away from the biological and into the psychological/spiritual interface, where science has less direct relevance. Jung, who mapped this interface perhaps more fully than any other psychologist, himself recognized that recall and interpretation of dreams may not be necessary for their function to be achieved: 'It is often objected that the compensation [function of dreams] must be ineffective unless the dream is understood. This is not so certain, however, for many things can be effective without being understood.'[14] In his view the effectiveness of dreams is, however, enhanced by interpretation and understanding.

In order to recognize the value of understanding our own dreams, it is perhaps important to distinguish the direct function of dreaming, primarily biological and not requiring any conscious involvement, from the active exploration of the psychological/spiritual interface. The direct function concerns biological mechanisms essentially involved in the maturation of the brain and in some aspect of processing in relation to memory. It is very doubtful whether understanding of dream content plays any role as far as this function is concerned. Bearing in mind that this direct biological function is common to many animals, it would be difficult to understand how it could have evolved if conscious reflection on dream content were important to its function. When it comes to the more overtly psychological and spiritual dimensions, however, such reflection on dream content may have a part to play. As in many spheres, it seems that a 'higher' function has been grafted on to a 'lower' function in human evolution. Whilst the lower, biological function is essential to brain processes, especially those involved with memory, involvement in the higher function may be more a matter of choice. Not everyone becomes engaged in conscious exploration of the psychological/spiritual interface; there is no substantive price to pay for ignoring this realm of our lives. Moreover, dream content is not the only material to which we may turn in this regard. As discussed in previous chapters, active imagination is instrumental in such exploration of our inner worlds, and dream material is only one of several sources for scrutiny. Other products of the imagination, including the images explored in visualization work and those that are encountered in myths, may similarly hasten our advance into this territory.

If we wish to find a single word that epitomizes the function of dreaming it must be *healing*. Healing encompasses both the biological and the psycho-spiritual dimensions. The quest of life is a quest for wholeness, and that is what the word 'healing' means. Biologically, dreaming and visualization have been demonstrated to promote physical wellbeing. Psycho-spiritually, active imagination can help us find our true sense of belonging in the world. Ullman has stressed this role of dreams with regard to healing. The dream is a 'magic mirror' to reflect aspects of ourselves which may need attention: '. . . any dream image that succeeds in finding its way into the waking state [is] a potentially healing instrument. Once we connect with its metaphorical content it can put us in touch with more of the truth about ourselves than we are ordinarily aware of.'[15]

At the nether end of our framework, we are faced with the famous question as to what is dream and what is reality. Malamud discusses the implications of becoming *lucid* in dreaming. This is a situation in which the dreamer knows that the current activity is a dream, and may even be able to direct the flow of dream content. She captures precisely, to my mind, the value of becoming conscious of our own dream imagery:

The richness and strangeness of our dreams are glaring reminders that we hardly know who we are in our roles as creators of our dream worlds. For me, the challenge of becoming lucid is to discover how and why I create my dreams. I am not seeking another method to interpret the 'foreign language' of dreams, but rather, to get in touch with that state of my own consciousness in which dream language is not foreign, but native, so that I can understand directly my intentions as the creator of my dreams.[16]

Malamud speculates on the intriguing symmetry between dreaming and waking life. With regard to dreaming, it is possible for one to become lucid, at which time one recognizes that the world being then experienced is illusory, a creation from oneself fulfilling some particular need. Is there not an analogous situation in waking life? One may 'awaken', become truly conscious, and realize that one's normal world is equally a subjective construction. Such an awakening Malamud equates with the mystic experience. As she writes, '*Awakening* would mean becoming experientially aware of a seemingly more objective reality and of the *Self* who *Dreams* our waking lives.'

THE ROYAL ROAD REVISITED

The closest to a common denominator amongst the many psychological theories concerning the function of dreaming is the stress placed on their role in relation to memory. As succinctly stated by Greenberg, 'We see dreaming as integrating information from current experience with past memories in order to produce schemas that are organizers of complicated behavioral tasks.'[17] And such a perspective can be viewed as consonant with the more biological view of Jouvet and others. Whereas in early development sensory and motor systems themselves are presumed to undergo modification during REM sleep, at later ages we might expect such modification to be restricted to more general associative regions of the brain.

Can we be more specific in relation to the nature of this integrative function? I believe that the answer to this question will be found in considering the 'I-tags' which I have postulated as somehow attaching to our memories of past events. Perhaps it is worth reviewing briefly the relevant concepts.

In my discussion of memory (Chapter 3), I suggested that

voluntary recall of some particular episode from memory involves effecting connection between the current 'I' and the 'I' that experienced the episode in the first place – that episode's 'I-tag'. In Chapter 4, the nature of 'I' was explored further. The *identity plane* is an amalgam of 'I-tags' attaching to memories currently being activated through resonance with our present situation. A single focus within this identity plane is established by the *interpreter*, the left hemisphere brain module which constructs a coherent interpretation of ongoing activity. This sense of coherence comes about precisely because ongoing activity is continually projected on to a single actor, the 'I' of immediate experience. This 'I' is, falsely, regarded as the receiver of impressions and the instigator of actions.[18] I have postulated further that, when this 'I' is dethroned, the individual may become aware of a *higher plane* which represents their involvement with the pure memory process devoid of 'I-tags'.

The key to everyday, voluntary memory access must concern the organization of 'I-tags'. Quite simply, we can envisage that REM sleep gives the brain an opportunity to sift through 'I-tags', perhaps instituting a greater degree of order than would otherwise exist.

There is widespread agreement amongst psychologists and neurophysiologists that some kind of 'indexing' of memories must occur. The only really 'new' idea in the suggestions I am putting forward concerns the nature of 'I' and the 'I-tags' attached to specific memories. As I have argued in earlier chapters, these suggestions are advanced in relation to the notion that there is a pure memory process which is not personal. If, like Bergson and Sheldrake, we view this memory process as somehow beyond the brain, then we would argue that the brain constitutes an input–output device. The brain's concern is with the nature of self in relation to that pure memory process. Alternatively, if we view this pure memory process as in some way brain-dependent, access via 'I-tags' is still the key. Memories may be widespread through the brain, but there must be some kind of central index of 'I-tags'. This index is employed during voluntary recall. As discussed in Chapter 3, such voluntary recall incorporates the appropriate 'I-tags' into the current construction of 'I', bringing the required memories into consciousness. A situation such as prosopagnosia – loss of memory for faces – for example, comes about because damage to the specific cortical region involved interferes with the 'I-tags' which would normally attach to remembered faces. As we saw in Chapter 3, the patient may still manifest face recognition in an implicit (outside of 'I') manner. The problem in such a patient is that the interpreter's current construction of 'I' is unable to connect with the 'I-tags' for faces.

A recent theory[19] with regard to indexing of memories views the hippocampus as housing records for the locations of specific engrams (memory traces) in the cortex of the brain. The hippocampus becomes a kind of master catalogue, or map, for all memories. The evidence for the centrality of the hippocampus in this role is indeed strong from both experimental studies on animals and human neuropsychological cases. Relating these ideas of hippocampal function to the model developed here, it seems quite conceivable that the hippocampus maintains connections to all the 'I-tags'. This, I would argue, is the nature of its master catalogue. It does not index all memories; it indexes the organism's involvement with those memories. Its concern is with self.[20] Periodic updating of this index is presumably necessary, and this function may be connected with dreaming. It could well be that the hippocampal theta, characteristic of REM sleep, is the outward sign of the limbic system's updating of 'I-tags' during REM.

I envisage that activation of the cortex during REM sleep triggers particular 'I-tags' and, therefore, associated memory images. The left hemisphere's interpreter is engaged during this time in establishing a coherent story-line to link the diverse images aroused through widespread cortical activation. It is characteristic of dreams that, although they may appear bizarre upon later reflection, at the time of dreaming they flow with a coherence of their own. This is the hallmark of the interpreter: it spins a good story. The only difference between the 'I' in dreaming and when awake is that when awake it maintains its coherence in relation to external events; it is oriented to outer reality.

There has been a great deal of interest in the question as to which of the two cerebral hemispheres is more active during REM sleep. Claims have been made for dominance of the left by some, and of the right by others.[21] Antrobus[22] arrives at a position similar to the one I am arguing here. He reviews many studies and comes down in favour of the left hemisphere having a predominant role. The right hemisphere is certainly not quiescent, and is perhaps responsible for many specific images. However, the primary characteristic of dreaming – the dramatic and coherent narrative – seems to be a left hemisphere function. Evidence is therefore consistent with a central role for the interpreter during REM sleep.

The other obvious characteristic of dreaming is that our dreams are readily forgotten. How many times do we awake with a theme in our head, only to find it gone later?[23] I see no reason for supposing this amnesia to be essentially any different from the other amnesias considered earlier. The reason we cannot generally remember our dreams is that the current 'I' cannot connect with the 'I' that experienced the dream. We do not need to postulate some psychological entity specific to dreaming. The same general principles that we have established apply here. Putting the point technically, 'I' is *state specific*. The 'I' of the dream is not consolidated over time by the limbic system. If we do remember a dream on waking and make the effort to hold on to it (for instance by writing it down), then continuity between the dreaming 'I' and waking 'I' is established. In this case we can generally retrieve the dream at any time subsequently.

My hypothesis, then, is as follows. During waking, the interpreter generates our moment-to-moment sense of 'I', establishing its continuity through self-commentary in relation to interactions with the external world. At the same time, the limbic system establishes the continuity of this 'I' with previous 'I's (giving rise to the feeling of 'I', as discussed in Chapter 5). During REM sleep, the interpreter does much the same as it does whilst awake, except that there is no involvement with the external world. The limbic system, however, is occupied with updating its index of 'I-tags'. The images occurring in the dream are a consequence of this need for updating. But, *unlike its role in the waking state*, the limbic system is not engaged in consolidating the output of the interpreter. In other words, the functions become somewhat time-reversed. During waking, the limbic system follows on the heels of the left hemisphere's interpreter; whereas in the REM state, the relationship is reversed. The interpreter synthesizes a story from the images which the limbic system has been indexing. This hypothesis is depicted in figure 6.3.

The updating of 'I-tags' concerns in particular those that escaped incorporation into 'I' during the previous day. This would involve experiences that occurred at the fringes of our awareness (subliminal), or that were in some measure actively excluded (repressed). Here we begin to connect with more standard psycho-analytical approaches to dreams. The images thrown up during this updating of 'I-tags' will reveal aspects of ourselves that were inconsistent with the ongoing construction of 'I'. Exploring

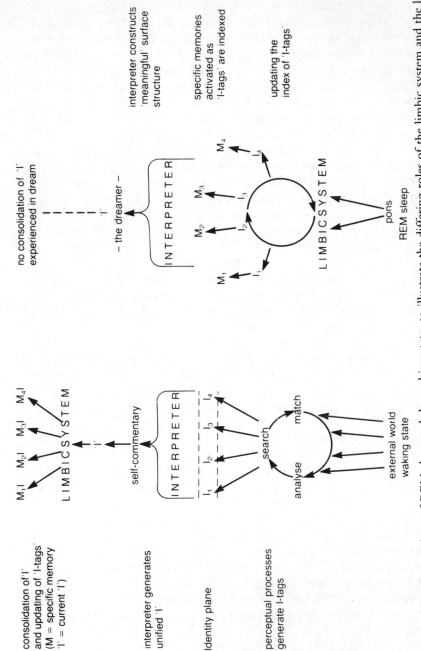

Figure 6.3: Comparison of REM sleep and the waking state, to illustrate the differing roles of the limbic system and the left hemisphere's interpreter. As with earlier figures, the dynamic, interactive nature of these processes cannot be conveyed in the figure. The processes are not so unidirectional as the figure suggests.

the reasons for such inconsistencies would be an important source of self-knowledge. The Jungian view that dreams embody a compensatory view of psychic life is particularly consonant with the hypothesis advanced here. Aspects of ourselves excluded from 'I' constitute precisely what Jung specified as the *shadow*. Jung discusses the ways in which dreams may portray images of the shadow to the dreamer. In Jungian terms, personal development would require *conscious* integration of such material.

A major tenet of Freud's insight into the nature of dreams is the distinction between latent and manifest content. The latent content is the unconscious motive underlying the imagery of which we are aware in the dream. Perhaps, in the differentiation I am proposing between limbic concern with 'I-tags' and the interpreter's construction of the 'I' at the centre of the dream's narrative, we have the basis of the latent–manifest distinction. The interpreter employs material 'to hand' in constructing the narrative. Such material may be significant in relation to the dreamer's everyday experiences, but it is relatively superficial by comparison with the core material with which the limbic system is concerned. Manifest content is thus essentially cortical, whereas latent content reflects subcortical activity.[24]

Another major feature of Freud's view of dreams concerns the essential sexuality of psychic energy, or *libido*. The emphasis on sexuality won Freud many enemies and led to the break with major disciples such as Jung and Adler. It is quite common to read theorists today rejecting this notion that sexuality is the primary driving force behind dreams. It is worth noting, however, that 90 per cent of REM sleep episodes in men are accompanied by penile erection, whilst only 10 per cent of dreams recounted on awakening from REM sleep are of an explicit sexual nature.[25] REM sleep episodes in women are similarly frequently accompanied by clitoral engorgement. There is clearly some kind of sexual dimension intrinsic to the REM state.

In considering this sexual dimension, let us bear in mind the brainstem initiation of the events of REM sleep. Thus far I have considered the role of the limbic system and cortex in dreaming. Why should the brainstem be the initiator? After all, reptiles which possess a brainstem analogous to ours display no REM sleep. If the function of dreaming was only concerned with learning and memory, it is difficult to see why the processes of REM could not involve only the limbic and cortical brain levels.

In Chapter 5, I examined the underpinnings of the sense of

self. I conceive of the self as a kind of hierarchy in which successively higher levels of the brain add their own specific aspect to the primary differentiation, that of self from nonself. This primary differentiation was hypothesized to be the domain of the brainstem. It is in this context that I think we may understand the sexual nature of the libido. It is not that dreams necessarily generate specifically sexual themes. Rather, underlying all dreams is the will to maintain the integrity of 'I'. This, in itself, is bound up with sexuality which is integral to the self–nonself divide. The primary energy of the psyche is directed towards the aim of establishing this divide, which gives rise to the ego as understood in Freudian terms. Paradoxically, this energy is also directed towards the reconciliation of the divide, through union with an other. This paradox lies at the heart of our sexuality, concerned, as it is, with both the assertion of individuality and the drive to self-transcendence in the loss of individuality. It is, of course, analogous to the paradoxes we have discussed in relation to mysticism.

Freud's initial interests in the mind were as a neurologist. The limited understanding of the brain and its mechanisms in his day led him to abandon his original intention to couch his theories in neurological terms. We can only speculate as to how he would have responded to the biolgical data on REM sleep so important to theories today. That they would have impacted on him as a neurologist there can be little doubt. The 'royal road to the unconscious', as he referred to dreams, may still be trodden without regard to biology; one may simply attend to the psychological messages they bear. But if our interest ranges more widely into the workings of the mind, the challenge becomes that of understanding the knot which binds psychology and physiology. In a practical sense, we need to sift the essential insights that Freud made from the ideas which were, perhaps, more related to his own circumstances, those of his time and place. Hindsight certainly helps us here. But all ages, including our own, have their prejudices. It is, I believe, the scientific advances made over recent years that, more than any other material, allow us to revisit Freud's royal road and emerge with an enriched view.

DESCENDING IN ORDER TO ASCEND

> Why do we say, 'it ascended in thought', rather than use the term, 'descended'? For surely we say that one who gazes into the vision of the *chariot* descends and subsequently ascends. . . . It is because thought includes no vision whatsoever and has no end. And in relation to that which has no end or limit 'descent' is inappropriate.[26]

This quotation is another cryptic paragraph from the *Bahir*. It is referring to the oldest recorded mystical practice in Judaism, *ma'ase merkavah*, translated as the *work of the chariot*. This practice, records of which date from the first century BCE, involves the mystic gaining a vision of the chariot depicted in the Book of Ezekiel. The chariot becomes a vehicle for the mystic to attain direct knowledge of the heavenly realms, or 'palaces'. The question addressed here concerns the distinction that is drawn between the vision of the chariot itself and the knowledge (that is, thought) of the higher regions that is gained by means of the chariot.

Before considering the answer to the question, let us try to understand what exactly is being asked. Clearly, visionary experience has played a major part in all the world's religions. The chariot experience itself undoubtedly involved an altered state of consciousness, presumably analogous to other kinds of trance or shamanistic states which are claimed to confer special knowledge. But there is nothing intrinsically special about visions. In itself a vision may be little more than a glorified daydream. Even worse, it may be as much a symptom of a deranged mind as a harbinger of some 'higher knowledge'. So where exactly does the gossamer film between mysticism and madness begin and end? On what grounds may we distinguish the pursuit of 'higher knowledge' from the indulgence in delusion which is the hallmark of madness?

Terms analogous to 'descent' are habitually used in respect of trance states. We 'go under' into a hypnotic trance, 'fall' asleep, become 'submerged' in the unconscious. In more physiological terms, the deeper, older parts of the brain seem to dominate in those states where imagery is strong. In addition to direct physiological evidence for the role of old brain structures in REM sleep and states rich in waking imagery, there are anecdotal, subjective reports which may support an association of mystical imagery with lower brain regions. Mavromatis[27] draws on the descriptions of several writers who claimed to have travelled in an 'astral body', an experience apparently equivalent in many respects to that of the 'descenders to the chariot'. Of some note is the observation by these writers of a sensation of activation in the *medulla oblongata*, a region of the lower brainstem. Whatever the status of such reports as evidence, more compelling physiological data including the brainstem events associated with sleep and dreaming seem to support the view that entering a trance involves a descent from cortical to brainstem regions. Moreover, the preparations for the chariot experience included adopting a special posture with the head bent down and held between the knees. This posture constituted a very tangible physical 'descent'.

In Chapter 5 I discussed the centrality of 'regression' to primitive states for any effective work on oneself. We saw that real self-change comes about through an encounter with the deeper strata in what I called the archaeology of self. In this respect, it is also relevant to note that the descenders to the chariot were adopting a posture which the rabbis understood as that adopted by the foetus in the womb.[28]

The emphasis on descent is therefore understandable. In a physical, experiential and neurological sense, the mystic descends into a visionary trance state. Such a state was evidently viewed not as an end in itself, but as a means to reach a higher state (he 'descends and subsequently ascends'). Moreover, the *Bahir* seems to be suggesting that in order to achieve the desired end the mystic has to remain 'above' the vision throughout. It is as if one part of the mystic descends into the trance state, but another part actually holds on to the reins of control.

The *Bahir* conveys this central point by means of a quote from Isaiah. The relevant passage begins with the instruction to set a watchman – 'Let him declare what he sees!' What he does see is a chariot, and then, 'As a lion, he called out: I stand on the watchtower continually by day, and in my guard I am stationed throughout the whole of the nights.' (Isaiah 21:8.) Clearly, this episode is being used to imply that the mystic should maintain a state of vigilance during his visionary work. In other words, from 'the watchtower' he looks *down* into the vision; he does not become submerged in the vision. Some part of him, the 'watcher', remains in control, detached, using the chariot as one would use any other tool.

In attempting to understand these ideas in more contemporary, psychological terms, let us first stress the similarity to *lucid dreaming*. As pointed out above, the lucid dreamer maintains a watching role whilst dreaming; it is very much as if the lucid dreamer is 'above' the dream, looking down on the proceedings. The relevance of this to mystical experience was apparently distilled in certain practices of Tibetan yoga. According to LaBerge and Gackenbach,[29] these yogis developed a technique to enable them to enter a state of lucid dreaming directly from the waking state. The parallel with chariot mysticism is striking. Whilst not overtly entering sleep, the chariot mystics cultivated a variety of procedures which are conducive to trance states. These included prolonged fasting, repetition of finger movements and divine names, and chanting. Holding the special posture, with the head between the knees, for a prolonged period would undoubtedly affect the blood supply to the brain, which is also likely to hasten the onset of some kind of trance state. At the same time, great attention was placed on the need to memorize complex formulae to be used as the mystic confronted various angels or guards on his 'journey'. Pages and pages of the classical texts of this period, the *Hekalot* literature, are devoted to these formulae. There can be no doubting the seriousness with which the enormous memory task involved would have been taken.

Thus, we have two aspects to the chariot experience. One aspect promoted a 'letting go', a descent into trance; the other stressed the importance of 'holding on' to a complex mind-set, rationally induced prior to the descent. The first aspect brought the dangers of madness; the second, implying a controlled intrapsychic dissociation, was the protection against madness. Whilst the language of the *Hekalot* texts is very much couched in terms of its own complex imagery, references to what we would call madness are indeed made. If the various protective formulae were not remembered or employed correctly, dire consequences were in store. And, to quote a clear reference to madness, 'If one was unworthy to see the King in his beauty, the angels at the gates disturbed his senses and confused him. And when they said to him: 'Come in,' he entered, and instantly they pressed him and threw him into the fiery lava stream.'[30]

In the previous section, I discussed the brain activity associated with REM sleep in relation to the model of the mind developed over previous chapters. In short, I suggested that the interpreter is engaged in synthesizing a 'story' out of the fragmentary images associated with 'I-tags' which are in process of being indexed by the limbic system. The phenomenology of lucid dreaming would suggest that the lucid dreamer is observing the operation of the interpreter from a separate region of the mind. Our interest here naturally focuses on the *higher plane*. I suggest that, whilst the normal dreamer is centred in the identity plane, the lucid dreamer is somehow able to witness the dream events from the vantage point offered by the higher plane. The nature of this higher plane will be discussed further in Chapter 7.

Just as the lucid dreamer is centred in the higher plane observing their own dreams, so I envisage the chariot mystic to be centred in the higher plane observing their visionary exploits. Similarly with all creative use of imagery: the individual has to develop that fine balance between, on the one hand, rigid control of imagery and, on the other, indulgence in the 'picture shows' for their own sake. As mentioned already on more than one occasion, working with the free-flowing state of mind characteristic of trance-like states is the key to the quest for human potential. But it has to be a disciplined state. We have both to 'let it happen' and to 'control it' at the same time. Here again is one of those paradoxes which seem impossible to convey sensibly. Yet it is a paradox that practical study of any of the established mystical techniques will reveal. I have focused on chariot mysticism. We could equally have discussed the visualization techniques of tantric yoga, or the cultivation of certain states used in the shamanistic traditions. The emphasis on the mental discipline of the trainee is necessarily strong.

Central to my line of argument is the notion that there is a continuity between the dream state and the waking state in which imagery or visions may be explored. There is good evidence in support of this notion. First, none of the physiological processes associated with REM sleep is actually unique to the REM state. In Vertes' detailed review of the events of REM sleep he presents a great deal of evidence supporting this view, arguing that 'the function(s) served by REM overlap to a significant degree with functions carried out in other states'.[31] Second, there is good psychological evidence to suggest a regular oscillation between an imagery-rich state and one rich in more rational mentation throughout both sleep and waking. During sleep this manifests as the switch between REM and non-REM sleep. But the cycle continues during the waking state, giving rise, for example, to daydreaming cycles which have the same time course as does REM activity in sleep.[32] It seems that imagery is fundamental to the mind. Whether the imagery manifests as dreams during sleep or 'fantasy' when awake is essentially a question of degree and not one of absolute difference.

Finally, we can draw on the mystic's own experience, for waking visions are often described in terms of sleep dreams. Here, for example, is a passage from the writings of Rabbi Shem Tov ben Abraham Ibn Gaon (late thirteenth to fourteenth century), cited by Idel:

> One who is engaged in the secrets of the Chariot . . . will see that there is no end to his intellect, and he shall delve deeply into the secrets of the Chariot and the structures of Creation, to the place where the mouth is unable to speak and the ear is unable to hear. Then he will see visions of God, as one who dreams and whose eyes are shut, as it is written [Song of Solomon 5:2], 'I am asleep but my heart is awake. . . .'[33]

LaBerge and Gackenbach suggest that lucid dreaming may be useful in 'mapping out the dream world.' I think it is highly likely that this is precisely what the chariot mystics, as well as Tibetan yogis and other schools engaged in regular imagery work, were concerned with. In the quotation above, the mystic is said to delve into the structures of creation, whilst the early chariot literature is full of resplendent descriptions of the heavenly palaces. Are these not to be understood in psychological terms as projections of the archetypal world of the psyche? Such a thoroughly 'modern' view was evidently presaged in the eleventh century by Rabbi Hai Gaon, who writes that the mystic 'perceives *within himself and in the chambers [of his heart]* as if he saw the seven palaces with his own eyes'.[34] As Idel comments on this passage, 'The scene of revelation is thus no longer the supermundane hierarchy of palaces, but the human consciousness.'

Ma'ase merkavah, the work of the chariot, was a partner in this first recorded phase of Jewish mysticism to *ma'ase bereshit*, the work of creation. The work of creation was of a more intellectual character, involving speculations on the process of creation and its various stages. It is not unrealistic to compare this partnership to that between psychology and physics in our day. Physicists speculate on the nature of reality, and the process of cosmogony; psychologists are concerned with the visions of that reality as it manifests in the human psyche. These endeavours, couched as they are within the prevailing scientific world view, have largely squeezed the spiritual from their vocabulary. Yet the terminology is not important. What is common across all ages is the quest to discern our place in the scheme of things. When all is stripped to basics, there is not much that is new under the sun.

7

The Watcher Who Sleeps Not

> One higher than another watches, and there is one higher than them.
>
> Ecclesiastes 5:7

> The hidden part . . . is not a hypnotized part of the self. It knows all parts.
>   The hidden observer is watching, mature, logical, has more information.[1]

The concept of some kind of higher self, or more knowing inner self, is practically universal in mystical literature. We met earlier Gurdjieff's term, the *real I*. According to Ouspensky, one of the foremost chroniclers of Gurdjieff's philosophy, it was introduced thus in one of Gurdjieff's talks:

> A man must realize that he indeed consists of two men.
>   One is the man he calls 'I' and whom others call 'Ouspensky', 'Zakharov', or 'Petrov'. The other is the real *he*, the real *I*, which appears in his life only for very short moments and which can become firm and permanent only after a very lengthy period of work.[2]

The work to which Gurdjieff refers involves intense self-observation directed to the goal of liberating one's essence from the more superficial trappings of personality. The latter amount to stories we tell ourselves, and others tell us, about ourselves. These stories are bound up with our name, and are largely accidents of personal history. Essence, on the other hand, runs deeper, being our true centre of gravity and the seed of the *real I*. As one continues to 'work on oneself' so one develops what is termed 'objective consciousness', which brings an expanded vision, a more effective operation of mind. Compared to the mundane state of consciousness, the objective state registers perceptions more rapidly, giving the impression of a change in timescale. The perceptions are, furthermore, more accurate, being free from adulteration by our own wishes and desires. Things begin to be seen as they are, and not as we imagine them to be.

It is the sense of personal evolution that is most striking here. It is true that much hard work is said to be required; nevertheless the goal of a more enriched state is one which shines with the aura of fulfilment. Many psychologists in their various systems and therapies have also stressed the carrot of a higher, or more embracing, state which may be arrived at through self-knowledge. Jung's concept of the *self* is a prime example. For Jung, the self is the totality of the psyche, embracing unconscious as well as conscious elements, and is the goal to which psychic development is directed. The journey to self-realization is one of liberation from the restricted vision of the ego, and brings the individual into more direct relationship to the world:

> . . . there arises a consciousness which is no longer imprisoned in the petty, oversensitive, personal world of the ego, but participates freely in the wider world of objective interests. This widened consciousness is no longer that touchy, egotistical bundle of personal wishes, fears, hopes, and ambitions which has always to be compensated or corrected by unconscious countertendencies; instead, it is a function of relationship to the world of objects, bringing the individual into absolute, binding, and indissoluble communion with the world at large.[3]

Although self-realization may be a long and arduous process, the self is not to be conceived of as something that has to be created from scratch by our work. As Jung said, 'The beginnings of our whole psychic life seem to be inextricably rooted in this point.' The self is the archetype of wholeness, and therefore ever-present. Our 'task' is to integrate into consciousness those contents of the collective unconscious into which the self extends. The central issue thus concerns the ego's relationship to the self: how closely the ego approximates to the self. In fact, the individual can never be completely conscious of the self for it necessarily includes unconscious elements. But the ego may grow to the extent that it recognizes that it is a part of a richer totality – the individual has an intimation of the self.

Deikman makes the important point that mystical and psycho-therapeutic paths have in common an emphasis on observation. Despite the variety of differing theoretical formulations and belief systems, almost all psychotherapies are underpinned by simple, unbiased observation of mind processes. Similarly, mystical systems stress not only mindfulness but also unclouded observation of external objects in contemplation. This emphasis on observation, Deikman argues, is designed to direct us away from the contents of consciousness to awareness itself. The term 'contents of consciousness' refers to those thoughts, feelings and perceptions which normally occupy our minds – things that we can witness. But that which witnesses, the *observing self*, is transcendent to those contents. The observing self is 'the transparent center, that which is aware'. It is 'prior to thought, feeling, and action, for it experiences these functions'.[4] For Deikman, the observing self should be our goal. If our aim is to understand ourselves, then we must experience the observing self directly, rather than focus only on those contents which it observes.

It is difficult to assess whether the self as conceived of by Jung is the same as Deikman's observing self, or indeed whether these may be identified with the *real I* in Gurdjieff's philosophy. I think this matters little, the substantive issue being which system of thought is most appealing to a given individual. And these are just three of many! Whichever particular formulation we may prefer, there is impressive agreement in positing some kind of apparent duality within. There is the part of us with which we are habitually identified, the ego or 'I'. At the same time, a fuller, richer self operates but is largely obscured from the former part.

Whilst the unanimity of these voices, of psychologists and mystics alike, and from the diverse cultures of humankind, could be said to lend credence to this notion of a richer inner self, the acid test comes with personal involvement. Is the discipline of observation and the associated spiritual and/or therapeutic work worthwhile? Does the individual who embarks on such a path find the kind of fulfilment proferred? Inasmuch as the changes likely to be effected in the individual have some affinities with those involved in brainwashing, as discussed in Chapter 5, it is important that any individual embarking on a path of this nature does ask such questions. Indeed, any worthwhile school or therapist would encourage a questioning attitude.

Here I wish to consider whether the fruits of experimental

science can reinforce the implication that there is some kind of deeper part to the individual – an inner watcher, as I shall call it. In the model of mind developed over these pages I have argued that memory images activated by current preoccupations constitute a *higher plane* of mind. Generally, an 'I' connection is then established with these images, giving rise to the *identity plane*. The higher plane is ever-present, but normally unknown to the individual on account of their identification with one or another 'I' owing to the operation of the interpreter. Clearly, this hypothesis of the higher plane is consonant with the various forms of the observing, or higher, self concept. But there is no point in simply pushing terminology. What is the evidence for the higher plane?

Throughout this book we have met the evidence in the many studies which have demonstrated that we know more than we think we know. Whatever terminology we wish to employ, there is undoubtedly some organization of information at a level at which 'I' has no connection. We may call this level 'subconscious' since 'I' cannot directly reach it. More accurately, it is preconscious in that it comes into being before the interpreter generates 'I'. Moreover, it is 'higher' in the sense that the information is not distorted by contact with 'I'. It is uncontaminated by the tricks of the interpreter. As discussed earlier, it embodies our contact with the pure memory process and, as such, has a broader vista on things; it embraces all possibilities, whereas 'I' sees only those things which fit into a current and consensual interpretation of events.

The details which support the above assertions, including subliminal perception, implicit memory and so on, have been covered in preceding chapters. Here I wish to focus on this notion of an inner watcher in relation to studies using hypnosis. In what has arguably been the most discussed and influential book concerning hypnosis over recent years, Hilgard[5] posits the presence of a *hidden observer* within the hypnotized individual. The hidden observer monitors events which the hypnotized 'part' of the individual misses as a consequence of following the hypnotist's instructions. In Hilgard's first demonstration of this effect, a highly hypnotizable subject was given instructions, under hypnosis, that he would not hear anything. The subject became hypnotically 'deaf', as evidenced by his not answering questions addressed to him and not reacting to loud bangs close to his head. However, when he was given the suggestion that 'perhaps there is some part of you that is hearing my voice and processing the information', the response was positive: the subject signalled that there was such a part to him. Subsequently that part, the hidden observer, was able to report accurately on sounds 'heard' during his hypnotically induced deafness.

A major problem here is that of untangling what is subjective from what is objective. Obviously the hypnotized subject in this situation is not deaf in any organic sense. But we cannot know exactly what goes on inside him from his reports alone. The issue goes to the heart of questions about the nature of hypnosis itself. What is it about our mental make-up that brings about the kinds of major changes seen following hypnotic induction procedures? Basically, two rival approaches have been advanced. One holds that the explanation primarily concerns the social relationship between hypnotist and subject. The subject wishes to comply with the hypnotist and acts accordingly; hypnosis is thus a sophisticated form of role-play. The other view holds that a deeper change is brought about, so that the subject's mind undergoes a dissociation. The hypnotic trance is an altered state of consciousness in which the integration of disparate processes within the subject's mind has become disturbed by comparison to the normal state. These two competing views revolve around the question of what exactly it is about the individual that is manipulated during hypnosis. On the former view, the hypnotist manipulates the individual's behaviour; on the latter view the hypnotist manipulates the individual's mind.

In the case of the hypnotically induced deafness, the former view holds that subjects actually continue to hear but, in order to comply with the hypnotist's will, react in a manner that will indicate deafness. It is in this way that subjects fulfil their social role of compliance to the hypnotist. The alternative, dissociationist, view holds that the part of the individual that is actually experiencing the world at the time becomes deaf. Hilgard's metaphor of a hidden observer lies firmly within this latter view. The concept of dissociation suggests that different systems within consciousness may become separated; in this case the part experiencing hypnosis is dissociated from the hidden observer. Such a view is consistent with my earlier discussion of the multiplicity of 'I'. An increasingly acrimonious argument rages between the proponents of these two views.

In a recent demonstration of the effect, Zamansky and Bartis employed two critical tests, both in the form of negative hallucinations (hallucinating that something is not present when it actually is). First, their hypnotized subjects were given a bottle of ammonia to sniff following the suggestion that they would not smell anything. Second, following a suggestion that they would see nothing, they were shown a sheet of paper on which a number was clearly displayed. Subjects who passed these tests – that is, succumbed to the suggestion and reported no smell or number – were later tested further. They were informed that when hypnotized 'you have a hidden part of you that knows reality, what is really going on'. When the hypnotist counts to three, 'this hidden part will no longer be hidden and you will be aware of things that you were not aware of or did not know before'.[6] The results indicated that ten out of eleven subjects were indeed able to retrieve information about the ammonia and the number, although they had passed those tests previously. Evidently their 'hidden observers' had witnessed the real stimuli at the time, despite their contrary reactions.

The weakness of such demonstrations lies in the fact that the hidden part has to be accessed through suggestion. By suggesting that subjects have 'hidden parts', the hypnotist is perhaps encouraging them to behave accordingly. As Hilgard's arch-critic, Spanos, writes:

> A social psychological account of the reports . . . eschews the positing of esoteric psychological processes like the 'unconscious seeing' of supraliminal stimuli [stimuli above threshold and therefore easily perceived under normal circumstances]. Our account suggests that subjects who passed the negative hallucination suggestion saw the stimulus number but, in response to the compliance pressures of the suggestion, denied having done so. Later, the hidden observer instructions altered instructional demands.[7]

There is certainly an impasse here. The hidden observer cannot be accessed without giving the hypnotized subject instructions about its nature; but, in giving these suggestions, the seeds of doubt as to its validity are sown. As with many such debates, the two camps construe the evidence to fit their own viewpoint. If it were a valid approach to the state of mind in hypnosis, then the hidden observer concept would offer some fruitful parallels with the ideas, discussed above, of some kind of inner self. In particular, Deikman's view that the observing self transcends the contents of consciousness would gain credence. Whilst the contents of consciousness may be manipulated by the hypnotist's magic spell, the watcher within remains in touch with the world beyond the trance.

A different experimental approach and possible way forward considers the physiological changes brought about by hypnosis. Spiegel, Cutcomb, Ren and Pribram[8] recorded the visual evoked response in the brain generated when subjects were watching a coloured grid flashing on and off. The subjects were hypnotized and, amongst other conditions, were given the suggestion to see a cardboard box which would obscure their perception of the screen on which the grid was being presented. The box was, of course, not really there. The central issue here concerns the effect of this manipulation on the brain's response to the real stimulus, the coloured grid, when obscured only by an imagined stimulus, the box. Results showed that the later components of the evoked responses were clearly suppressed under this condition in highly hypnotizable subjects. Early components were not significantly affected.

The first point to make in regard to these results is that it is difficult to see how the social explanation of the hypnotic state could fit. The specific wave of the evoked response which was suppressed is one referred to as P300 (since it is a positive deflection occurring roughly 300 milliseconds following the onset of the stimulus). This wave has been invoked as relating to a subject's conscious awareness of sensory stimuli: '. . . whenever P300 occurs, the subject is conscious of the task-relevant information carried by the eliciting stimulus'.[9] Since, in Spiegel's study, it was suppressed, it seems likely that subjects' failure to 'see' the obstructed stimulus had a genuine physiological basis in terms of brain activity. The situation is, in fact, analogous to the one we met earlier in discussing evoked responses under anaesthesia. Surely, no one would wish to argue that the patient under anaesthesia really continues to feel pain but, in compliance with the wishes of the anaesthetist, conceals it.

The second point of interest arising from this study follows from the fact that the early components of the evoked responses were not affected by the hypnotic manipulation. These early components reflect the sensory analysis itself. Evidently, the hypnotic hallucination does not affect the direct analysis of the sensory input; it only suppresses the subsequent interpretation, and consequent presentation of that input in the identity plane. There is a parallel here with the manner in which subliminal stimuli are processed in the brain. Libet, Alberts, Wright and Feinstein[10] recorded directly from the brain cortex in their subjects to assess the form of evoked responses to sensory stimuli. In this case, the stimuli were electrical pulses to the skin. The strength of the pulses was varied so that some were too faint to be felt (subthreshold). The evoked responses to the subthreshold stimuli differed from those to the felt stimuli. Subthreshold-evoked responses were completely lacking in the late components, whilst early components were intact but of reduced amplitude by comparison with the evoked responses to those stimuli which the subjects consciously experienced. The authors noted that the early components could not of themselves correspond to, or indicate, conscious sensory experience. Such experience seemed to correlate specifically with the late components. Again, these electrophysiological data are consistent with the argument that the processing of subliminal signals leads to activity in the higher plane, but that presentation of a meaningful interpretation in the identity plane is attenuated.

In the light of these physiological details we may understand the basis of the hidden observer phenomenon in the following way. As we have discussed in previous chapters, the sensory analysis activates the pure memory process and generates the higher plane. So far the process is preconscious. Normally, an 'I' relation to the object is next established in the identity plane through the work of the interpreter. This is a consequence of the dynamic quest for meaning described in Chapter 2, and leads to phenomenal awareness – that is, I 'see' the object. It is precisely this quest for meaning that is at the heart of the subject–hypnotist relationship. The subject accepts the meaning imposed by the hypnotist. Presumably, this state of affairs comes about because the hypnotist's suggestions have their effect on the subject's interpreter. The interpreter will generate an 'I' that witnesses according to those suggestions. The subject does not see the grid obscured by a box, or the number written on a piece of paper, or whatever the hypnotist's instructions inculcate. But at the higher plane there is awareness – here is the watcher. Later, under hidden observer instructions, a different 'I' is generated, one that can say what the number was, or whatever may be called for. The new 'I' is as fickle as the other 'I'; it is not 'higher' at all. But its uncovering of hidden information points to an awareness that is higher in the sense of being more inclusive and more objective. Thus is the higher plane revealed.[11]

As far as the operation of mind is concerned, there is little difference between the trance of hypnosis and the 'trance of everyday life', as it has been called. In both cases we experience the world secondhand, as it were. Only the higher plane experiences reality directly. As soon as 'I' am, an interpretation of that reality has taken place.

The difference between the normal and the hypnotic condition concerns the checking of perceived reality that characterizes the normal state of mind. Orne[12] has referred to a characteristic of the hypnotic state as 'trance logic', whereby the hypnotized subject may tolerate mutually contradictory perceptions. In his classic demonstration, the so-called double hallucination test, a hypnotized subject is given the posthypnotic suggestion to see a certain person sitting in a chair. Later, after the hallucination is established, the subject's attention is drawn to the real person who is actually standing to one side. So now the subject sees two versions of this person – a hallucinated one in the chair, and the real one standing. According to Orne, it is characteristic of hypnotized subjects that they are not unduly disturbed by this. They have no need to establish a resolution to this impossibility. Trance logic means that both versions can coexist simultaneously.

This is reminiscent of the paradoxes we examined in relation to mysticism in Chapter 5. As discussed there, paradox is inevitable owing to the undifferentiated nature of things in the mystical state. It would appear that the hypnotized subject draws from this same undifferentiated state, according to the demands of the hypnotist. A crucial difference between the two cases concerns the individual's awareness. The hypnotized subject is completely unaware of the undifferentiated source of the hallucinations affecting his perception of reality. The mystic, on the other hand, *is* aware of the undifferentiated state, and reverts to paradox only when attempting to describe it. Under hypnotism, the double hallucination can be sustained because the subject has tacitly given control of their identity plane to the hypnotist. As discussed in Chapter 6, in entering into a world of imagery (bordering on hallucination) the mystic both lets go and maintains control at the same time. The mystic becomes centred in the higher plane. The hypnotized subject, on the other hand, is firmly entrenched in the identity plane, under manipulation from the hypnotist. Nevertheless, the 'letting go' aspect is similar in the two cases and involves, so we may speculate, a 'descent' to the brainstem region and consequent loosening of the bonds of self.

IN SEARCH OF THE PERSON

Returning to the ongoing debate about the nature of hypnosis, Spanos, as we have seen, criticizes the notion that some form of 'unconscious' perceiving of supraliminal stimuli takes place. But what about stimuli perceived under anaesthesia, or stimuli perceived and later recalled only implicitly by an amnesic patient? Are these not being perceived 'unconsciously'? The debate really focuses on the nature of the person, and on what is meant by describing a process as 'unconscious'. These are the very issues to which this book is centrally directed. The reason for the debate in the first place is that there is something unsettling, even threatening, in the notion that we are actually not as unified as we think. If there is some hidden, or unconscious, part, then who is in control? Who is responsible for our deeds? And where exactly does the cherished notion of free will fit in? Is it not safer to view the manipulations of hypnosis as simply playing with the subject's compliance, and not with the very composition of their mind?

The many lines of evidence supporting the model advanced over these pages, with its emphasis on the multiplicity of 'I' in the identity plane, suggest, however, that the questions really should be turned around. If there is no firm 'I', then how can there be any notion of responsibility unless there is in fact a higher part which transcends the shifting sands of identity? When we consider what it is that actually makes the person, and where we may assign responsibility, we must look to the upper storey of personality, the higher plane.

The point is not merely academic. There has been much debate recently over the issue of responsibility in a legal sense. In one dramatic case,[13] a man suffered a night terror (a kind of intense nightmare occurring during non-REM sleep) in which he experienced himself being chased by two Japanese soldiers intent on killing him. One of the soldiers was brandishing a knife, the other a gun. When they caught up with him, he became entangled in a fierce struggle with the soldier bearing the knife. As they fell to the floor, he got his hands around the soldier's neck and tried to strangle him. But the other soldier approached and fired. . . . As he awoke from this ordeal, sweating and in a panic, he found his wife dead on the floor. She had been strangled. It was his hands, the same hands that had been locked around the soldier's neck in his sleep experience, which had dealt the mortal blow. In the subsequent legal case this man was acquitted on the grounds that his actions had been 'sane automatisms'. This phrase means that he was not insane, and therefore did not require to be detained in a suitable institution, yet bore no responsibility for the action which he committed. In effect, the killing occurred with no involvement of the perpetrator's will.

The problem with this is that it assumes a model of the person which is not necessarily accurate. The notion that we are all characterized by a multiplicity of 'I' implies that one 'I' could do something which is somehow out of step with what we construe as our major personality. In fact, this is not such a rare occurrence. We have all, at one time or another, said or done things which we immediately realize somehow came from a part which 'wasn't me'. How often do we hear that 'I wasn't myself', or that 'I couldn't help myself'? It is as if the words or actions squeezed their way out, as it were automatically, from some kind of darker self, the Mr Hyde lurking within. But it is not the case that we can disown these words or actions so readily. On closer examination, as Freud has demonstrated so clearly in *The Psychopathology of Everyday Life*, they are in fact precisely motivated, and do reflect some meaningful part of the totality which is us.

In this context it is significant that comparisons between the condition of the normal, psychologically healthy individual and the multiple-personality patient have often been made. Here is Beahrs on the subject:

> . . . we are all actual multiple personalities in perhaps a more meaningful sense than the way the term is used psychiatrically. Every individual has many internal subparts, each with its own conscious experience, even if unperceived by his executive self and therefore relegated to the unconscious.[14]

Roper makes the important further point that an act carried out whilst asleep may well reflect an intention set prior to sleep. He cites the case of a patient suffering from *bulimia*, a condition that manifests in compulsive eating. The patient would sleep-walk to her refrigerator and gorge herself on whatever was there. In treating her, Roper employed the fact that she had a latent snake phobia. As part of the patient's therapy, the patient's husband was instructed to place a toy snake on the kitchen table before retiring to bed. This proved highly effective and the nightly visits to the refrigerator ceased. However, during the thirty months of this procedure the husband forgot to place the snake on the table for a total of six nights. On each of these nights the bulimia returned, suggesting that the patient's intent to eat was still present but would only manifest when the conditions were 'safe' (that is, no snake). Roper draws the implication that 'In the same way a previously formed intent to commit a crime could lead to it being carried out during sleepwalking under certain circumstances.'[15]

Beahrs, in the passage quoted above, assumes that there is an executive self. He seems to view such an executive as a part of ourselves which delegates the control of particular aspects of behaviour to other subsidiary selves as appropriate, much as the conductor of an orchestra cues the various instrumental groups in order to achieve the desired output of music. This seems reasonable since, assuming a model involving a multiplicity of 'I', there must surely be a psychological mechanism to bring some kind of order to this multiplicity. As Beahrs writes, the 'issue at hand is how executive control is determined and who or what has executive control'.[16] He further hints at the possibility that there is an 'overall self', an executive that includes not only those 'I's that regularly come in and out of operation, but also those that have become split off from the major personality. Surely it is here – in relation to the overall self – that we must endeavour to focus our definition of the 'person' psychologically and, if it comes to it, legally. The immediate sense of individuality, the 'I' of everyday experience, is hardly robust enough, nor is it fully inclusive of the brain modules which may have precipitated specific actions. In fact, it is only in the context of the overall self that we may meaningfully talk of free will and responsibility.

The problem is that it is not immediately clear that the overall self is conscious in the normal sense in which we use the term. As Beahrs implies in the passage quoted earlier, different parts of us may have their own conscious experience but, if they are not recognized by the executive self, remain effectively unconscious. The overall self, which is posited as including *all* parts, cannot therefore be fully conscious. Or can it? The issue of terminology, confronted in Chapter 1, seems to be still haunting us. Words, of course, only have meanings by convention and usage. What is important is that we should understand the issues here, and not be caught on a particular use of words. Put simply, the various studies reviewed in this book are best explained assuming a model of the mind in which different parts, what I have been calling different 'I's, come in and out of operation. Given such multiplicity, it seems reasonable to assume further that there needs to be some form of integration of these parts – an overall self.

In Chapter 1 I argued that the notion of accessibility is central to what is meant by the term 'consciousness'. But in the light of the many studies reviewed so far the situation has become more complicated. What is doing the accessing? We may either attribute consciousness to the immediate 'I' of experience, calling everything else 'unconscious', or we could call the overall self 'conscious', viewing individual 'I's as parts of the conscious totality. It seems to me that the strongest argument for the latter position is this issue of free will and responsibility. The term 'conscious', should, I believe, refer to that within us which does have free will and responsibility. The overall self, which I identify with the higher plane (see below), is therefore conscious, even though a given 'I' may not be conscious of the overall self.

The issue here is actually not one of science, but one of moral philosophy. The individual *is* responsible for their actions, because at some level they exercised their free will in a conscious decision to act. However, at the level of 'I', which may be equated with the trance of everyday life, they may not be aware of the conscious part that made the decision. In that sense only, the higher level may be referred to as 'unconscious'. But this designation of the higher part as unconscious seems to imply that the individual was somehow not responsible for their actions. It should not. On the contrary, the part we call 'I' can hardly be considered responsible since it comes about *after* an action is initiated. Here we return to the *terra firma* of scientific investigation, for this assertion concerning the timing of actions is made in relation to some ingenious research by Libet.

Libet asked his subjects to produce a simple movement of the wrist or fingers 'at will'. Other than the fact that they were instructed to do this at some stage during the experimental period, they were free to choose when to act. The movement was thus a 'conscious, endogenously willed motor action'.[17] Subjects were instructed to pay attention to their own mental processes and to attempt to detect the moment of onset of the 'urge, desire, or decision' to act. During the course of the experiment subjects watched a spot of light revolving around a screen depicting a clock face. The intention was that they would subsequently recall precisely where the light spot had been at the time that they became aware of 'wanting to move'. Thus the timing of the conscious event could be determined.

Two physiological measures were recorded with the intention of relating the timing of the subjective experience to the objective physical occurrence. One was a measure of the electrical activity in the muscles to be moved (EMG), and the other was the brain electrical activity recorded from the scalp. The latter was averaged over forty trials to maximize the signal strength.

The brain electrical activity associated with voluntary acts takes the form of a slow negative shift in potential which has been called the *readiness potential*. The key result from Libet's work was that the readiness potential onset was on average 535 milliseconds before the activation of the muscle as indexed by the EMG, and *345 milliseconds before the reported time of the subject's conscious intention to act* (figure 7.1). The brain's initiation of the movement evidently preceded the subject's conscious intent as indexed by the 'clock face' method described above. Libet concludes that:

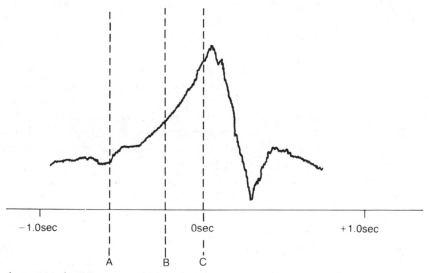

−1.0sec   0sec   +1.0sec

                  A   B   C

A = onset of readiness potential
B = conscious intention to act (as reported by subject)
C = onset of EMG response (i.e. activation of muscle)

Figure 7.1: Brain electrical activity during a conscious, voluntary movement. (Adapted by permission of Cambridge University Press from Libet, 'Unconscious cerebral initiative and the role of conscious will in voluntary action', *The Behavioral and Brain Sciences*, 1985, 8, 531.)

Some neuronal activity associated with the eventual performance of the act has started well before any (recallable) conscious initiation or intervention is possible. This leads to the conclusion that cerebral initiation even of a spontaneous voluntary act of the kind studied here can and usually does begin *unconsciously*.

Although the act studied here, a simple flexion of the finger was itself quite trivial, the conclusion may have general relevance. What the individual conceives of as actions performed consciously – acts of will – may in fact have been initiated unconsciously. This raises important issues pertaining to the nature of will.

Before returning to the implications of Libet's study, let us consider movements which can be seen more easily as goal-directed and complex. Take the example of riding a bicycle. We all know that the complex of specific muscular movements involved in such a task are performed automatically. Indeed, thinking about how to do it may well detract from our efficiency of performance. We would generally say that we (consciously) decide to ride the bicycle and then our brain (automatically) controls all the muscle groups in generating the co-ordinated movements required. The initial decision to ride the bicycle was an act of will on our part; the performance of the actions themselves, being simply automatic, does not involve the will.

But this is an oversimplification. Why did we decide to ride the bicycle in the first place? If we consider the situation we will realize that one thing led to the next. 'I had to post a letter and decided to go by bike.' Here, you could argue, was the conscious decision, for presumably I could equally well have decided to walk (although even here it is probably more to do with habitual responses than with free will).[18] But this decision does not generate the movements for riding the bicycle. It sets a goal which at some future time will necessitate those movements. The subjects in Libet's experiment made a parallel decision in agreeing to participate in the first place. When it comes to the actual execution of the movements – riding the bicycle, or flexing a finger in the case of Libet's subjects – the goal becomes the master and the means is a sequence of appropriate muscular movements. What we perhaps do not realize is that here a complex operation of memory is implicated. To achieve a particular goal through action a whole array of memories concerning how specific muscular movements will bring about certain results must be activated. The situation parallels that in the case of perception, where the final percept is arrived at only after an interaction with memory via the higher plane. In the case of motor behaviour we may consciously hold a goal, but the execution of that goal is achieved, I hypothesize, via the higher plane's interaction with memory.

Just as we could not possibly be conscious of all the intricate operations involving memory schemata in the perceptual process, so too the array of schemata concerned with motor operation are activated preconsciously. To convey the point about the complex memory processes involved in motor behaviour, consider even a simple task like walking along a path. Imagine the complex of precise muscular adjustments that may be required from one moment to the next. If, for example, we see a slight bump in the path where our next step will land, there have to be decisions about changes to the muscle tension in the foot, ankles, legs and so on. How will those changes affect my balance? How should the arms, shoulders, fingers even, be adjusted to handle the change in balance? Each of these thousands of muscular movements must be calculated on the basis of complex memories of how they have operated in the past.

The initiation of movement comes when the higher plane draws on the pure memory process according to the desired goal. The goal (as in my decision to ride the bike) may have been set previously. But the actual initiation of action comes with this involvement of the higher plane. This is the moment in which the will operates. 'I', which is a construction of the identity plane, comes into being subsequently. In fact it may not come into being at all, with no apparent loss of motor efficiency. There are cases of epileptic patients suffering petit mal attacks and carrying on with tasks initiated prior to the attack with no disruption. Such attacks involve only what seems to be an 'absence' for a short time; the patient is described as 'losing consciousness' and, unlike grand mal epilepsy, there are no gross motor disturbances. One such case involved a concert pianist. The performance was quite up to the normal standard, but the pianist had no recollection of her performance for the period of the attack. In our terms, no 'I' connection was made to her automatic actions. Closer to home, any experienced driver can describe occasions when a journey was successfully completed, as it were, on automatic pilot. The driver has no subsequent recollection of the journey. 'I' was asleep, but the watcher was awake.

It is this distinction between the operation of the higher plane and the identity plane in physical activity which underlies the variety of meditative exercises involving willed action which spiritual disciplines have developed. The Gurdjieffian system places great emphasis on performing actions 'consciously'. One means deployed to give 'the possibility of getting out of the circle of automatism' is the 'stop' exercise. During the course of normal routine, the teacher calls 'stop' – at which command all pupils have to freeze their bodily positions:

> A man is walking, or sitting, or working. At that moment he hears a signal. A movement that has begun is interrupted by this sudden signal or command to stop. His body becomes immovable and arrested *in the midst of a transition from one posture to another, in a position in which he never stays in ordinary life.* Feeling himself in this state, that is, in an unaccustomed posture, a man involuntarily looks at himself from new points of view, sees and observes himself in a new way.[19]

Alternatively, our attention may be focused on what are normally automatic processes by performing them in unusual ways – walking deliberately slowly, using alternate hands for accustomed tasks, and so on. Through all such exercises runs the common thread of observation and the attempt to catch the ways in which the higher plane controls movements we take for granted.

Nowhere has this challenge been more beautifully described than in Herrigel's book *Zen in the Art of Archery*. To understand the Zen perspective on will we need to realize that the paradox concerning self inherent in the nature of the higher plane, discussed earlier, must hold here in relation to action as well. If will operates at the level of the higher plane, where there can be no 'I', whose will is it, or, indeed, how can 'I' know my will? The art of archery involves the finest decision of will: when to loose the arrow. And in that moment, for the Zen master, 'I' is dissolved; archer, bow, arrow and target – all are one in a single breath. There is no disturbance; will operates in silence.

> One day I asked the Master: 'How can the shot be loosed if "I" do not do it?'
> '"It" shoots,' he replied.
> 'I have heard you say that several times before, so let me put it another way: How can I wait self-obliviously for the shot if "I" am no longer there?'
> '"It" waits at the highest tension.'
> 'And who or what is this "It"?'
> 'Once you have understood that, you will have no further need of me. . . .'

'Do you now understand,' the Master asked me one day after a particularly good shot, 'what I mean by "It shoots", "It hits"?'

'I'm afraid I don't understand anything more at all,' I answered, 'even the simplest things have got in a muddle. Is it "I" who draws the bow, or is it the bow that draws me into the state of highest tension? Do "I" hit the goal, or does the goal hit me? Is "It" spiritual when seen by the eyes of the body, and corporeal when seen by the eyes of the spirit – or both or neither? Bow, arrow, goal and ego, all melt into one another, so that I can no longer separate them. And even the need to separate them has gone. For as soon as I take the bow and shoot, everything becomes so clear and straightforward and so ridiculously simple. . . .'

'Now at last,' the Master broke in, 'the bowstring has cut right through you.'[20]

In emergencies we all operate in a way similar to that cultivated by these spiritual disciplines. I well remember an occasion when my elder daughter, then only a baby, fell on the stairs. How I twisted backwards, calculating the only possible angle to catch her in an instant, at the same time balancing against my own fall as I caught her, I could not possibly say. But it happened – and it certainly didn't depend on 'I'. We know of similar feats when an emergency comes whilst driving. Or consider the sprinter's response to the starter's gun. The 50–100 milliseconds it takes to set off is certainly faster than the time required for a stimulus to become consciously recognized. Again, the operation is devoid of 'I', presumably instigated by the higher plane before the interpreter generates the 'I' that hears the gun and thinks it started running. In fact, all top-class sports require such swift action without conscious deliberation.

Having considered the role of will in relation to significant actions, it is time to return to the work of Libet. But let us change one small detail. The movement under consideration is still a slight flexion of the finger; but let us suppose that that finger rests upon the trigger of a gun pointing at another person. Like I said, only a small change!

First, as with the bicycle example, presumably a decision has been made previously: the potential killer resolved to kill. Whether or not we call that a conscious decision is not the issue here, for our concern is with responsibility. If the finger does not flex, there is no murder. Now, to my mind, any separation between responsibility and will must be artificial. As has been said, 'By their deeds shall you know them.' The only will that can be of any interest is that operating at the time of action.

It is the same in the case of Zen archery. Decisions made previously ('I will practise archery this afternoon') are of no practical consequence to the real issue of the will in relation to the action in the moment. So too with Libet's subjects. Trivial as they are, I conclude that these movements are instigated by that within us which can access the detailed 'muscular' memories required to bring about the goal intended. It is, accordingly, the higher plane, and not 'I', which we should identify with the will.

Earlier I characterized the higher plane as a kind of inner watcher. It comprises our direct response to the world of the senses in which we are embedded. But, as I have now suggested, it is, in addition, the origin of our will. There is a certain symmetry here. On the perceptual side, stimuli are received and generate resonance through the pure memory process prior to 'I' coming into the picture. On the motor side, as Libet's studies demonstrate, a voluntary, willed action is instigated prior to any awareness that 'I' set the process in motion. Just as the 'I' that perceives is a result of a drive to interpret my reality as cohering around a unified self-image, so too the 'I' that acts is a construct which attempts to reinforce the illusion that this self-image is in control. 'It is illusion to say our movements are voluntary,' writes Ouspensky,[21] 'All our movements are automatic.'

Since the higher plane is thus the receiver of impressions and the instigator of action, it seems reasonable to equate it with what Beahrs called the 'overall self'. Furthermore, it represents our interface with the pure memory process and therefore encompasses the various associations that are made to any situation in which we find ourselves. Our essential nature is completely bound up with the form of these associations. We *are* the totality of those associations, whereas 'I' is a subset of the associations, a subset that enters time as we know it as 'the stream of consciousness'.

Yet there remains something of a paradox. The term 'higher plane' implies that there is no real substantiality to this entity. It is only a 'plane' of the mind. The term 'self' on the other hand, seems to conjure up a complex, organized structure. A self could be an executive, in control; a plane is just a geometrical construct. As previously noted, in relation to the mind all terms are of course essentially metaphorical; the mind has no dimensions of space. I chose to refer to 'planes' in this context to reflect an experiential aspect. To me, it 'feels' like I have occasionally shifted from one level to another, from one plane of mind to another. In the lower plane my experience centres on my personal identity; in the higher, what identity I could specify, is larger, less personal. Hence the terms 'identity plane' and 'higher plane'.

But what, in any case, is self? Stace quotes the Mandukya Upanishad, an ancient Indian metaphysical work. It describes four states of consciousness. These include normal consciousness, dreaming, dreamless sleep and the fourth, which is 'pure unitary consciousness wherein awareness of the world and of multiplicity is completely obliterated. It is ineffable peace. It is the Supreme Good. It is One without a second. It is the Self.' Stace comments as follows:

> . . . the word 'self' as thus used in the Upanishads – and the passage quoted is typical and not exceptional – is systematically double-meaninged. It is in the first instance the individual self. It is I who have reached my pure I-ness. But it is also the Universal or Cosmic Self, which is the absolute or ultimate reality of the world. This double meaning is not due to confusion of thought or verbal muddle. It is deliberate. The reason is that . . . the individual self and the Universal Self are not two existences but are identical. I *am* the Universal I.[22]

As we approach the true nature of the person, the real self, then like some will-o'-the-wisp its substantiality seems to fade. Perhaps it is here that the relation between physics and psychology that we met in Chapter I is most relevant. Bohm's concept of the implicate order encapsulates the notion that at the 'higher' level all is one in a 'sea of holism'. If this is so, then, as we become aware of our root in the implicate order, we would simultaneously and necessarily become aware of our root in the Universal Self. Is this, then, the nature of the person: as it were, a portal into the ultimate unity of all things?

Returning to the prosaic world of physiological studies of willed action, it is interesting to note that the readiness potential begins as a symmetrical wave over the whole brain. If the target movement is a flexion of the right finger, then the potential focuses on to the left motor region of the brain (brain control of bodily muscles is crossed left to right) around the time that conscious awareness comes into the picture.[23] Could it be that the widespread, symmetrical stage corresponds to the operation of the higher plane? Although it is not yet possible to specify the biological basis of the higher plane, I envisage that it involves holistic features of the brain. It encompasses the multiple memories that are engaged in both perception and willed action. The sheer magnitude of the processing involved must be enormous, and it would be difficult to envisage its operation by some serial process. It could be that the widespread origination of the readiness potential reflects the 'unfolding' of explicate from implicate levels of reality. Localization of function to discrete areas of the brain is an explicate reality; at the implicate level the whole brain is integrated with the universal 'holomovement'.

To continue in this vein of 'informed speculation', a threefold model of mind may be entertained:

1. The primary base of mind is the pure memory process. It underscores everything we can perceive and do, and enables patterns of information to come into being which become our personal memory structures, our psyches. But it is not limited by those patterns; it is simply their ground. The view of memory as a fundamental reality, much as I have in mind here, is articulated in the words of the Mexican writer and poet Octavio Paz: 'Memory is not that which we remember, but that which remembers us. Memory is a present that never stops passing.'[24] This pure memory process may be identified, I propose, with activity at the implicate level. It is not personal in any sense. Such an identification between the fundamental nature of memory and the implicate order seems also to have been considered by Bohm. In a discussion with Sheldrake, he stressed the role of the implicate order in relating past to present moments: 'If we extended quantum mechanics through the implicate order, we would bring in just that question of how past moments have an effect on the present.'[25] Such connectivity over time is, of course, the most basic expression of memory.

2. The higher plane comes into being as the interface between implicate and explicate orders. It is that unfoldment of implicate reality which becomes my brain and my mind. It therefore has two faces; that of non-self as it faces the implicate level, and that of real self as it faces the explicate.

3. Finally, the explicate order is the localized functional specialization of the brain: distinct parts for distinct operations. We experience the explicate order as the separate 'I's of the identity plane; as the self on being cast out of Eden.

THE HIGHER PLANE, MEMORY AND EMOTION

I was drawn from my reflections by the warbling of a thrush perched upon the highest branch of a birch tree. At that instant the magical sound brought my paternal estate before my eyes; I forgot the catastrophes of which I had been a witness and, transported suddenly into the past, I saw again that country where I had so often heard the thrush sing.

Chateaubriand, *Mémoires d'Outre-Tombe*

This description by Chateaubriand is of an experience of a kind which we can all surely recognize. It is a special kind of memory experience – but so different from everyday memory, when we voluntarily search for some particular thing that we know to be in storage, that it necessitates a deeper understanding of the nature of memory. Proust termed these special memories *involuntary* memories. They come unbidden. But their impact can be enormous. Why? What can they tell us about ourselves?

The quotation from Chateaubriand includes the major hallmarks of involuntary memories. They are 'magical'; they appear to arrive in an 'instant'; and they seemingly 'transport' us into the past. A further feature, so fully described by Proust in his *Remembrance of Things Past*, is the quality of emotion they access. It is as if we become flooded with an intensity of emotion which accompanies the quality of presence which these memories bring. Indeed, the emotion may be even more intense in an involuntary memory than in the original scene. And these are not any old emotions – these are the emotions that make us feel alive. A feeling beyond words, but one which we all recognize: 'Subjectively the feeling is miraculous, miraculous as a moment of love, the first sight of a newborn healthy baby to a mother, the sudden light of understanding of your idea in another person's eyes, or a moment of recognition of beauty in a work of art or scientific theory.'[26]

And it is in these moments when we feel most acutely alive that we can have a sense of true selfhood. In discussing the experience that Chateaubriand had on hearing the thrush singing, Mein suggests that as a child, 'He must have poured, however unconsciously, a vital part of his innermost self into a sound heard so often on the very edge of perception.'[27] And this would seem to capture the essence of involuntary memory, for the joy in the experience is not necessarily the joy inherent in the event we recall; it is the joy which comes with effecting connection to a larger self. This is its magical quality: involuntary memory drags us into a moment of consciousness of the higher plane. Normally it passes almost immediately. But that moment offers a 'window of opportunity' in which to explore our inner make-up.

It is this quest for the underpinnings of involuntary memories which becomes the backbone to Proust's work. The intense emotion is an intimation of some poignant memory which in turn may be followed to unearth something essential about our self. In one instance, Proust describes the effect thus brought about by the taste of a cake soaked in tea. Following one unsuccessful effort to unlock the memory, he tries for a second time:

> I place in position before my mind's eye the still recent taste of that first mouthful, and I feel something start within me, something that leaves its resting place and attempts to rise, something that has been embedded like an anchor at a great depth; I do not know yet what it is, but I can feel it mounting slowly; I can measure the resistance, I can hear the echo of great spaces traversed.
>
> Undoubtedly what is thus palpitating in the depths of my being must be the image, the visual memory which, being linked to that taste, has tried to follow it into my conscious mind.[28]

The visual memory brings us into direct alignment with the past events. In this instance the taste of the cake serves as the bridge to a time when, as a boy, he was given a similar cake dipped in tea by an aunt. The initial, involuntary connection opens the door to the visual memory which vividly brings details of his boyhood life into his mind's eye. For Proust, this alignment with the past enables a direct experience of the self precisely because time is transcended. We do not simply remember the events, as in everyday, voluntary memory. We effect connection with the self that observed the events. In the transection of past and present events, the self is experienced directly as the observer which is restricted to neither the past nor the present. The self, then, is outside of passing time:

> I experienced them [events recollected following involuntary memory] at the present moment and at the same time in the context of a distant moment, so that the past was made to encroach upon the present and I was made to doubt whether I was in the one or the other. The truth surely was that the being within me which had enjoyed these impressions had enjoyed them because they had in them something that was common to a day long past and to now, because in some way they were extra-temporal, and this being made its appearance only when, through one of these identifications of the

present with the past, it was likely to find itself in the one and only medium in which it could exist and enjoy the essence of things, that is to say: outside time.[29]

It is our experience of everyday, passing time that is transcended in these experiences. Through 'the miracle of an analogy' of the present moment to the past, Proust's being apprehends 'a fragment of time in the pure state'. And such contemplation of eternity, as he calls it, provides the 'only genuine and fruitful pleasure that I had known'. Memory, for Proust, goes beyond normal temporal existence and reveals both the essence of things around us and our own essence, our 'extra-temporal being'.

> From this metaphoric relationship between two impressions there has finally surged up the self; not a present self, without content, at the disposal of time and death; and not a past self, lost, and hardly retrievable; but an essential self, liberated from time and contingency, a primal and perpetual being, the creator of itself. . . . It is thus that, leaving the moment and having made an immense voyage across lost time, the existence travelling in search of its essence finds it in timelessness.[30]

It is beyond the scope of this book to delve deeply into that mystery we call time. Let me simply say that in my own experience, and in that of many with whom I have worked, this notion of a dimension outside passing time certainly has its place. Indeed our concept of eternity, not as endless time but as a kind of infinite fullness of time in the present moment, derives, I believe, from human experience and not from some abstract conception of theologians. At the end of his masterly survey *Man and Time*, Priestley describes his own experiences in which his mind was released from 'an egocentric relation with passing time'. These descriptions strike a chord with me, as I am sure they will with any individual who has been moved at some stage to examine the deeper meaning of his or her experiences.

> Whether it came at moments of great danger, in contemplating works of art, or with 'the aesthetic feeling' about certain aspects of life, the first kind of experience put things into slow motion, detached my consciousness from passing time, and transformed me while it lasted into an almost selfless observer, existing outside any sphere of action.
> The second kind of experience did not withdraw me from action but flung me into it, did not turn me into a detached observer but into a creator working like a man possessed, lending me energy and

imagination and a creative will. But I write 'me' for convenience; actually in this experience there is an absence of any feeling of self. . . .[31]

The altered experience of time coupled with selflessness that Priestley captures is, I believe, complementary to the intense experience of self outside time that Proust describes. Both experiences are focused in the higher plane. I suspect that it is in the pure memory process, out of which the higher plane emerges, that these altered conceptions of time have their basis.[32]

What of the emotion that accompanies the involuntary memories? Undoubtedly the emotion, be it of joy or indeed of fear, lends heart to these experiences, spiritualizes them. But the emotion is not simply a result, an output from the involuntary memory connection, which we may savour. It is the emotion itself that drives us forward to explore the connection. Maritain takes this line of argument a stage further in recognizing that such emotion becomes an 'instrument of intelligence'. As we experience the joy or fear, so the deeper meaning of the memory has already been known, but only preconsciously. Things are 'grasped and known obscurely' by emotion.[33] I equate Maritain's use of 'preconsciously' in this context to the operation of the higher plane in the terms advanced in this book. Such an emotion, a *higher*, or *creative* emotion, is not connected to 'I'. The joy or fear that 'I' feel is already one stage removed from the pure emotion. The emotion bears a numinous quality which cannot be pinned down in the identity plane. It intimates a fullness of meaning, as in the case of involuntary memories, which can be known only from the higher plane. Perhaps that is the function of such emotion in our lives – to launch us on a Proustian quest for meaning.

It should be noted that Maritain also distinguishes creative emotion from subjective emotions or feelings. The latter comprise our everyday drives and desires but have no major part to play in our creative life. Creative emotion, on the other hand, is the dynamic of poetic intuition which Maritain views as epitomizing all creative endeavour. In this, Maritain again parallels Proust in viewing the creative vision involved in generating a work of art as being one and the same as that vision which enables us to discover our deepest self.

I have dwelt at some length on these literary figures because their descriptions (and many others like them) seem to me the best evidence we have for the reality of the higher plane. Brain science and psychology may point us to the fact that there is an organization of information which is both prior to, and more inclusive than, that of which we are generally aware. It is, however, only personal experience that can remind us that consciousness actually attaches to that organization; that the higher plane gives access to knowledge and not mere information.

The work of the poet in particular, and the artist in general, is directed towards manifesting such knowledge in a form accessible not only to others, but also to the poet himself. It is as if the poem was somehow already present from the moment of inspiration, but in some concealed form. The knowledge inherent in that inspiration has to be uncovered, conveyed by the lines for which the poet gropes. The power of words is not that of communicating information; this they do, but it is not their power. The power of words lies in their ability, through the resonance of sound, rhythm and metaphor, to lead the mind into that state in which the inspiration was born. The true poet not only describes the beauty of the rose; he transports us into the presence of the rose. The beauty comes in our own act of recollection.

> . . . the soul,
> Remembering how she felt, but what she felt
> Remembering not, retains an obscure sense
> Of possible sublimity, whereto
> With growing faculties, she doth aspire,
> With faculties still growing, feeling still
> That whatsoever point they gain, they yet
> Have something to pursue.
>
> Wordsworth, *The Prelude*, II: 315–22.

8

Imagination, Mind and Reality

Meaning is the essence of reality. . . . Meaning organizes everything.[1]

The central characteristic of the human mind, its quest for meaning, may be discerned in a very simple tendency, that of *gap-filling*. In both perception and memory, the brain readily extrapolates information to cover whatever gaps may have been present. In the case of visual perception, for example, we are all faced with 'holes' in the visual field all the time, but of course we do not notice them. I have in mind the blind spot in each eye where the optic nerve leaves the eyeball. There is no visual sensitivity in this spot, as can be demonstrated by viewing with only one eye two dots displaced horizontally. In normal vision the 'holes' are filled in, since, as already mentioned, the brain does not faithfully copy the sensory input but constructs an image of the scene. The image need not portray every detail inclusive of the 'holes'. Indeed, patients who have sustained relatively small areas of damage to the visual region at the back of the brain may actually be unaware of the scotomata ('holes' in the visual field) which result. As the eyes are continually moving around, whatever may have been obscured due to the scotoma in one moment will be revealed in the next. We may envisage that the brain extrapolates not only spatially but also temporally in integrating the visual information received. In this way the gaps become filled.

The same gap-filling tendency is apparent when it comes to perceiving briefly exposed stimuli. For example, a circle with a gap in it may be seen as a whole circle, and an array of dots forming a square pattern may be perceived as a complete square design even if one of the dots is missing or slightly out of position. These are the kinds of observations that were made by psychologists of the gestalt school earlier this century. They considered that this tendency to fill gaps was a manifestation of a more basic feature of mind – the drive to perceive wholes rather than accretions of parts.

When it comes to memory, the seminal observations of Bartlett[2] established the nature of gap-filling when material to be remembered included what amounted to 'holes' – that is, meaningless or incomplete ideas. In one of his many studies, he asked subjects to remember stories which came from foreign cultures and were difficult to assimilate. When they were later asked to recall the stories, changes had been introduced which rationalized the stories and rendered them meaningful in terms of the subjects' own knowledge. What was remembered was the meaning that the subject had found in the story, not the story itself. More directly related to gap-filling were instances of subjects supplying a cause or an elaboration to some isolated element in the story. The sentence 'That Indian has been hit', for example, was recalled as 'An Indian was wounded by an arrow' or 'An Indian was shot'. As Gregory says, 'Gap-filling is basic in memory and perception. It seems that vacuums are as abhorrent to Mind as to Nature!'[3]

As we have seen earlier in this work, the drive to attribute explanations and causes to events is not restricted to perception and memory alone. It is fundamental to the sense of 'I' itself. 'I' arises through the work of the interpreter, which operates in precisely such a fashion: 'The left brain is constantly and reflexively generating theories to explain the internal and external events that occur around us. And it is because of that structure that we always attribute causes to everything that happens to us.'[4] It is precisely because the mind is motivated towards meaning that an episode which lacks a perceived, or inferred, cause is effectively a gap to the mind. In filling in these gaps the interpreter is not exercising a specific function all of its own; it is manifesting the fundamental gap-filling tendency according to its own specific operation. The point is that this gap-filling tendency is absolutely central to the nature of mind. We may, however, observe differing expressions of this tendency according to the level of mind, or specific module of the brain, under examination.

The very beginning of the sense of self – the seed of self, as I called it – can be understood within the same framework. The drive to closure, to make a whole from parts, brings about the most primitive sense of the organism's integrity. This sense is the equivalent in mind to the body's defence of its physical integrity. The self–nonself divide is a necessary consequence of this drive, since the organism can only sense itself as an integral whole by experiencing a separation from what is not self. The seed of self therefore carries within it the paradox of separation from the greater whole. Here lies the most fundamental root of the duality between *eros* and *thanatos*. On the one hand there is the drive to perpetuate selfhood, to reinforce the psychological forces that assert the integrity of the organism. On the other hand we have the drive to union with the greater whole that may only come through the dissolution of self. In a fundamental sense, sexuality is the resolution of this duality.[5] This ambivalence in the drive to wholeness becomes the central paradox of mind, manifest throughout the levels of self. Thus the 'I', as the fullest or most meaningful expression of the drive for continuity and integration in self, itself becomes the most substantive block to the alternate desire for union with the world beyond self.

The two forms of knowledge that we met in Chapter 2 represent the two sides of this divide. Analytical knowledge reinforces the integrity of 'I' by emphasizing the subject–object differentiation. Intimate knowledge dissolves that differentiation, fusing self to object in the act of knowing. The various forms of imagery that have been discussed throughout this book are valuable in their power to promote the second mode of knowledge. Ullman argues that dreaming in particular may be understood as our most regular encounter with this second mode, which he characterizes as 'aesthetic–creative'. This second mode 'serves man's need for unity, togetherness and harmony',[6] and the place of dreaming in our lives is, accordingly, that of reminding us of the price we may be paying for the emphasis on separateness in our daily lives:

> This view of dreams suggests that we are capable of looking deeply into the face of reality and of seeing mirrored in that face the most subtle and poignant features of our struggle to transcend our personal, limited, self-contained, autonomous selves so as to be able to connect with, and be part of, a larger unity.

The larger unity towards which we struggle has a double aspect. It is, at one and the same time, the self, that wholeness of Being of which 'I' is but a fragment, and the world beyond self encountered as we realize our root in the universal flux of implicate reality. And the paradox comes back to the nature of memory, for what can 'I' do when it is confronted, point blank as it were, with a Proustian involuntary memory? As discussed in relation to Bartlett's work, 'I' remembers meaning. But the meaning of an involuntary memory is only to be found in the continuity of self, not in the immediate meaning with which 'I' operates. The typical response of 'I' may be to dismiss the numinous quality of the experience, to paper over the gap that had opened up between the present and the past. But the gap (in other words, why do I experience this sense of familiarity now?) can only be fully filled by penetrating the deeper connections between the past and present. And, as we saw in the previous chapter, this brings the experience of self in its wake.[7]

Thus we find gap-filling as the central dynamic of mind at all levels. I identify this central dynamic, as did Coleridge,[8] with *imagination*. It is not simply the ability to arrive at novelty, as we may commonly think of imagination, but the absolute centre of the quest for meaning. Without imagination there could be no meaning, and without meaning there could be no mind. Warnock expresses the point with characteristic precision following her thorough examination from the philosophical perspective:

> Imagination is our means of interpreting the world, and it is *also* our means of forming images in the mind. The images themselves are not separate from our interpretations of the world; they are our way of thinking of the objects in the world. We see the forms in our mind's eye and we see these very forms in the world. We could not do one of these things if we could not do the other. The two abilities are joined in our ability to understand that the forms have a certain meaning, that they are always significant of other things beyond themselves. We recognize a form as a form *of* something, as Wittgenstein said. It seems to me both plausible and convenient to give the name 'imagination' to what allows us to go beyond the barely sensory into the intellectual or thought-imbued territory of perception.[9]

I proposed in Chapter 7 that the pure memory process operates at the implicate level. Since the implicate order is characterized by undivided wholeness, all things have the potential to be interconnected on account of their root in that order. This gives the basis to memory, for memory is fundamentally concerned with the relationships between events. We may describe the nature of those relationships in terms of physical forces as we know them, be it reverberation or resonance, for example. But such properties are only on the surface. The deep structure of memory is precisely this interconnectedness in the implicate order. Memory as we experience it – that is, personal memory – depends on the subset of connections that unfolds into explicit reality as the individual's brain and mind. The role of the brain, as we have seen, is focused on the nature of self; different levels in an evolutionary sense contributing different levels of complexity to self. Memory as we experience it is therefore an unfoldment of those interconnections that intersect with self. Explicit memory includes those memories that connect with 'I'. Implicit memories, although devoid of such a connection to 'I', still connect with deeper levels in the hierarchy of self. The individual mind/brain is thus a subset of the pure memory process unfolded into the explicate order. It may perhaps be compared to a constellation superimposed on the amorphous backdrop of stars. Looking at it from the other direction, the brain enfolds the memories connected to self back into the implicate order. In effect, the brain thereby limits our contact with the pure memory process. It acts primarily to guard the limits of self, much as Bergson and Huxley have argued.

Just as the recognizable operation of memory reflects a root principle at the implicate level, so too with imagination. Imagination, in the fundamental sense in which I have discussed it in this chapter, is evident throughout the operations of mind precisely because it is a second aspect of the pure memory process at the implicate level. The first aspect is holism, which gives rise to the connections of memory. But this alone would constitute, as it were, a frozen sea. It would be static. As Bohm argues, there is always movement: 'The new form of insight can perhaps best be called *Undivided Wholeness in Flowing Movement*. This view implies that flow is, in some sense, prior to that of the 'things' that can be seen to form and dissolve in this flow.'[10] This flow is the fundamental dynamic of reality. And in the unfoldment into explicate reality it becomes the imagination in all the guises we have been discussing. It is the flow of mental information covering the gaps in the most basic processes of mind; and it is the flow that generates those intuitive leaps which may illumine the world as some recondite gap in our knowledge is bridged with insight.

These two, connectivity and imagination at the explicate level, holism and flow at the implicate, are the yin and yang of memory. The pure memory process, far from being frozen, is a sea of life. We recognize that life as thought, for in its unfoldment it becomes the life of the mind. But it is just as much thought before it unfolds, and therefore not limited to the individual mind. The thinking of the pure memory process is the trigger that lies behind the thought forming in the individual mind. It is the silence that precedes manifestation; the presence filling the space vacated by 'I' in those rare moments of sublime inspiration. And wherever there is thought there is also the quest for meaning.

Epilogue

Do not investigate into that which is miraculous to you; and into that which is concealed from you, do not probe. Where you have authority, seek to understand. But it is not for you to delve into mysteries.[1]

But what is a mystery? The brain hides its functions from our eyes. Unlike other organs in the body, the logic of its operation cannot be discerned from its appearance. Whilst the heart is clearly built like a pump, or the kidneys like filtration units, the brain displays nothing of its function to a cursory investigation. Over the ages we have probed according to the limits of our understanding. When we sought for vapours we found them; when we sought for electricity we found it; and when we sought for chemical transmission we found that. When we expected to find functions localized in specific regions of the brain, such localization of function appeared as the intrinsic logic of brain structure. When we aspired to the power of computers in the framework within which we viewed the world, the brain was indeed a computer. Now, when we are entranced by the sophistication of holography, the brain has been quick to oblige and manifests the appropriate patterns of activity. Who knows, but when we seek for wings the brain won't bear us into the furthest reaches. . . ?

I am reminded of the manna sent with the crystalline dew to nourish those whose path took them through the desert. According to tradition, its taste varied according to the aspirations of those who ate it: to the child it tasted like milk; to the youth, like bread; to the old, like honey. In fact 'What is it?' became its name (Exodus 16:15). It was, of course, all of these and more, because it was 'ground by the angels in heaven'.

Humankind has always delved into that which appeared mysterious, and in our age science has substituted much explanation for myth. Yet wherever we may deem it to be, there is always a border between the known and the unknown. There is always that which is just beyond the sensitivity of our most powerful instruments. Of course it is humanity's greatest dignity to bring light where there was darkness; that is not in question. The question really concerns our approach to that which remains unknown. 'Thirty spokes share one hub. Adapt the nothing therein to the purpose in hand, and you will have the use of the cart.'[2]

I have drawn on the symbolism of Hebrew letters more than once in this book. Let me do so one more time. The first letter of the alphabet, *alef*, as we have seen, is silent. Its shape embodies the principle of balance, and it symbolizes the unknown. The next three letters give the Hebrew word for clothing, *beged*. And here, quite simply, is the teaching. We can know only the clothing.

There is a delicate balance to be struck between the egocentricity of our quest for meaning and the openness we must cultivate in order that the unexpected may not be missed. This is the balance we strike between the security of 'I' and the deeper sense of self associated with the higher plane. When it comes to brain research, our understanding has led to many insights. But, however rich those insights, let us not obscure the space wherein the mystery unfolds.

And so it is with human potential. In closing this book, let me make the point that the place of mysticism within our lives is very much misunderstood. Mysticism is not the indulgence of a select few outsiders who chart the limits of human experience according to their vocations. It is the heritage of anyone who pauses from time to time to ask questions of themselves. Certainly, mysticism has developed systematizations of thought in the form of signposts to guide the individual who goes beyond simple questions. But, as the juxtaposition in this work of insights from mysticism with those from brain science indicates, the basic concern is very much with the ordinary person in the here-and-now. Each of us confronts the unknown at every turn. That is the major theme of the model developed over these pages. What I have termed the higher plane is unknown to 'I'. But it is the ground from which 'I' is constructed. There is no final goal to which our potential is directed, as if the final victory would come with the complete surrender of 'I' (unless, of course, we consider death to be that goal). All we can do is give ourselves the space in which 'I' may acknowledge its own ground. In that way there is the potential for 'I' to grow, to become ever more inclusive in its role as wayfarer through the path of a life. Knowledge of self is the beginning and end of human potential.

Notes

INTRODUCTION

1. *Avot* 1:14. This is a tractate of the *Mishna*, rabbinical writings dating from the second century CE. Known in English as *Sayings of the Fathers*, it records significant teachings forming an unbroken line from the end of the era of the prophets until the time of its writing.
2. Throughout this book the term 'I' is preferred to 'ego', as used in psychoanalytical literature. There are two reasons for this preference. First, over the years differing shades of meaning have accompanied different authors' use of the word 'ego'. Second, when we speak of 'the ego', it can appear to many as somewhat clinical and distant. Although it may not roll off the tongue quite so well as 'ego', 'I' is a more direct term for English-speaking readers. It conveys what is intended – the personal sense of the experiencing self.

1: CONSCIOUSNESS, MIND AND BRAIN

1. *Zohar I* 15a. The *Zohar*, a book first circulated in the thirteenth century, has become the major text of Jewish mysticism.
2. Cassirer (1955); Neumann (1954).
3. Neumann (1954), p.104.
4. Schnapper (1980), p.202.
5. The exegesis of the biblical story of Adam and Eve draws especially on Horowitz's *Shnei Luchot Habrit*, first published 1649, Amsterdam.
6. Jung (1969), p.508.
7. Maritain (1953), pp.98–9.
8. The way in which the universe is described as tangible may require some comment. By 'tangible' I mean that we can, more or less, form

an image of the thing concerned. Whilst the universe as a whole is not observable directly in the way in which the other two are, it is tangible to the intellect in a way that 'consciousness' is not.

9. Minsky (1988), p.160.
10. Sperry (1969), p.533.
11. Schrödinger (1964), p.37.
12. De Chardin (1965), p.56.
13. Aristotle (1984), p.1698.
14. Stace (1960), p.14.
15. Cohen and Phipps (1979), p.93.
16. Cohen and Phipps (1979); Hardy (1979); Hay (1982).
17. Capra (1975); Davies (1983); LeShan (1974); Zukav (1979).
18. Zukav (1979), p.101.
19. Bohr (1934), cited in Zukav (1979), p.118.
20. Deikman (1973), p.319.
21. Bohm (1980), p.175.
22. Davies (1983), p.111.
23. Bohm (1980), p.117. Passages cited in next paragraph, pp.195 and 178.
24. The relevance of Bohm's theory positing two orders of reality to the world view of mysticism has been questioned by Wilber (1982). In Wilber's view, the testimony of mysticism argues against a simple dichotomy of levels. In particular, it is suggested that the mystic ascending beyond the normal, ego-based consciousness passes through several diverse transcendent states. By equating such diversity of states of consciousness with diversity of levels of reality, Wilber proposes a scheme somewhat more complex than that envisioned by Bohm. The orders of reality become multiple rather than twofold.
25. Bohm (1980), p.209. Next passage, p.209.
26. James (1976), p.4.
27. Von Franz (1974), p.156.
28. See, for example, Wilber (1977).
29. Wigner (1972), pp.133–4.
30. The notion that consciousness could have been presaged in the big bang with which the universe began derives from the so-called *anthropic principle*. Briefly, the argument is that for life as we know it to come about, the origin of the universe had to adhere to certain parameters, in terms, for example, of the speed and power of the initial explosion. On a chance basis, it seems to be highly unlikely that these parameters would have been met. Had they not been met, the order of the universe, including the laws of science as we know them, could not have ensued. Consequently, the conditions for life as we know it to develop could never have come about. The strong anthropic principle suggests that the incredible odds against

a universe such as ours coming into being were overcome because the nature of the big bang was not determined randomly. It was conditioned according to an 'intended' outcome – the generation of life forms with powers of observation. In other words, the universe began in the way it did *in order that observers such as ourselves would evolve*. This is an argument for some kind of design underlying our universe, and the drive towards observation, or consciousness, becomes a determining factor. In some way, then, this drive was present in the inception of the universe. See Barrow and Tipler (1988).

31. Bloom and Lazerson (1988), p.303.
32. Oliver (1987), p.50.
33. Bergson (1978); Huxley (1954); Sheldrake (1981).
34. Schürmann (1978), p.134.
35. Jeffrey (1986), p.275.
36. In defining my terms I am particularly aware that such definitions involve assumptions that have a moral impact. This, it seems to me, is a fact too little recognized in psychology. It may be argued, for example, that the current interest in animal rights stems from a realization that the previously upheld theological and philosophical distinction between 'man and beast' is untenable in the light of evolution. Our Victorian ancestors were able to inflict their will on animals for purposes of entertainment or casual research not because they were inherently more cruel than us, but because their world view held there to be an unbridgeable gap between the human soul and that of animals. Thus, we can see that assumptions underlying a world view have very direct implications for the distinction between what is, and what is not, acceptable behaviour. As the divide between human and animal has receded in our day, so too it seems that the divide between human and machine is currently under threat. The view, discussed earlier, that super-complex machines would be conscious is an example of this. As I have argued, the central issue here, the distinction between mind and mechanism, is not available to scientific enquiry. It is, however, an issue with profound moral implications. It often happens that scientists, raised in a tradition hostile to moral philosophy, tend by default to deny the distinction. This has already happened in the case of the human–animal divide. Philosophy today tends to be under the spell of science. Philosophers would, however, do well to ponder the implications of further erosion of the 'moral order' which separates man from machine. As has often been said, today's science fiction can all too easily become tomorrow's reality.
37. Deikman (1973), pp.317–18.

2: PERCEPTION: GATEWAY TO THE MIND

1. The recognition of the symbolic mode and the non-dual mode of knowing also figures prominently in the work of Henri Bergson (intellect vs. intuition), Abraham Maslow (intellectual vs. fusion knowledge), Trigant Burrow (ditention vs.cotention), Norman O. Brown (dualistic vs. carnal knowledge – 'carnal' because subject and object become one in the act of knowing), Andrew Weil (straight vs. stoned), Krishnamurti (thought vs. awareness), Wei Wu Wei (outseeing vs. inseeing), Spinoza (intellect vs. intuition) . . . and these to name but a very, very few.
    [Wilber (1977), pp.45–6.] See also Bogen (1969).

2. It is no accident that we describe such an experience as 'moving'. As we shall see in later chapters, we generally operate with consciousness centred in our sense of identity, the *identity plane*. This plane defines our horizons in terms of ego–strengthening goals: it embodies the 'Cain mode' of operation. An experience such as that described here 'moves' us, as it were, beyond this identity plane. As will be discussed later, spatial terms can only be metaphorical in relation to mind since the mind is not dimensional – it is not a spatial entity. Language simply reflects the way in which our experience focuses on this metaphor of space as the only way in which we may grasp features of mind. Thus we *under-stand*, *fall* into reverie, or even experience a *narrowing* or an *expansion* of consciousness. See Thass-Thienemann (1968a), pp.360–9.

3. Haith (1980), p.107.

4. Fantz (1961).

5. Hubel and Wiesel (1979); Hubel (1988).

6. Heron, Doane and Scott (1956).

7. Shurley (1960), p.543.

8. Reed (1979), p.164.

9. See Clarke and Dewhurst (1972).

10. Zeki (1978); Zeki and Shipp (1988).

11. Perrett, Mistlin and Chitty (1987).

12. Hubel (1988).

13. Coren and Porac (1984).

14. Gregory (1977).

15. Held (1965). For a more detailed discussion of perceptual adaptation see Welch (1978).

16. Yeats (1961), p.159.

17. Maritain (1953), pp.111–12.

18. Deikman (1963).

19. Shelley (1880), pp.139–40.

20. Segal (1972).
21. The conclusion derived from studies such as those by Segal described here – that imagery activates mechanisms which are actually a part of the normal perceptual process – has been criticized on the grounds that the effect may be due to more general parallels between imagery and perception. The two processes may share cognitive demands which are not necessarily perceptual in nature, for example attention. It has further been suggested that subjects may employ strategies in their imagery task which, at an unconscious level, draw on their knowledge of perception. Thus, according to this view, it is not that imagery and perception share mechanisms, but that the subject makes an unconscious comparison between the two. I would argue, as does Farah (1988), that the neurophysiological evidence cuts through such criticisms since it points to the precise loci where such sharing of mechanisms between imagery and perception is observed.
22. Segal (1971), p.195.
23. For reviews see Finke (1985, 1986); Shepard (1984); Shepard and Cooper (1982).
24. Farah (1988, 1989).
25. Bisiach and Luzzatti (1978).
26. The neuronal input model must be hierarchically constituted. We can imagine how successive groupings of features may be incorporated in the model, starting with the simplest elements such as lines, and building up to complex 'mosaics' incorporating colour, motion and shape. A good example of such hierarchical processing is found in the case of our perception of faces, as discussed by Perrett, Mistlin and Chitty (1987).
27. Oatley (1978), p.166.
28. Zeki and Shipp (1988).
29. For the purposes of distinguishing the four experiences depicted in figure 2.7 it is convenient to contrast the role of the sensory input. As discussed in the text, perception and contemplation focus on the present input, while visualization and hallucination do not. This is not to imply, however, that visualizations and hallucinations owe nothing to current sensory input. There is good evidence that, at least in some cases, hallucinations develop from normally inhibited features of the visual input, such as images of the blood vessels of the retina or of the structure of the lens of the eye (for discussion see Horowitz (1978)). In figure 2.7, however, we are interested in the situation as construed by the subject.
30. Luria (1969).

3: MEMORY: THE TAPROOT OF MIND

1. McCarthy and Warrington (1988), p.429.
2. Pribram (e.g. 1971, 1981).
3. Bergland (1985), p.106. Earlier quote from p.120.
4. In some of his writings, Pribram seems to imply that holographic storage, although centred on properties of the brain as far as our memories are concerned, is not limited to the brain alone. The 'wave-form domain', into which the distribution of information in the brain leads, is identified with the implicate order we met in Chapter 1 and is, therefore, a connection between the individual and the universe as a whole: 'Mental properties are the pervasive organizing principles of the universe, which includes the brain.' (Pribram (1982), p.30.)
5. Sheldrake (1988), p.199. See also Sheldrake (1981).
6. Thompson (1986).
7. Bergson (1978), p.321.
8. Yeats (1961), p.50.
9. Gray, Konig, Engel and Singer (1989).
10. Raikov (1983).
11. Cohen (1980), p.105.
12. Cohen (1980), p.101.
13. The *Bahir* is a kabbalistic work which is thought to have been edited in Provence during the twelfth century.
14. Scholem (1961), pp.135–6.
15. Bohm and Peat (1989), p.8.
16. Hebrew letters are used as numbers (*alef* as one, *bet* as two and so on) in addition to their normal linguistic use. It follows that a given word has a numerical value. Many commentators have assumed that equivalence of numerical value between words implies some connection with regard to the meaning of the words. Such an endeavour to find meaningful connection on the basis of number is called gematria.
17. Eagle, Wolitzky and Klein (1966).
18. Fisher (1954); Kaser (1986).
19. Levinson (1965); Blacher (1987).
20. Evans and Richardson (1988).
21. *Lancet*, 1 November 1986, pp.1019–20.
22. Picton and Hillyard (1974); Thornton, Catley, Jordan, Lehane, Royston and Jones (1983).
23. When viewing figure 3.4 the reader should bear in mind that, as Marcel (1980) points out, a stimulus processed nonconsciously activates more than one meaning simultaneously. The search of memory is not a sequential process. It most probably involves some complex form of parallel activations. As far as figure 3.4 is

concerned, the process appears sequential only due to the limitations of diagrammatic representation.

24. Murch (1969).

25. Sacks (1986), p.105. Subsequent passages quoted are from pp.110 and 104–5.

26. The topic of implicit memory has been reviewed by Schacter (1987) and Schacter, McAndrews and Moscovitch (1988).

27. Graf, Squire and Mandler (1984).

28. De Haan, Young and Newcombe (1987), p.412.

29. Renault, Signoret, Debruille, Breton and Bolgert (1989); Tranel and Damasio (1985).

30. Glisky, Schacter, and Tulving (1986).

31. Marcel (1988), p.140.

32. A discussion of infantile memories and their impact on the adult may be found in Janov (1977).

33. The centrality of self to memory has been recognized by many philosophers. In particular, it is fruitful to read Mary Warnock on this matter. The ideas she arrives at in the following extract come very close to my hypothesis of 'I-tags' and their role in recall:

> Any truly recalling memory . . . must contain the idea of self. Whether through images or through direct knowledge, to count as a memory a cognitive experience, or thought, must contain the conviction that I myself was the person involved in the remembered scene. The image, if there is one, must be labelled not only 'this belongs to the past' but also 'it belongs to *my* past'. The knowledge, if it is to be so described, must be knowledge that *I* had the earlier sensation or performed the earlier act. The knowledge is a kind of self-knowledge. It is in myself that the truth to be uncovered by recollection must lie.
> [Warnock (1987), pp.58–9.]

34. In this dichotomy of thought we approach what was arguably Freud's greatest insight: the distinction between secondary and primary processes. Freud recognized that these two processes of thought are active in the mind simultaneously, the primary 'beneath' the secondary. The secondary process is effectively what we recognize as normal thinking. It is logical, goal-directed and predominantly verbal in nature. The primary process, by comparison, is generally unconscious. It is nonlogical, proceeds through images, lacks a time base, and is symbolic in content. Freud considered dreams, for example, to be manifestations of primary process thinking. I would argue that the pure memory process is ultimately non-personal, but manifests in the individual as primary process thought when outside the realm of 'I' (cf. implicit memory). Secondary process thinking comes about with the involvement of 'I' in memory access (explicit memory). The primary process is therefore to be identified with the

higher plane, to be introduced in Chapter 4. Freud's seminal discussion of primary and secondary processes may be found in *The Interpretation of Dreams*, pp.588–610.

4: IDENTITY AND BEYOND

1. Jaspers (1963), p.766.
2. The *Zohar*, Book of Concealment: 1. The dynamic of creation is conceived in this work as an interplay between two different divine 'countenances'. These may best be understood as being centres of organization in the emanations from God. One countenance is viewed as transcendent; the other, a lower reflection of the first, is immanent. The Book of Concealment is largely concerned with exploring the detailed correspondence which exists between the two countenances.
3. Jung (1963), p.371. Passage that follows, pp.284–5.
4. Lao Tzu (1963), p.66.
5. The *Bahir*, paragraphs 70 and 79.
6. Idel (1988a), p.12.
7. Quoted in Wilber (1977), p.321.
8. Kubie (1958), p.137.
9. Lowell (1952), p.109.
10. Representative of the range of recent works exploring the nature of multiplicity in the person are those by Beahrs (1982); Elster (1986); Gazzaniga (1985); Hilgard (1986); Parfit (1984); Quen (1986); and Rowan (1990).
11. Parfit (1984, pp.502–3) cites a number of Buddhist texts in support of his advocacy of the 'bundle' theory of mind which encompasses the notion of multiplicity. The following captures the essential point:

    Buddha has spoken thus: 'O Brethren, actions do exist, and also their consequences, but the person that acts does not. There is no one to cast away this set of elements, and no one to assume a new set of them. There exists no Individual, it is only a conventional name given to a set of elements'.

    And in the West we have, for example, a statement from the Church Father, Origen, quoted by Jung: 'You will see that a man who seems to be one is not one, but as many different persons appear in him as he has attitudes.' (Cited in Rowen (1990), p.12.)
12. For a historical view see Carlson (1986); Ellenberger (1970).
13. Beahrs (1982), p.52.
14. Gazzaniga (1985), p.135.
15. Gazzaniga and LeDoux (1978); Gazzaniga (1985, 1988a and b); LeDoux (1985). The studies described in the remainder of this section are from Gazzaniga (1988a).

16. Gazzaniga (1988b), p.219.
17. Gazzaniga (1989), p.950.
18. Bellugi, Poizner and Klima (1989), p.387.
19. Whorf (1956), p.55.
20. Jerison (1985), p.5.
21. Hermelin (1978).
22. Leslie (1987).
23. Rowan (1990), p.8.
24. Weiskrantz (1986), p.170.
25. Weiskrantz, Warrington, Sanders and Marshall (1974).
26. Marcel (1988).
27. Wickes (1968), p.ix.
28. The quotations are from Nicoll (1984), pp.1553–4, 1721, 1723, 1396 and 1266.
29. Stace (1961), p.87.
30. Jung (1953), p.238.
31. For a contemporary discussion of the Buddhist theory of 'no-self' see Kolm (1986).
32. The two passages on mindfulness are from Schumacher (1978), p.84.
33. Mavromatis (1987), p.270.
34. Jung (1967), p.16.
35. Coleridge (1956), p.167.

5: THE ARCHAEOLOGY OF SELF

1. Armstrong (1982), p.232.
2. Critchley (1979), p.103.
3. Mandell (1980).
4. Stace (1961), p.53.
5. Underhill (1922), p.77.
6. James (1960), pp.487 and 490.
7. Kissin (1986).
8. MacLean (1970), p.347.
9. Mueller (1983), p.99.
10. Sacks (1986), p.107.
11. Proust (1949), p.61.
12. Sacks (1986), p.107.
13. MacLean (1977), p.313.
14. Gott, Hughes and Whipple (1984), p.71.
15. Csikszentmihalyi (1975). The quotations are from pp.50, 53 and 45.
16. Any given psychological state is unlikely to reflect an exclusive involvement of one hemisphere or the other. Obviously, the issue here is one of relative activation. When the operation of the interpreter

is attenuated, as in these 'flow' states, other resources of the left hemisphere may nevertheless be active. Thus, for example, when playing chess analytical processes presumed to reside in the left hemisphere would be crucially involved. Similarly, musical composition may well depend on left hemisphere involvement as far as the 'language' of musical notation is concerned. In both examples, right hemispheric processes would presumably operate on the overall pattern of the game/music. The central issue is the distinctive quality lent to the state when the interpreter is silenced. Since the interpreter is an exclusively left hemisphere module, the state reflects a relative decrease in left hemispheric involvement.

17. Bogen and Bogen (1969).
18. The comments by Taub appear in a discussion of a paper by Scheibel and Scheibel (1977). For a fuller discussion of the role of subcortical brain areas in meditation, see in particular Mavromatis (1987).
19. Scheibel (1980), p.63.
20. Melzack (1989), p.4.
21. Lilly (1981), p.175.
22. Stace (1961), p.305.
23. Sagan (1977).
24. Thass-Thienemann (1968a), p.65. The following quotations are from pp.161 and 302.
25. *Sefer Yezirah*: 18. The *Sefer Yezirah* is believed to have been compiled between the second and sixth centuries. The book's centrality to Jewish philosophical and mystical thought is well conveyed by the myth which holds its contents to have been taught in the first place by an angel to Adam in the Garden of Eden. Others hold that it was written by the patriarch Abraham.
26. Stace (1961), p.297.
27. Rothenberg (1971), p.198.
28. Yeats (1961), p.255.
29. Jung (1969), p.508.
30. Midrash is the collective term for voluminous early rabbinical writings dealing with largely homiletic interpretations of the scriptures. These interpretations are often based on the Hebrew forms of particular words where alternative meanings could be extracted. The instance cited here is found in *Genesis Rabba* on Genesis 2:3. The discussion concerns Adam's response to his first experience of darkness (on the night of the sixth day). Understandably, Adam was terrified, not knowing that the darkness would ever pass. In order to comfort him God made him find two flints and produce fire. Hence, 'night is light in my Eden'. The deeper message of Midrashic texts is left for the reader to extract. The point here is not the superficial issue of Adam fearing night and being comforted with light, but the deeper meaning of the sixth day and its relationship to the

seventh, the sabbath. Human creativity, in partnership with God, derives light from darkness in the final 'stage' before the cessation of creative endeavour. Fire is the archetypal symbol of creativity, and it is the gift of creativity which cements the relationship between God and humankind. Fire is, at the same time, the great destroyer. Fire thus depicts the tension of opposites – creation and destruction – and heralds the sabbath which becomes the time for the unification of opposites.

31. Continuing in the 'honey-gold' complex is the name of the bee, a recurrent personal name of women: in Hebrew *Deborah*, the name of Rachel's nurse; in Greek *Melissa* or *Melitta*, the name given to the priestesses of Delphi, of Demeter, and of Artemis. In the language of Neo-Platonic philosophy 'bee' is the name of any pure soul coming to birth. Moreover, the idea of the bee being the fetus in the womb is further implied in both *meli-pais-symblos*, 'the hive with its honey-children', and *simbl-euo*, 'to shelter as in a hive'. The infantile fantasies about the beginning of life during the Golden Age are present in all these words. The 'queen wasp' is called in Greek *metra*, 'womb'. In Hungarian the 'womb' is called *meh* or *anya-meh*, 'bee' or 'mother-bee'. These repressed fantasies are also present in such formulas as the Latin *luna mellis*, i.e., 'honeymoon'. On the reality level such words may be ridiculed as sheer nonsense, yet they are meaningful in terms of the unconscious fantasies implied.
[Thass-Thienemann (1968b), p.195–196.]

32. The Talmud is the record of rabbinical discussions, dating from the third to the fifth century, which largely moulded the development of Judaism in its post-Temple form. In addition to establishing the regulations governing social and religious conduct, it is a repository of early 'scientific' and mythical ideas such as that quoted here concerning the embryo in the womb (*Niddah* 30b).

33. James (1960), p.257.

34. McKenzie (1981).

35. Lifton (1966), p.208.

36. Koestler (1967), MacLean (1969).

37. Hobson (1988), p.93.

38. When it comes to questions of causation, the balance between biological and psychological factors in mental disturbance has long been an issue of some contention. In the case of autism both sides have their protagonists, some holding that the condition is attributable to psychological pressures within the family (psychological), others pointing to abnormal brain development (biological). The psychological view was highly influential until about the mid-seventies. Since then, and with increasing evidence to support it, the biological viewpoint has tended to prevail. With hindsight we can discern an unfortunate touch of cruelty in the attempt to inflict on parents

already suffering for their children's sake the added burden of guilt associated with the onset of autism when this was attributed solely to familial factors.

39. Possible biological determinants of autism have been reviewed recently by Frith (1989); Schopler and Mesibov (1987); and Wing (1988).
40. Ornitz (1985).
41. James and Barry (1980).
42. Gaffney, Kuperman, Tsai, Minchin and Hassernein (1987).
43. Despert (1946), p.246.

6: DREAMING AND THE BRAIN

1. Aserinsky and Kleitman (1953).
2. Kissin (1986); Winson (1985).
3. Cohen (1979).
4. Jouvet (1975).
5. Vertes (1984), p.279.
6. Jouvet (1975), pp.511–12.
7. Morrison (1983).
8. Kasamatsu and Pettigrew (1976).
9. Jung (1954), p.117.
10. Winson (1985), p.209.
11. Crick and Mitchison (1983).
12. See, e.g., Fishbein (1981).
13, Scrima (1984), p.215.
14. Jung (1960), p.294.
15. Ullman (1987a), p.120.
16. Malamud (1986), pp.600–1. Passage that follows, p.609.
17. Greenberg (1987), p.48.
18. The idea that 'I' is not actually the instigator of our actions will receive fuller consideration in Chapter 7, where issues relating to voluntary control and responsibility will be explored.
19. Teyler and DiScenna (1986).
20. An issue that has not been directly addressed is that of the sense of self in animals. This is an issue which seems to excite a great deal of interest but which, necessarily, depends on much speculation. As far as the theory developed here is concerned, the argument that REM sleep is a time for the organization of 'I-tags' implies that animals displaying REM sleep have memory systems operating through the use of 'I-tags', as in humans. This does not, however, imply any sense of self-awareness in animals. I envisage that self-awareness only comes about through the work of the interpreter, presumably uniquely human. An 'I-tag' is not an experience of self; it is simply

the individual organism's reference to an event in memory. Whilst a cat, for example, may have no sense of an inner 'I' as a focus of its experience and the cause of its behaviour, it may be envisaged that indexing of memories still involves its sense of integrity as a single being, achieved via 'I-tags'. In other words, the cat is not devoid of a sense of self, but this sense is presumably one that is more primitive than that generated by the interpreter.

21. Gabel (1987, 1988), for example, reviews many studies leading to his conclusion that REM sleep reflects greater activation or efficiency of the right hemisphere. Such studies include several that examine cerebral blood flow and EEG patterns during the REM/non-REM cycle. The majority of these studies have suggested a right hemisphere – REM relationship. However, Antrobus (1987) criticizes the EEG studies and suggests that the picture from these studies is, at best, uncertain. The argument for an important left hemisphere involvement in dreaming rests heavily on studies of brain-damaged patients. In cases where such patients have reported a loss of dream recall, damage has been found invariably in the left hemisphere (Greenberg and Farah, 1986). Perhaps the equivocal nature of the evidence is best attributed to the fact that dreaming is certainly a complex process and presumably involves many intra- and inter-hemispheric activities.

22. Antrobus (1987).

23. The ability to remember dreams may be considerably improved by setting the intention to do so. For example, placing a pen and paper next to one's bed with the intention of writing down dreams upon waking not only enables us to remember those we do write down in the morning, but also seems to increase the number we may recall at the time of waking.

24. Over recent years, Freud's distinction between latent and manifest content has tended to be ignored. Thus, for example, in a survey of four psychoanalytical journals, Warner (1987) found that, out of fifty-seven dreams discussed, the latent content was employed as the major source for interpretation in only two dreams. A major feature of Freud's notion of these two levels in dreams concerns the role of the *censor*. The latent content may be unacceptable to the dreamer and the censor 'sanitizes' the material in generating the manifest content. Whether such a feature of Freud's model is sustainable today is for psychoanalysts to decide. My view of the role of the limbic system and that of the interpreter in relation to the dream is confined to the notion of different levels within the imagery. The story-line (interpreter) is a form of surface structure to the deep structure of specific images of concern to the limbic system.

25. Fisher, Gross and Zuch (1965).

26. *Bahir*: 88.

27. Mavromatis (1987), pp.245–6. It is also worth noting the emphasis that Ullman (1987b, p.389) places on the concept of descent in relation to dream images: 'I use the term descent advisedly because, for too long, we have been misled into thinking that dream content ascends into consciousness from a primitive substratum of our personality. I believe the opposite to be the case.'

28. 'What does an embryo resemble when it is in the bowels of its mother? It resembles a folded writing tablet. Its hands rest on its two temples, its two elbows on its two legs, and its two heels against its buttocks. Its head lies between its knees. . . .' (Talmud, *Niddah* 30b.)

29. LaBerge and Gackenbach (1986).

30. This text, quoted by Scholem (1961, pp.52–3) is an elaboration of a famous talmudic story concerning four who entered Paradise (i.e. engage in *ma'ase merkavah*). One of the four, Ben Zoma, is said to have gazed and become stricken. This is interpreted to mean that he lost his sanity. In fact only one of the four, Rabbi Akiba, entered and returned intact. A further point worth noting in relation to this story is the Talmud's use of the word *hitzitz*, translated here as 'gazed'. This word also means 'to blossom' and is used for the 'plate' which Aaron wore on his forehead and on which was written 'holiness to the Lord' (Exodus 28:36–8). Is the gazing cultivated during the descent to the chariot to be identified with the blossoming of the third eye in the forehead found in various spiritual traditions? Surely, a common foundation of experience is implied here.

31. Vertes (1984), pp.275–6.

32. Kripke and Sonnenschein (1978).

33. Idel (1988a), p.119.

34. Cited in Idel (1988b), p.90. Italics added.

7: THE WATCHER WHO SLEEPS NOT

1. Reports by Hilgard's subjects concerning their experiences of a hidden observer within themselves whilst hypnotized. The concept of the hidden observer is discussed in this section. See Hilgard (1986), p.209.

2. Ouspensky (1950), p.147.

3. Jung (1953), p.176. Passage that follows, p.236.

4. Deikman (1982), p.94.

5. Hilgard (1986).

6. Zamansky and Bartis (1985), p.245.

7. Spanos, Flynn and Gwynn (1988), p.9.

8. Spiegel, Cutcomb, Ren and Pribram (1985).

9. Donchin, McCarthy, Kutas and Ritter (1983), p.112.

10. Libet, Alberts, Wright and Feinstein (1967).

11. In saying that the 'I' generated under hidden observer instructions is fickle I also have in mind some studies by Spanos in which the 'knowledge' of the hidden observer was manipulated. For example, in a modified replication of Zamansky and Bartis' study, Spanos (1988) suggested to subjects that the hidden observer sees things reversed. Sure enough, these subjects reported that the number on the card during the earlier negative hallucination condition was 81 when it had in fact been 18. To Spanos this implies that compliance rules the subjects' behaviour. However, the issue as I see it concerns the original awareness of the number, not its subsequent fate. As Zamansky writes, in his reply to Spanos' criticism, 'If the notion of the hidden observer is, in any reasonable sense, a valid one, it must be considered to refer to what is actually *perceived* ('observed'), not merely to what is reported.' (1988, p.12)

12. Orne (1959).

13. Schatzman (1986).

14. Beahrs (1982), p.80.

15. Roper (1989), p.796.

16. Beahrs (1982), p.60.

17. Libet (1985), p.530. Passage that follows, p.536.

18. The whole question of free will is problematic and has generated many heated arguments amongst both philosophers and psychologists. Essentially, any action may be reduced to the balance of circumstances that precede it. Had the circumstances been different, then I might have acted differently. Was the action, then, conditioned by those circumstances, or did I make my decision based on a 'free' evaluation of those circumstances? The situation is, of course, further complicated if we bring the notion of an unconscious into the argument. Freud, whilst accepting that we have a *conviction* of free will, considered that an apparently 'free' decision at the conscious level is nevertheless determined by the unconscious: '. . . what is . . . left free by the one side receives its motivation from the other side, from the unconscious; and in this way determination in the psychical sphere is still carried out without any gap'. (Freud (1966), p.254.)

19. Ouspensky (1950), p.353.

20. Herrigel (1953), pp.73 and 85–6.

21. Ouspensky (1950), p.352.

22. Stace (1961), p.90.

23. Goldberg (1985).

24. Paz (1973), p.97.

25. Sheldrake and Bohm (1982), p.45.

26. Salaman (1982), p.50.

27. Mein (1962), p.46.

28. Proust (1949), p.60.

29. Proust (1970), p.229. Passages in following paragraph from pp.229, 230 and 234.

30. Poulet (1962), p.171.
31. Priestley (1964), pp.290–1.
32. In my studies of Jewish mysticism, the insights somehow embedded in the Hebrew language have never ceased to intrigue me. On this notion of time and the nature of self, the language is particularly revealing. The word *ad* means eternity. It is related to the word for 'religious festival', the link reflecting a view of time which differs from our common view. A festival is a commemoration of a particular event not in the simple historical sense, but in the sense that the event transcended passing time and is therefore still, as it were, present in eternity. Eternity constitutes a separate dimension of time, but nevertheless one with which the yearly cycle intersects. Hence, religious events correspond to appropriate seasonal events (Passover, a time of rebirth, in spring; the period of self-examination and atonement in autumn when the surface layer of leaves is falling away, etc.). Related to *ad* is the word *ed*, meaning 'witness'. True testimony comes from the higher plane which has access to the eternity of the pure memory process. Moreover, these relationships are hinted at in the central prayer of Judaism, the *shema*, in which the two letters comprising the word *ed* are deliberately enlarged. The relevance of these relationships becomes more explicit in the meditative traditions which surround that prayer. See Kaplan (1985)

    A second word translated as 'eternity' is *olam*, which originally referred to a more spatial concept meaning 'world' or 'universe'. In mystical thinking the two concepts were indeed one, depicting a transcendental reality. A cognate root means 'concealed', a juxtaposition interpreted to mean that the transcendental sphere in which space and time fuse is a 'concealed' dimension of our everyday reality. The famous poem in Ecclesiastes depicting the nature of time ('To every thing there is a season; and a time to every purpose under heaven. . . .') ends with an obscure sentence (3:11) which is only penetrable once the pun is decoded: 'Also He has placed the world [*olam*] in their hearts, without which man could not find the work which God has made from beginning to end.' *Concealed* in the heart is our connection to *eternity*, a holistic sphere in which beginnings and ends, space and time, are One. This seems to me a very clear depiction of what I refer to metaphorically as the higher plane and its connection to the pure memory process.
33. Maritain (1953), p.123.

8: IMAGINATION, MIND AND REALITY

1. Statements made by David Bohm in an interview with Weber (Weber (1987), pp.441 and 443).

2. Bartlett (1932).
3. Gregory (1981), p.36.
4. Gazzaniga (1985), p.188.
5. As is well known, Freud identified the sexual instinct with the life force. This identification underscored his choice of the term *eros*. Many have disputed this pillar of Freudian theory, both in the early years of psychoanalysis and more recently. It is beyond the scope of this book to go deeply into this debate. However, I would just stress the point argued in the text, both here and earlier in Chapter 6 (p.152), that I consider sexuality to occupy a special position in relation to self in that it includes both the drive to self-assertion and that to self-dissolution. If the two primary drives might be characterized as one towards life and the other towards death, then I do not identify sexuality with the former alone; accordingly, I would have difficulty in assigning the life force the name *eros*. The frequent use of sexual imagery in mystical literature may only be fully understood in terms of this duality inherent in human sexuality.
6. Ullman (1987b), p.387. Passage that follows, p.390.
7. It is worth noting in this context that meditation, as the operation of mind directed most explicitly to the experience of self in both personal and transpersonal guises, has a strong relation to remembrance. Wilber (1982, p.163 notes that 'all meditation is called remembrance or recollection (Sanskrit *smriti*, Pauli *sati*, as in *satipatthana*, Plato's *anamnesis*, Sufi *zikr* – all are precisely translated as 'memory' or 'remembrance').'
8. The imagination then I consider as primary or secondary. The primary imagination I hold to be the living power and prime agent of all human perception, and as a repetition in the finite mind of the infinite I AM. The secondary I consider as an echo of the former, co-existing with the conscious will, yet still as identical with the primary in the kind of its agency, and differing only in degree, and in the mode of its operation. It dissolves, diffuses, dissipates, in order to re-create; or where this process is rendered impossible, yet still, at all events, it struggles to idealize and to unify. It is essentially *vital*, even as all objects (as objects) are essentially fixed and dead.
   [Coleridge (1956), p.167.]
9. Warnock (1976), p.194–5.
10. Bohm (1980), p.11.

EPILOGUE

1. Talmud, *Chagiga* 13a.
2. Lao Tzu (1963), p.67.

Bibliography

Antrobus, J., 'Cortical hemisphere asymmetry and sleep mentation', *Psychological Review*, *94*, 359–68, 1987.

Aristotle, *The Complete Works of Aristotle*, revised Oxford Translation, ed. J. Barnes, Princeton University Press, 1984.

Armstrong, K., *Through the Narrow Gate*, Pan, 1982.

Aserinsky, E. and Kleitman, N., 'Regularly occurring periods of eye motility and concomitant phenomena during sleep', *Science*, *118*, 273–4, 1953.

The Babylonian Talmud, ed. I. Epstein, Soncino Press.

Bahir, English translation by A. Kaplan, Weiser, 1979.

Barrow, J. D. and Tipler, F. J., *The Anthropic Cosmological Principle*, Oxford University Press, 1988.

Bartlett, F. C. *Remembering*, Cambridge University Press, 1932.

Beahrs, J. O. *Unity and Multiplicity: Multilevel Consciousness of Self in Hypnosis, Psychiatric Disorder and Mental Health*, Brunner/Mazel, 1982.

Bellugi, U., Poizner, H. and Klima, E. S., 'Language, modality and the brain', *Trends in Neuroscience*, *12*, 380–8, 1989.

Bergland, R., *The Fabric of Mind*, Viking-Penguin, 1985.

Bergson, H., *Matter and Memory*, trans. N. M. Paul and W. S. Palmer, Harvester Press (first published 1911), 1978.

Bisiach, E. and Luzzatti, C., 'Unilateral neglect, representational schema and consciousness', *Cortex*, *14*, 129–33, 1978.

Blacher, R. S., *The Psychological Experience of Surgery*, Wiley, 1987.

Bloom, F. E. and Lazerson, A., *Brain, Mind, and Behavior*, second edition, Freeman, 1988.

Bogen, J. E., 'The other side of the brain II: an appositional mind', *Bulletin of the Los Angeles Neurological Societies*, *34*, 135–62, 1969.

Bogen, J. E. and Bogen, G. M., 'The other side of the brain III. The corpus callosum and creativity', *Bulletin of the Los Angeles Neurological Societies*, *34*, 191–220, 1969.

Bohm, D., *Wholeness and the Implicate Order*, Routledge & Kegan Paul, 1980.

Bohm, D. and Peat, D. *Science, Order and Creativity*, Routledge, 1989.

Bohr, N., *Atomic Theory and the Description of Nature*, Cambridge University Press, 1934.

Capra, F., *The Tao of Physics*, Wildwood House, 1975.

Carlson, E. T., 'The history of dissociation until 1880', in J. M. Quen (ed.), *Split Minds/Split Brains: Historical and Current Perspectives*, New York University Press, 1986.

Cassirer, E., *The Philosophy of Symbolic Forms*, Vol. 2: *Mythical Thought*, Yale University Press, 1955.

Clarke, E. and Dewhurst, K., *An Illustrated History of Brain Function*, University of California Press, 1972.

Cohen, D. B., *Sleep and Dreaming: Origins, Nature and Functions*, Pergamon Press, 1979.

Cohen, J., *The Lineaments of Mind in Historical Perspective*, Freeman, 1980.

Cohen, J. M. and Phipps, J.-F., *The Common Experience*, Rider, 1979.

Coleridge, S. T., *Biographia Literaria*, J. M. Dent & Sons (first published 1817), 1956.

Coren, S. and Porac, C., 'Structural and cognitive components of the Muller-Lyer illusion assessed via Cyclopian presentation', *Perception and Psychophysics*, *35*, 313–18, 1984.

Crick, F. and Mitchison, G., 'The function of dream sleep', *Nature*, *304*, 111–14, 1983.

Critchley, M., *The Divine Banquet of the Brain*, Raven Press, 1979.

Csikszentmihalyi, M., 'Play and intrinsic rewards', *Journal of Humanistic Psychology*, *15*, 41–63, 1975.

Davies, P., *God and the New Physics*, Penguin, 1983.

De Chardin, P. T., *The Phenomenon of Man*, revised edition, Collins (first published 1959), 1965.

De Haan, E. H. F., Young, A. W. and Newcombe, F., 'Face recognition without awareness', *Cognitive Neuropsychology*, *4*, 385–415, 1987.

Deikman, A. J., 'Experimental meditation', *Journal of Nervous and Mental Disease*, *136*, 329–43, 1963.

Deikman, A. J., 'The meaning of everything', in R. E. Ornstein (ed.), *The Nature of Human Consciousness: a Book of Readings*, Freeman, 1973.

Deikman, A. J., *The Observing Self: Mysticism and Psychotherapy*, Beacon Press, 1982.

Despert, J. L., 'Discussion of paper by L. Kanner: Irrelevant and metaphorical language in early infantile autism', *American Journal of Psychiatry*, *103*, 242–6, 1946.

Donchin, E., McCarthy, G., Kutas, M. and Ritter, W., 'Event-related brain potentials in the study of consciousness', in R. J. Davidson, G. E. Schwartz and D. Shapiro (eds), *Consciousness and Self-Regulation: Advances in Research and Theory*, Vol. 3, Plenum Press, 1983.

Eagle, M., Wolitzky, D. L. and Klein, G. S., 'Imagery: effect of a concealed figure in a stimulus', *Science*, *151*, 837–9, 1966.

Ellenberger, H., *The Discovery of the Unconscious*, Basic Books, 1970.

Elster, J. (ed.), *The Multiple Self*, Cambridge University Press, 1986.

Evans, C. and Richardson, P. H., 'Improved recovery and reduced postoperative stay after therapeutic suggestions during general anaesthesia', *Lancet*, 27 August 1988, 491–3, 1988.

Fantz, R. L., 'The origin of form perception', *Scientific American*, *204*, 66–72, 1961.

Farah, M. J., 'Is visual imagery really visual? Overlooked evidence from neuropsychology', *Psychological Review*, *95*, 307–17, 1988.

Farah, M. J., 'The neural basis of mental imagery', *Trends in Neuroscience*, *12*, 395–9, 1989.

Finke, R. A., 'Theories relating mental imagery to perception', *Psychological Bulletin*, *98*, 236–59, 1985.

Finke, R. A., 'Mental imagery and the visual system', *Scientific American*, *254*, 76–83, 1986.

Fishbein, W. (ed.), *Sleep, Dreams and Memory*, MIT Press, 1981.

Fisher, C., 'Dreams and perception. The role of preconscious and primary modes of perception in dream formation', *Journal of the American Psychoanalytical Association*, *2*, 389–445, 1954.

Fisher, C., Gross, J. and Zuch, J., 'Cycles of penile erection synchronous with dreaming (REM) sleep', *Archives of General Psychiatry*, *12*, 29–45, 1965.

Freud, S., *The Interpretation of Dreams*, ed. J. Strachey, standard edition, Vols. 4 and 5, The Hogarth Press (first published 1900), 1953.

Freud, S., *The Psychopathology of Everyday Life*, trans. A. Tyson, Ernest Benn Ltd (first published 1901), 1966.

Frith, U., *Austism: Explaining the Enigma*, Basil Blackwell, 1989.

Gabel, S., 'Information processing in rapid eye movement sleep: possible neurophysiological, neuropsychological, and clinical correlates', *Journal of Nervous and Mental Disease*, *175*, 193–200, 1987.

Gabel, S., 'The right hemisphere in imagery, hypnosis, rapid eye movement sleep and dreaming', *Journal of Nervous and Mental Disease*, *176*, 323–31, 1988.

Gaffney, G. R., Kuperman, S., Tsai, L. Y., Minchin, S. and Hassanein, K. M., 'Midsagittal magnetic resonance imaging of autism', *British Journal of Psychiatry*, *151*, 831–3, 1987.

Gazzaniga, M. S., *The Social Brain*, Basic Books, 1985.

Gazzaniga, M. S., 'Brain modularity: towards a philosophy of conscious experience', in A. J. Marcel and E. Bisiach (eds), *Consciousness in Contemporary Science*, Clarendon Press, 1988a.

Gazzaniga, M. S., 'The dynamics of cerebral specialization and modular interactions', in L. Weiskrantz (ed.), *Thought Without Language*, Oxford University Press, 1988b.

Gazzaniga, M. S., 'Organization of the human brain', *Science*, 245, 947–52, 1989.

Gazzaniga, M. S. and LeDoux, J. E., *The Integrated Mind*, Plenum Press, 1978.

Glisky, F. L., Schacter, D. L. and Tulving, E., 'Computer learning by memory-impaired patients; Acquisition and retention of complex knowledge', *Neuropsychologia*, 24, 313–28, 1986.

Goldberg, G., 'Supplementary motor area structure and function: review and hypothesis', *The Behavioral and Brain Sciences*, 8, 567–616, 1985.

Gott, P. S., Hughes, E. C. and Whipple, K., 'Voluntary control of two lateralized conscious states: validation by electrical and behavioral studies', *Neuropsychologia*, 22, 65–72, 1984.

Graf, P., Squire, L. R. and Mandler, G. 'The information that amnesic patients do not forget', *Journal of Experimental Psychology: Learning, Memory, and Cognition*, 10, 164–78, 1984.

Gray, C. M., Konig, P., Engel, A. K. and Singer, W., 'Oscillatory responses in rat visual cortex exhibit inter-columnar synchronization which reflects global stimulus properties', *Nature*, 338, 334–7, 1989.

Greenberg, M. S. and Farah, M. J., 'The laterality of dreaming', *Brain and Cognition*, 5, 307–21, 1986.

Greenberg, R. 'The dream problem and problems in dreams', in M. L. Glucksman and S. L. Warner (eds), *Dreams in New Perspective: the Royal Road Revisited*, Human Sciences Press, 1987.

Gregory, R. L., *Eye and Brain: the Psychology of Seeing*, third edition, Weidenfeld & Nicolson, 1977.

Gregory, R. L., *Mind in Science: a History of Explanations in Psychology and Physics*, Weidenfeld & Nicolson, 1981.

Haith, M. M., *Rules that Babies Look By: the Organization of Newborn Visual Activity*, Lawrence Erlbaum, 1980.

Hardy, A. C., *The Spiritual Nature of Man*, Clarendon Press, 1979.

Hay, D., *Exploring Inner Space*, Penguin, 1982.

Held, R., 'Plasticity in sensorimotor systems', *Scientific American*, 213, 84–94, 1965.

Hermelin, B., 'Images and language', in M. Rutter and E. Schopler (eds), *Autism: A Reappraisal of Concepts and Treatment*, Plenum Press, 1978.

Heron, W., Doane, B. K. and Scott, T. H., 'Visual disturbances after prolonged perceptual isolation', *Canadian Journal of Psychology*, 10, 13–18, 1956.

Herrigel, E., *Zen in the Art of Archery*, trans. R. F. C. Hull, Routledge & Kegan Paul, 1953.

Hilgard, E. R., *Divided Consciousness: Multiple Controls in Human Thought and Action*, expanded edition, Wiley, 1986.

Hobson, J. A., *The Dreaming Brain*, Basic Books, 1988.

Horowitz, M. J., *Image Formation and Cognition*, Appleton-Century-Crofts, 1978.

Hubel, D. H., *Eye, Brain, and Vision*, Scientific American Library/ Freeman, 1988.

Hubel, D. H. and Wiesel, T. N., 'Brain mechanisms of vision', *Scientific American*, *241*, 130–44, 1979.

Huxley, A., *The Doors of Perception*, Chatto & Windus, 1954.

Idel, M., *Studies in Ecstatic Kabbalah*, State University of New York Press, 1988a.

Idel, M., *Kabbalah: New Perspectives*, Yale University Press, 1988b.

James, A. L. and Barry, R. J., 'A review of psychophysiology in early onset psychosis', *Schizophrenia Bulletin*, 6, 506–25, 1980.

James, W., *The Varieties of Religious Experience: a Study in Human Nature*, Collins (first published 1902), 1960.

James, W., *Essays in Radical Empiricism, The Works of William James*, ed. F. Burkhardt, F. Bowers and I. K. Strupskelis, Harvard University Press (first published 1912), 1976.

Janov, A., *The Feeling Child*, Sphere, 1977.

Jaspers, K., *General Psychopathology*, trans. J. Hoenig and M. W., Hamilton, Manchester University Press (first published 1923), 1963.

Jeffrey, F., 'Working in isolation: states that alter consensus', in B. B. Wolman and M. Ullman (eds), *Handbook of States of Consciousness*, Van Nostrand Reinhold, 1986.

Jerison, H. J., 'On the evolution of mind', in D. A. Oakley (ed.), *Brain and Mind*, Methuen, 1985.

Jouvet, M., 'The function of dreaming: a neurophysiologist's point of view', in M. S. Gazzaniga and C. Blakemore (eds), *Handbook of Psychobiology*, Academic Press, 1975.

Jung, C. G., 'The relations between the ego and the unconscious', in *Collected Works*, Vol. 7., *Two Essays on Analytical Psychology*, trans. R. F. C. Hull, Routledge & Kegan Paul (first published 1945), 1953.

Jung, C. G., 'Analytical psychology and education', in *Collected Works*, Vol. 17, *The Development of Personality*, trans. R. F. C. Hull, Routledge & Kegan Paul (first published 1926), 1954.

Jung, C. G., 'On the nature of dreaming', in *Collected Works*, Vol. 8, *The Structure and Dynamics of the Psyche*, trans. R. F. C. Hull, Routledge and Kegan Paul (first published 1948), 1960.

Jung, C. G., *Memories, Dreams, Reflections*, trans. R. and C. Winston, Collins (first published 1961), 1963.

Jung, C. G., 'Commentary on the Secret of the Golden Flower', in *Collected Works*, Vol. 13, *Alchemical Studies*, trans. R. F. C. Hull, Routledge & Kegan Paul (first published 1929), 1967.

Jung, C. G., 'Psychological commentary on the Tibetan Book of the Great Liberation', in *Collected Works*, Vol. 11, *Psychology and Religion: West and East*, trans. R. F. C. Hull, second edition, Routledge & Kegan Paul (first published 1954), 1969.

Kaplan, A., *Jewish Meditation: A Practical Guide*, Schocken Books, 1985.

Kasamatsu, T. and Pettigrew, J. D., 'Depletion of brain catecholamines: failure of ocular dominance shift after monocular occlusion in kittens', *Science*, *194*, 206–9, 1976.

Kaser, V. A., 'The effects of an auditory subliminal message upon the production of images and dreams', *Journal of Nervous and Mental Disease*, *174*, 397–407, 1986.

Kissin, B., *Conscious and Unconscious Programs in the Brain*, Plenum Press, 1986.

Koestler, A., *The Ghost in the Machine*, Hutchinson, 1976.

Kolm, S. G., 'The Buddhist theory of "no-self" ', in J. Elster (ed.), *The Multiple Self*, Cambridge University Press, 1986.

Kripke, D. F. and Sonnenschein, D., 'A biologic rhythm in waking fantasy', in K. S. Pope and J. L. Singer (eds), *The Stream of Consciousness: Scientific Investigations into the Flow of Human Experience*, Wiley 1978.

Kubie, L. S., *Neurotic Distortion of the Creative Process*, Porter Lecture Series 22, University of Kansas Press, 1958.

LaBerge, S. and Gackenbach, J., 'Lucid dreaming', in B. B. Wolman and M. Ullman (eds), *Handbook of States of Consciousness*, Van Nostrand Reinhold, 1986.

Lao Tzu, *Tao Te Ching*, trans. D. C. Lau, Penguin, 1963.

LeDoux, J. E., 'Brain, mind and language', in D. A. Oakley (ed.), *Brain and Mind*, Methuen, 1985.

LeShan, L., *The Medium, The Mystic, and the Physicist*, Viking Press, 1974.

Leslie, A. M., 'Pretense and representation: the origins of 'theory of mind', *Psychological Review*, *94*, 412–26, 1987.

Levinson, B. W., 'States of awareness under general anaesthesia', *British Journal of Anaesthesia*, *37*, 544–6, 1965.

Libet, B., 'Unconscious cerebral initiative and the role of conscious will in voluntary action', *The Behavioral and Brain Sciences*, *8*, 529–66, 1985.

Libet, B., Alberts, W. W., Wright, E. W. and Feinstein, B., 'Responses of human somatosensory cortex to stimuli below threshold for conscious sensation', *Science*, *158*, 1597–600, 1967.

Lifton, R. J., 'Thought reform of Chinese intellectuals', in M. Jahoda and N. Warren (eds), *Attitudes: Selected Readings*, Penguin, 1966.

Lilly, J. C., 'The mind contained in the brain: a cybernetic belief system', in R. S. Valle and R. von Eckartsberg (eds), *The Metaphors of Consciousness*, Plenum Press, 1981.

Lowell, A., 'The process of making poetry', in B. Ghiselin (ed.), *The Creative Process*, University of California Press, 1952.

Luria, A. R., *The Mind of a Mnemonist*, Jonathan Cape, 1969.

McCarthy, R. A. and Warrington, E. K., 'Evidence for modality-specific systems in the brain', *Nature*, *334*, 428–30, 1988.

McKenzie, I. K., 'Hostage-captor relationships', *Bulletin of the British Psychological Society*, *34*, 161–3, 1981.

MacLean, P. D., 'The paranoid streak in man', in A. Koestler and J. R. Smythies (eds), *Beyond Reductionism*, Hutchinson, 1969.

MacLean, P. D., 'The triune brain, emotion, and scientific bias', in F. O. Schmitt (ed.), *The Neurosciences Second Study Program*, Rockefeller University Press, 1970.

MacLean, P. D., 'On the evolution of three mentalities', in S. Arieti and G. Chrzanowski (eds), *New Dimensions in Psychiatry: a World View*, Wiley 1977.

Malamud, P. J., 'Becoming lucid in dreams and waking life,' in B. B. Wolman and M. Ullman (eds), *Handbook of States of Consciousness*, Van Nostrand Reinhold 1986.

Mandell, A. J., 'Toward a psychobiology of transcendence: God in the brain', in J. M. Davidson and R. J. Davidson (eds), *The Psychobiology of Consciousness*, Plenum Press, 1980.

Marcel, A. J., 'Conscious and preconscious recognition of polysemous words: locating the selective effects of prior verbal context', in R. S., Nickerson (ed.), *Attention and Performance*, Vol. VIII, Erlbaum, 1980.

Marcel, A. J., 'Phenomenal experience and functionalism', in A. J. Marcel and E. Bisiach (eds), *Consciousness in Contemporary Science*, Clarendon Press, 1988.

Maritain, J., *Creative Intuition in Art and Poetry*, Princeton University Press, 1953.

Mavromatis, A., *Hypnagogia: the Unique State of Consciousness Between Wakefulness and Sleep*, Routledge & Kegan Paul, 1987.

Mein, M., *Proust's Challenge to Time*, Manchester University Press, 1962.

Melzack, R., 'Phantom limbs, the self and the brain', *Canadian Psychology*, *30*, 1–16, 1989.

Midrash Rabbah, English translation under editorship of H. Freedman and M. Simon, Soncino Press.

Minsky, M., *The Society of Mind*, Pan, 1988.

Morrison, A. R., 'A window on the sleeping brain', *Scientific American*, *248*, 86–94, 1983.

Mueller, J., 'Neuroanatomic correlates of emotion', in L. Temoshok, C. Van Dyke and L. S. Zegans (eds), *Emotions in Health and Illness: Theoretical and Research Foundations*, Grune & Stratton, 1983.

Murch, G. M., 'Responses to incidental stimuli as a function of feedback contingency', *Perception and Psychophysics*, *5*, 10–12, 1969.

Neumann, E., *The Origins and History of Consciousness*, Princeton University Press, 1954.

Nicoll, M., *Psychological Commentaries on the Teaching of Gurdjieff and Ouspensky*, Shambhala (5 vols) (first published 1955–6), 1984.

Oatley, K., *Perceptions and Representations: The Theoretical Bases of Brain Research and Psychology*, Methuen, 1978.

Oliver, L., *Meditation and the Creative Imperative*, Dryad Press, 1987.

Orne, M. T., 'The nature of hypnosis: artifact and essence', *Journal of Abnormal and Social Psychology*, *58*, 277–99, 1959.

Ornitz, E. M., 'Neurophysiology of infantile autism', *Journal of the American Academy of Child Psychiatry*, *24*, 251–62, 1985.

Ouspensky, P. D., *In Search of the Miraculous: Fragments of an Unknown Teaching*, Routledge & Kegan Paul, 1950.

Parfit, D., *Reasons and Persons*, Clarendon Press, 1984.

Paz, O., *Aquila o Sol? – Eagle or Sun?* trans. E. Weinberger, October House, 1973.

Perrett, D. I., Mistlin, A. J. and Chitty, A. J., 'Visual neurones responsive to faces', *Trends in Neuroscience*, *10*, 358–64, 1987.

Picton, T. W. and Hillyard, S. A., 'Human auditory evoked potentials, II: effects of attention', *Electroencephalography and Clinical Neurophysiology*, *36*, 191–200, 1974.

Poulet, G., 'Proust and human time', in R. Girard (ed.), *Proust: a Collection of Critical Essays*, Prentice-Hall, 1962.

Pribram, K. H., *Languages of the Brain: Experimental Paradoxes and Principles in Neuropsychology*, Prentice-Hall, 1971.

Pribram, K. H., 'The brain, the telephone, the thermostat, the computer, and the hologram', *Cognition and Brain Theory*, *4*, 105–22, 1981.

Pribram, K. H., 'What the fuss is all about', in K. Wilber (ed.), *The Holographic Paradigm and Other Paradoxes: Exploring the Leading Edge of Science*, Shambhala, 1982.

Priestley, J. B., *Man and Time*, Aldus Books, 1964.

Proust, M., *Remembrance of Things Past*, Vol. 1: *Swann's Way Part 1*, trans. C. K. Scott Moncrieff, Chatto and Windus (first published 1913), 1949.

Proust, M., *Remembrance of Things Past*, Vol. 12: *Time Regained*, trans. A. Major, Chatto & Windus (first published 1929), 1970.

Quen, J. M. (ed.), *Split Minds/Split Brain*, New York University Press, 1986.

Raikov, V. L., 'EEG recordings of experiments in hypnotic age regression', *Imagination, Cognition and Personality*, *3*, 115–32, 1983.

Reed, G. F., 'Sensory deprivation', in G. Underwood and R. Stevens (eds), *Aspects of Consciousness*, Vol. 1: *Psychological Issues*, Academic Press, 1979.

Renault, B., Signoret, J-L., Debruille, B., Breton, F. and Bolgert, F., 'Brain potentials reveal covert facial recognition in prosopagnosia', *Neuropsychologia*, *27*, 905–12, 1989.

Roper, P., 'Bulimia while sleepwalking, a rebuttal for sane automatism?', *Lancet*, 30 September 1989, 796.

Rothenberg, A., 'The process of Janusian thinking in creativity', *Archives of General Psychiatry*, *24*, 195–205, 1971.

Rowan, J., *Subpersonalities: The People Inside Us*, Routledge, 1990.

Sacks, O., *The Man Who Mistook His Wife for a Hat*, Pan, 1986.

Sagan, C., *The Dragons of Eden: Speculations on the Evolution of Human Intelligence*, Hodder & Stoughton, 1977.

Salaman, E., 'A collection of moments', in U. Neisser (ed.), *Memory Observed: Remembering in Natural Contexts*, Freeman, 1982.

Schacter, D. L., 'Implicit memory: history and current status', *Journal of Experimental Psychology: Learning, Memory and Cognition*, *13*, 501–18, 1987.

Schacter, D. L., McAndrews, M. P. and Moscovitch, M., 'Access to consciousness: dissociations between implicit and explicit knowledge in neuropsychological syndromes', in L. Weiskrantz (ed.), *Thought Without Language*, Oxford University Press, 1988.

Schatzman, M., 'To sleep perchance to kill', *New Scientist*, *110* (no. 1514), 60–2, 1986.

Scheibel, A. B., 'Anatomical and physiological substrates of arousal', in J. A. Hobson and M. A. B. Brazier (eds), *The Reticular formation Revisited: Specifying Function for a Nonspecific System*, Raven Press, 1980.

Scheibel, M. E. and Scheibel, A. B., 'The anatomy of constancy', *Annals of the New York Academy of Sciences*, *290*, 421–35, 1977.

Schnapper, E. B., *The Inward Odyssey: the Concept of the Way in the Great Religions of the World*, second edition, George Allen & Unwin, 1980.

Scholem, G. G., *Major Trends in Jewish Mysticism*, Schocken Books (first published 1941), 1961.

Schopler, E. and Mesibov, G. B. (eds), *Neurobiological Issues in Autism*, Plenum Press, 1987.

Schrödinger, E., *My View of the World*, Cambridge University Press, 1964.

Schumacher, E. E., *A Guide for the Perplexed*, Sphere Books, 1978.

Schürmann, R., *Meister Eckhart: Mystic and Philosopher*, Indiana University Press, 1978.

Scrima, L., 'Dream sleep and memory: new findings with diverse implications', *Integrative Psychiatry*, *2*, 211–16, 1984.

Sefer Yezirah, I. Gruenwald (ed.), *Israel Oriental Studies*, *1*, 132–77. The book has been translated into English by several authors.

Segal, S. J., 'Processing of the stimulus in imagery and perception', in S. J. Segal (ed.), *Imagery: Current Cognitive Approaches*, Academic Press, 1971.

Segal, S. J., 'Assimilation of a stimulus in the construction of an image', in P. W. Sheehan (ed.), *The Function and Nature of Imagery*, Academic Press, 1972.

Sheldrake, A. R., *A New Science of Life: The Hypothesis of Formative Causation*, Blond & Briggs, 1981.

Sheldrake, A. R., *The Presence of the Past*, Collins, 1988.

Sheldrake, A. R. and Bohm, D., 'Morphogenetic fields and the implicate order', *ReVision*, *5*, 41–8, 1982.

Shelley, P. B., *A Defence of Poetry*, *The Works of Percy Bysshe Shelley*, Vol. 7, ed. H. B. Forman, Reeves and Turner 1880.

Shepard, R. N., 'Kinematics of perceiving, imagining, thinking, and dreaming', *Psychological Review*, *91*, 417–47, 1984.

Shepard, R. N. and Cooper, L. A., *Mental Images and their Transformations*, MIT Press, 1982.

Shurley, J. T., 'Profound experimental sensory isolation', *American Journal of Psychiatry*, *117*, 539–45, 1960.

Spanos, N. P., Flynn, D. M. and Gwynn, M. I., 'Contextual demands, negative hallucinations, and hidden observer responding: three hidden observers observed', *British Journal of Experimental and Clinical Hypnosis*, *5*, 5–10, 1988.

Sperry, R. W., 'A modified concept of consciousness', *Psychological Review*, *76*, 532–6, 1969.

Spiegel, D., Cutcomb, S., Ren, C. and Pribram, K., 'Hypnotic hallucination alters evoked potentials', *Journal of Abnormal Psychology*, *94*, 249–55, 1985.

Stace, W. T., *The Teachings of the Mystics*, Mentor Books, 1960.

Stace, W. T., *Mysticism and Philosophy*, Macmillan, 1961.

Teyler, T. J. and DiScanna, P., 'The hippocampal memory indexing theory', *Behavioral Neuroscience*, *100*, 147–54, 1986.

Thass-Thienemann, T., *The Interpretation of Language*, Vol. 1: *Understanding the Symbolic Meaning of Language*, Jason Aronson, 1968a.

Thass-Thienemann, T., *The Interpretation of Language*, Vol. 2: *Understanding the Unconscious Meaning of Language*, Jason Aranson 1968b.

Thompson, R. F., 'The neurobiology of learning and memory', *Science*, *233*, 941–7, 1986.

Thornton, C., Catley, D. M., Jordan, C., Lehane, J. R., Royston, D. and Jones, J. G., 'Enflurane anaesthesia causes graded changes in the brainstem and early cortical auditory evoked response in man', *British Journal of Anaesthesia*, *55*, 479–86, 1983.

Tranel, D. and Damasio, A. R., 'Knowledge without awareness: an autonomic index of facial recognition by prosopagnosics', *Science*, *228*, 1453–4, 1985.

Ullman, M., 'The dream revisited: some changed ideas based on a group approach', in M. L. Glucksman and S. L. Warner (eds), *Dreams in New Perspective: the Royal Road Revisited*, Human Sciences Press, 1987a.

Ullman, M., 'Wholeness and dreaming', in B. J. Hiley and F. D. Peat (eds), *Quantum Implications: Essays in Honour of David Bohm*, Routledge & Kegan Paul, 1987b.

Underhill, E., *The Life of the Spirit and the Life of Today*, Methuen, 1922.

Von Franz, M-L., *Number and Time*, Rider, 1974.

Vertes, R. P., 'Brainstem control of the events of REM sleep', *Progress in Neurobiology*, *22*, 241–88, 1984.

Warner, S. L., 'Manifest dream analysis in contemporary practice', in M. L. Glucksman and S. L. Warner (eds), *Dreams in New Perspective: the Royal Road Revisited*, Human Sciences Press, 1987.

Warnock, M., *Imagination*, Faber & Faber, 1976.

Warnock, M., *Memory*, Faber & Faber, 1987.

Weber, R., 'Meaning as being in the implicate order philosophy of David Bohm: a conversation', in B. J. Hiley and F. D. Peat (eds), *Quantum Implications: Essays in Honour of David Bohm*, Routledge & Kegan Paul, 1987.

Weiskrantz, L., *Blindsight: A Case Study and Implications*, Clarendon Press, 1986.

Weiskrantz, L., Warrington, E. K., Sanders, M. D. and Marshall, J., 'Visual capacity in the hemianopic field following a restricted occipital ablation', *Brain*, 97, 709–28, 1974.

Welch, R. B., *Perceptual Modification: Adapting to Altered Sensory Environments*, Academic Press, 1978.

Whorf, B. L., *Language, Thought and Reality*, J. B. Carrol (ed.), MIT Press, 1956.

Wickes, F. G., *The Inner World of Childhood*, revised edition, Mentor Books, 1968.

Wigner, E. P., 'The place of consciousness in modern physics', in C. Muses and A. M. Young (eds), *Consciousness and Reality: the Human Pivot Point*, Avon Books, 1972.

Wilber, K., *The Spectrum of Consciousness*, Quest Books, Theosophical Publishing House, 1977.

Wilber, K., 'Physics, mysticism and the new holographic paradigm: a critical appraisal', in K. Wilber (ed.), *The Holographic Paradigm and Other Paradoxes: Exploring the Leading Edge of Science*, Shambhala, 1982.

Wing, L. (ed.), *Aspects of Autism: Biological Research*, Gaskell (Royal College of Psychiatrists), 1988.

Winson, J., *Brain and Psyche: The Biology of the Unconscious*, Doubleday, 1985.

Yeats, W. B., *Essays and Introductions*, Macmillan, 1961.

Zamansky, H. S., 'Contextual demands, negative hallucinations, and hidden observer responding: three hidden observers observed' (commentary on Spanos *et al.* 1988), *British Journal of Experimental and Clinical Hypnosis*, 5, 11–12, 1988.

Zamansky, H. S. and Bartis, S. P., 'The dissociation of an experience: the hidden observer observed', *Journal of Abnormal Psychology*, 94, 243–8, 1985.

Zeki, S. M., 'Functional specialisation in the visual cortex of the rhesus monkey', *Nature*, 274, 423–8, 1978.

Zeki, S. M. and Shipp, S., 'The functional logic of cortical connections', *Nature*, 335, 311–17, 1988.

Zohar, trans. H. Sperling and M. Simon, Soncino Press. (NB The Book of Concealment is not included in this translation.)

Zukav, G., *The Dancing Wu Li Masters: an Overview of the New Physics*, Rider, 1979.

Index